Transfer Pricing and Financing

Transfer Pricing and Financing

Edited by

Raffaele Petruzzi
Michael Lang

TAX
Institute for Austrian and
International Tax Law Vienna
WU Transfer Pricing Center

Wolters Kluwer

Published by:
Kluwer Law International B.V.
PO Box 316
2400 AH Alphen aan den Rijn
The Netherlands
E-mail: lrs-sales@wolterskluwer.com
Website: www.wolterskluwer.com/en/solutions/kluwerlawinternational

Sold and distributed by:
Wolters Kluwer Legal & Regulatory U.S.
920 Links Avenue
Landisville, PA 17538
United States of America
E-mail: customer.service@wolterskluwer.com

ISBN 978-94-035-4022-1

e-Book: ISBN 978-94-035-4033-7
web-PDF: ISBN 978-94-035-4034-4

Editors

Dr Raffaele Petruzzi, LLM, is the Managing Director of the WU Transfer Pricing Center at the Institute for Austrian and International Tax Law at WU (Vienna University of Economics and Business), Austria, and an advisor specializing in international tax and transfer pricing.

Raffaele has gained extensive experience in dealing with topics related to international tax and transfer pricing for many years, from both a professional and an academic side. On the professional side, he regularly advises clients across numerous industries on specific topics (e.g., international tax and transfer pricing issues related to services, permanent establishments, financing, business restructuring, intangibles, indirect taxes, valuation of companies and intangible assets), international tax and transfer pricing risk management and compliance, optimization of international tax structures, implementation of mechanisms of dispute avoidance (e.g., rulings and APAs) and dispute resolution (e.g., MAPs and arbitrations), and tax audit defence. On the academic side, he is a frequent speaker at international conferences and lecturer of numerous courses all over the world, as well as an author of many publications. Moreover, he regularly cooperates with professionals in advisory, the business community, governments and international organizations (e.g., OECD, United Nations, World Bank Group, International Monetary Fund, and European Commission). *Inter alia,* he regularly provides assistance on tax policy issues, capacity building for tax administrations, and advises governments on projects related to fight against tax evasion. Finally, among others, he is a member of the United Nations Subcommittee on Transfer Pricing, of the International Fiscal Association (IFA), and of Transfer Pricing Economists for Development (TPED).

Raffaele holds a Ph.D. in International Business Taxation at WU, Austria; an LLM in International Tax Law at WU, Austria; and an MSc in Business Administration and Law at Bocconi University, Italy. *Raffaele has contributed to Chapter 1 of this book.*

Prof. Dr DDr h.c. Michael Lang is the Head of the Institute for Austrian and International Tax Law of WU (Vienna University of Economics and Business), Austria and academic director of both the LLM Programme in International Tax Law and the

Doctoral Programme in International Business Taxation (DIBT) of this university. He is the president of the Austrian branch of the International Fiscal Association (IFA) and has been a visiting professor at Georgetown University, United States; New York University, New York; Sorbonne University, Paris; Bocconi University, Milan; Peking University (PKU), China; University of New South Wales, Sydney; and others.

Assistant Editor

Marcelo H. B. Moura, LLM, received his law degree from the University of São Paulo in Brazil and an LLM from the Ludwig-Maximilians-Universität München in Germany. He is a teaching and research associate at the Institute for Austrian and International Tax Law at WU (Vienna University of Economics and Business), Austria. He is pursuing a Doctoral Degree in Business Law from WU, Austria. Previously, he worked as international tax consultant in Brazil and Germany. *Marcelo has contributed to Chapter 3 of this book.*

Contributors

Andre Dekker is a director of the Amsterdam Transfer Pricing team. He joined Baker McKenzie Amsterdam in January 2013. Andre is an experienced transfer pricing professional with extensive experience in the design, planning and documentation of intercompany transactions for multinational clients. His expertise includes financial analysis, economic benchmarking, and business valuation analysis. He has performed transfer pricing work for clients in a wide range of industries, including the oil and gas, financial services and pharmaceutical, among other industries. Andre's main area of expertise is intercompany financing transactions and valuation analyses, performing economic and financial analyses and preparation of transfer pricing documentation. His analyses include cash flow modelling, pricing of financial derivatives and conducting credit rating analyses, in addition to general transfer pricing compliance and documentation projects. Furthermore, Andre specializes in intercompany finance structuring, debt pricing and cash pool analyses from a tax, transfer pricing and treasury perspective. He has also been involved in the negotiation and conclusion of APAs for a broad range of clients. Andre regularly publishes on transfer pricing for financial transactions and is a visiting lecturer on this topic at the IBFD and the International Tax Centre in Leiden. *Andre has contributed to Chapter 2 of this book.*

Andrew Hickman was Head of Transfer Pricing at the OECD between 2014 and 2016 and responsible for the G20-mandated BEPS outputs, including the 2017 revisions to the OECD Transfer Pricing Guidelines. Involved in transfer pricing for over thirty years, Andrew was a tax partner with KPMG in London, where he worked with major multinational clients and tax authorities on transfer pricing compliance, dispute resolution, and advance pricing agreements. For the first part of his career, Andrew was an official with the UK tax authority. During that time, he acted as Competent Authority in eliminating double taxation with treaty partners, introduced legislation for and managed the UK's Advance Pricing Agreement programme, and was UK delegate to the OECD's Working Party 6. Andrew now operates as an independent consultant and works on matters that he finds interesting, including disputes, arbitration, research, and has contributed to the work of the UN subcommittee on transfer pricing.

He holds a Doctorate from the University of Oxford, UK. *Andrew has contributed to Chapter 3 of this book.*

Antonio Russo is Transfer Pricing Partner, Chair of the Global Tax Practice Group with Baker McKenzie and co-heads the Amsterdam Transfer Pricing team, which has been awarded the International Tax Review Award for The Netherlands Transfer Pricing Firm of the year in 2005, 2006, 2007, 2010, 2012, 2014, 2015, 2018, 2019 and 2020. He has been ranked among the best experts in transfer pricing for several consecutive years on the *Euromoney Expert Guides*, *Legal 500* and *Chambers*. According to the latest *Legal 500* survey, Antonio Russo is 'by far one of the most qualified transfer pricing experts'. Antonio Russo is an established practitioner of international tax law. Antonio lectures at numerous seminars and conferences around the world, as well as contributes articles to several international tax reviews. He specializes in transfer pricing design, implementation and valuation of companies and intangible assets. He has extensive experience in tax planning/restructuring engagements, and has assisted clients in numerous industries. Antonio has also provided assistance to clients in developing strategies for the conclusion of APAs as well as tax audit defence in APAC, EMEA and North America. *Antonio has contributed to Chapter 2 of this book.*

Bipin Dodhia is a chartered accountant with over fifteen years of post-qualification experience in transfer pricing. Currently working with BSR & Co. LLP as Associate Partner. Bipin has worked on a wide variety of assignments that include transfer pricing planning, global documentation, and controversy resolution. Bipin has assisted several multinationals in planning their transfer pricing strategies, preparing documentation, and represented them in the course of their transfer pricing audits, appellate proceedings, and APAs. Bipin has closely worked on global transfer pricing documentation studies involving pan-European and Asia-Pacific searches. Bipin has written various articles on transfer pricing topics, including international case laws, safe harbour recommendations, among others. Bipin has serviced clients across various industries, including financial services, shipping, logistics, e-commerce, startups, IT/ITES, marketing support/business support services, investment advisory, telecommunications, pharmaceuticals, and consumer products. Bipin holds degrees in Chartered Accountancy and a Graduate in Commerce. *Bipin has contributed to Chapter 6 of this book.*

David Ledure is International Tax & Transfer Pricing Partner at PwC Belgium and leads PwC's global Financial Transactions TP network. He advises clients on many aspects of transfer pricing, including development of global policies, complex economic analyses and valuations, substance assessments, system implementations, and tax controversy & dispute resolution. Given his passion for treasury & financing, he is able to connect the dots between these various domains. He is a regular speaker at international seminars and publishes regularly in reputable international tax periodicals. David holds a Master's in Business Engineering and a Master-after-Master in Tax Law. He is also a certified tax consultant at the Belgian Institute of Tax Advisors and Accountants. *David has contributed to Chapter 5 of this book.*

Elias Sobotka is a senior associate in the transfer pricing service line of KPMG in Germany, based in Duesseldorf. His experiences include design and documentation of transfer pricing models. Elias primarily works in KPMG Germany's transfer pricing centre of excellence for financial transactions. He has assisted in various projects related to debt and treasury transactions, such as intra-group loans, guarantees and cash pooling arrangements. Elias holds a Master's in Economics from the University of Maastricht, the Netherlands. *Elias has contributed to Chapter 4 of this book.*

Dr Georg Dettmann is a senior economist in the Transfer Pricing team of Copenhagen Economics in Stockholm, Sweden. Georg is dealing with transfer pricing aspects in both a professional and an academic context. He has extensive experience in advising international corporations, financial institutions, energy companies and businesses at the forefront of the digital economy across Europe, the Americas, Asia and Africa. He regularly provides support on the transfer pricing aspects of financial services and the valuation of intellectual property. Georg's recent professional work includes the structuring of transfer pricing insurances, the valuation of intellectual property for IT companies and supporting asset management companies in their transfer pricing. One of the focus points of his work is providing transfer pricing expertise in litigation cases. Prior to joining Copenhagen Economics, Georg worked as a principal at NERA Economic Consulting. From the academic side, Georg has lectured at several universities and held training for international tax authorities. Georg has published articles in industry-leading journals (e.g., *ITR*, *Bloomberg BNA*, among others) and co-authored some of the standard books on transfer pricing and IP valuation in both English and German. Georg holds a Ph.D. in Economics and Finance from the University of Verona, Italy and an MSc in Economics from the University of Bonn, Germany. *Georg has contributed to Chapter 8 of this book.*

Lucie Hovorkova is a tax practitioner at Deloitte Australia, fully dedicated to transfer pricing. She started her career at the Czech Ministry of Finance in 2004. As a head of the Transfer Pricing Section, she was involved in the introduction of transfer pricing documentation requirements and advanced pricing agreements in the Czech Republic and had regularly participated in meetings of the EU Joint Transfer Pricing Forum. Lucie has worked for Deloitte Prague since 2006 and moved to Deloitte Brisbane in 2018. During her professional career, she participated in a number of transfer pricing projects such as transfer pricing risk analysis and assessment, transfer pricing methodology modelling and documentation (global and local projects), advanced pricing agreements, mutual agreement procedures, tax audits and country-by-country reporting. She was also involved in lecturing for university students and the Czech tax administration. Lucie has a Master's in Economy and Management from Charles University in Prague. She is also a registered tax advisor certified by the Czech Chamber of Tax Advisors and the transfer pricing court expert registered by the Municipal Court of Prague. *Lucie has contributed to Chapter 7 of this book.*

Marc Oliver Birmans is a partner in the transfer pricing service line of KPMG in Germany, based in Cologne. He has been working in transfer pricing for more than eighteen years. His experiences include design, documentation and implementation of transfer pricing models, and he covers all advisory services along the transfer pricing life cycle. Marc Oliver has worked on valuation projects for business restructurings, the transfer pricing of intangibles and the creation and profit allocations to permanent establishments. In the post-BEPS world, his work is even more increasingly orientated in conducting value chain analysis together with his clients in particular in the context of business restructurings. In 2008, he was seconded for nine months to the Financial Services Transfer Pricing Team of KPMG LLP in London. Marc Oliver leads KPMG Germany's transfer pricing centre of excellence for financial transactions. He has managed various projects related to debt and treasury transactions, such as intra-group loans, guarantees and cash pooling arrangements. He advises tax and treasury departments of corporate clients on all financial services-related transactions. In this regard, his experience also includes debt structuring for PE investors, real estate property as well as alternative investments. One of his further focus items is tax audit defence as well as controversy and (alternative) dispute resolution (German tax court proceedings and bilateral MAPs/APAs). Marc Oliver is regularly consulted across Germany and beyond to support tax audits related to intra-group funding issues. Marc Oliver is also a member of KPMG's core M&A transfer pricing team supporting sell-side and buy-side due diligences as well as delivering deal and post-deal structuring support. Marc Oliver holds a Master's in Economics from the University of Bonn, Germany. *Marc Oliver has contributed to Chapter 4 of this book.*

Pooja R. Shah, Chartered Accountant, is a manager in the Transfer Pricing practice of BSR & Co. LLP. She has around ten years of post-qualification experience in transfer pricing and has specialized in transfer pricing matters associated with the financial services sector and financial transactions. She has assisted clients on diverse matters, including transfer pricing planning, risk management and compliance, documentation, audit and appellate support and implementation of dispute avoidance mechanisms (APAs). She has been contributing to articles/chapters in reputed professional journals and has in the last two years also undertaken knowledge management role within the Team. Pooja holds degrees in Chartered Accountancy from the Institute of Chartered Accountants of India, Company Secretary from the Institute of Company Secretaries of India and is a Graduate in Commerce. *Pooja has contributed to Chapter 6 of this book.*

Rahul Mitra is a practising Chartered Accountant, with thirty years of experience in handling taxation matters in India. He specializes in transfer pricing, supply chain management projects, international taxation, BEPS, profit attribution to permanent establishments, among others. He was a tax partner with PwC and KPMG in India for an aggregate period of twenty years, having served both the organizations as the leader of their national transfer pricing practices. Rahul has been nominated by Financier Expert Worldwide as among the leading global corporate tax experts in its directory for 2021. He received the 'International Tax Contributing Author of the Year' award on the subject of transfer pricing in 2019 from Bloomberg Tax. Rahul was invited by the OECD to speak at the 2012 Paris roundtable conference on developing countries' perspective on APAs. He was the country reporter on the topic, 'Non-Discrimination in international tax matters', for the IFA Congress held in Brussels in 2008. Rahul is a member of the global editorial board of the international web-based tax magazine *Bloomberg Transfer Pricing Forum*. He has been consistently rated as a leading transfer pricing professional and tax litigator in India by *Euromoney* and *International Tax Review* since 2010. Rahul was nominated as among the 'International Who's Who of Professionals' by the 'Who's Who Historical Society' for the year 2012. He has authored a book on transfer pricing, styled as *Decoding Transfer Pricing for Selling (Distribution and Agency) Functions*. Rahul has authored individual chapters for various books on transfer pricing published by the Vienna University of Economics and Business, Austria. He was invited by the Tax Tribunal and the Indian Revenue Board on several occasions to impart training on the topic of transfer pricing to Members of the Tax Tribunal and Senior Officials of the Indian Revenue, respectively. Rahul holds degrees in Chartered Accountancy and Honours Graduate in Commerce. *Rahul has contributed to Chapter 6 of this book.*

Rocío López is a Director at PwC with more than ten years of experience. She specializes in transfer pricing but has also assisted the international tax service and M&A practices. Since the beginning of her career at PwC, Rocío has focused on financial transactions, including design and implementation of inter-company financing policies, analysis and documentation of existing financial transaction transfer pricing structures, valuation, and dispute resolution, among others. She also has contributed to the development and enhancement of several technology tools for transfer pricing analyses. Rocío has a bachelor's degree in Economics and a postgraduate specialization in Finance. *Rocío contributed to Chapter 5 of this book.*

Sherif Assef is a principal in the Washington National Tax practice of KPMG in the United States, based in New York City. He has over twenty-five years of transfer pricing experience and has been named one of the world's leading transfer pricing professionals by Legal Media Group. Sherif has extensive experience advising clients on a variety of transfer pricing matters, working with companies in the financial services, publishing, commodities, software, retail goods, telecommunications, energy, engineering, and construction industries. He has analysed a variety of related party transactions, including loans and guarantees, cash pooling arrangements, global trading of financial instruments, asset management services, brokerage services, insurance and reinsurance transactions, management and support services, manufacturing and retail transactions, and the sharing of banking fees. Sherif has also performed valuations of intangible property and other assets. *Sherif has contributed to Chapter 4 of this book.*

Dr Stanley Hales, PhD, is a transfer pricing economist in the Deloitte Sydney Australia office. With experience working in Australia, the USA, and Brazil, he specializes in cross-border transfer pricing of transactions between related parties. Examples of transfer pricing projects with multinational companies in the insurance industry include tax valuation portfolio transfers, captive reinsurance ceding commissions, insurance premium and expense ratio/combined ratio benchmarking, reinsurance capital return analyses, transfer pricing controversy, negotiations of advance pricing agreements with revenue authorities, and transfer pricing documentation. Over the years, he published articles covering transfer pricing topics in the *International Tax Review, BNA Transfer Pricing International Journal, Tax Management International Journal, Euromoney, Management Issues*, and other channels. Stan also authored comments to tax and transfer pricing legislation and/or guidance and draft rulings submitted to the Internal Revenue Service, the Australian Tax Office, and the OECD. Stan taught university-level courses in economics, statistics, money and banking and transfer pricing. He was a doctoral fellow at the Rheinische Friedrich-Wilhelms-Universität Bonn, Germany and earned MA and PhD in Economics from The Ohio State University of Columbus, USA, with a primary focus on the valuation of foreign currency futures options. *Stan has contributed to Chapter 7 of this book.*

Tim Böhne is an associate in Baker McKenzie's Amsterdam office. He focuses on transfer pricing and international tax law. He joined Baker McKenzie Amsterdam in 2017 and has an educational background in international tax law and business economics. Within Baker McKenzie's tax practice, Tim focuses on transfer pricing and international tax law. Tim advises clients on the design of transfer pricing policies, transfer pricing compliance, as well as transfer pricing audits and dispute resolution. He works with a variety of international clients that are active in the technology, consumer goods and healthcare, among other industries. Furthermore, Tim has extensive experience in the field of intra-group financing transactions. He advises clients on all aspects of financial transactions, including, but not limited to, intra-group loans, cash pool structures and intra-group guarantees. Tim also regularly contributes to publications on financial transactions and is a visiting lecturer on this topic at the International Tax Centre in Leiden. *Tim has contributed to Chapter 2 of this book.*

Tomás Hermida is a Senior Associate at PwC Aregentina specializing in Financial Transactions Transfer Pricing for companies all around the world. His experience includes assisting in the design and implementation of intercompany financial transactions (analysing existing structures, defining future transfer pricing policies, valuations), preparation of transfer pricing documentation, and assisting in tax controversy and dispute resolution. Tomás has a bachelor's degree in Economics. *Tomás contributed to Chapter 5 of this book.*

Waman Y. Kale, a practising Chartered Accountant, is a partner with BSR & Co. LLP and is the Firm's lead for financial services transfer pricing. He has over twenty-five years of post-qualification experience and has specialized in transfer pricing since the introduction of Indian transfer pricing regulations in 2001. He has assisted various multinational clients on global transfer pricing matters, including planning, documentation, audit defence and controversy resolution. Waman has significant experience in representing clients at various appellate forums, including Tax Tribunal, Dispute Resolution Panel, Commissioner (Appeals). Waman has advised several clients in successfully negotiating APAs. He has been consistently featured for several years in the list of highly regarded/leading tax advisors released by ITR World Tax. He is a regular speaker at various professional forums. He also contributes articles/chapters on a regular basis to various national and international publications. Waman holds a Bachelor's in Commerce and Economics, holds qualification as Chartered Accountant from the Institute of Chartered Accountants of India and the Institute of Chartered Accountants in England and Wales and holds qualification as Chartered Management Accountant from the Chartered Institute of Management Accountants, UK (CIMA). *Waman has contributed to Chapter 6 of this book.*

Wouter Moelands is a director in PwC's New York Metro Transfer Pricing practice with more than fifteen years of international transfer pricing experience. Before joining PwC New York, Wouter was with PwC London's Financial Services Transfer Pricing practice and PwC Amsterdam's Transfer Pricing practice. Over the years, Wouter has developed a specialization in financial services and financial transactions transfer pricing. His experience includes different segments such as traditional and alternative asset management, banking & capital markets, (re)insurance and finance & treasury. Wouter has performed numerous transfer pricing consultancy projects on topics including management services, financial transactions, intellectual property, threshold permanent establishment and profit attribution. Furthermore, Wouter regularly has assisted clients in obtaining agreements with tax authorities. Wouter has presented on transfer pricing topics such as intangibles, financial transactions and PE profit attribution (including at the IBFD, IBC and BNA), and published articles (including in BNA). Wouter has a Master's in International Business and Economics. *Wouter has contributed to Chapter 5 of this book.*

Summary of Contents

List of Figures

List of Tables

List of Abbreviations

APA	Advance Pricing Agreement
APR	Annual Percentage Rate
ATO	Australian Tax Office
AUM	Assets under Management
BEPS	Base Erosion and Profit Shifting
bps	Basis Points
CAPHL	Chevron Australia Holdings Pty Ltd
CAPM	Capital Asset Pricing Model
CDM	Cargo Deutschland Manufacturing GmbH
CE	Capital Employed
CFA	Committee on Fiscal Affairs
CFC	Controlled Foreign Company
CI	Capital Insurer
CoCo	Contingent Convertible
CPL	Cash Pool Leader
CPM	Cost-Plus Method
CTFC	Chevron Texaco Funding Corporation
CU	Currency Unit
CUP	Comparable Uncontrolled Price
DCF	Discount Cash Flow
EBIT	Earnings Before Interest and Tax
EBITDA	Earnings Before Interest, Tax, Depreciation and Amortization
EONIA	Euro Overnight Index Average

ETF	Exchange Traded Fund
EU	European Union
EURIBOR	Euro Interbank Offered Rate
GCP	Group Credit Profile
IAS	International Accounting Standards
ICR	Issuer Credit Rating
IP	Intellectual Property
IRC	Internal Revenue Code
IRS	Internal Revenue Service
LIBOR	London Inter-Bank Offered Rate
MCR	Minimum Capital Requirements
MNE	Multinational Enterprise
NACE	Statistical Classification of Economic Activities in the European Community – *Nomenclature statistique des activités économiques dans la Communauté européenne*
[year] OECD TPG if a reference to the latest version, just OECD TPG	OECD Transfer Pricing Guidelines for Multinational Enterprises and Tax Administrations
OEM	Original Equipment Manufacturer
OLS	Ordinary Least Squares
P&C	Property and Casualty
P&L	Profit and Loss
PIK	Payment-in-Kind
PLI	Profit Level Indicator
PS LA	Practice Statement Law Administration
PSM	Profit Split Method
RCF	Revolving Credit Facility
REIT	Real Estate Investment Trust
ROA	Return on Asset
ROC	Return on Capital
ROCE	Return on Capital Employed
ROECE	Return on Equity Capital Employed
ROTC	Return on Total Costs
RPI	Related Party Insured
RPM	Resale Price Method
SACP	Stand-Alone Credit Profile
SCR	Solvency Capital Requirement

SWOT	Strengths, Weaknesses, Opportunities and Threats
TCC	Tax Court of Canada
TER	Total Expense Ratio
TNMM	Transactional Net Margin Method
TPSM	Transactional Profit Split Method
UK	United Kingdom
UN	United Nations
[year] UN TPM if a reference to the latest version, just UN TPM	United Nations Practical Manual on Transfer Pricing for Developing Countries
US	United States
WACC	Weighted Average Cost of Capital

Preface

In recent years, the interpretation and implementation of transfer pricing regulations of intra-group transactions involving financing functions increased proportionally as one of the main priorities of both taxpayers and governments.[1] The relevance of the transfer pricing analysis of such transactions derives from several factors. The first is the fact that money as an economic good is a highly movable asset that can often be shifted around the world without significant effort and almost immediately. Second, these issues are complex and thus require comprehensive knowledge not only of the applicable tax codes but also of other areas such as corporate finance, corporate law, and macroeconomics and microeconomics, among others. The third is the well-known debt-equity conundrum that has been historically subject to important discussions among tax experts.

The significant relevance of these topics along with the justified need to address them has attracted the attention of international organizations for a long time. The OECD Committee on Fiscal Affairs already acknowledged in 1972 that this field of study demanded a closer and more thorough examination. Consequently, the 1979 OECD Transfer Pricing Report included an entire chapter solely to address the issues concerning loans, and the OECD Report on Thin Capitalization focused on a number of similar related subjects in 1986. Nevertheless, the first version of OECD Transfer Pricing Guidelines was issued only in 1995, and it avoided the discussion and did not consider a chapter on these issues; the reasons for such an exclusion are unknown.

Twenty-five years later, the OECD finally released its Transfer Pricing Guidance on Financial Transactions that became Chapter X of the OECD Transfer Pricing Guidelines in February 2020. Not long after, the United Nations included these topics in Chapter 9 of its Practical Manual for Developing Countries in 2021.

The guidance provided by both international organizations is aligned with the best practices developed on the topic around the world. It clearly accentuates that the

1. According to the monitoring activity of case law conducted by the WU Transfer Pricing Center, cases dealing with financial transactions amounted to 39% in the biennium 2020–2021, confirming the trend of previous years.

accurate delineation and recognition of the actual transactions are of vital importance when analysing the transfer pricing aspects of intra-group financial transactions in different scenarios. Some relevant case law that will be explored in this book already confirms that these will be at the core of the discussions between taxpayers and tax administrations in the upcoming years.

Moreover, various methodologies have been proposed regarding pricing, and they are all very beneficial in practice. However, the manner in which they should be implemented in concrete cases remains a controversial issue as the following chapters will illustrate. Considering this environment, this book is the outcome of continuous efforts from the WU Transfer Pricing Center at the Institute for Austrian and International Tax Law at WU (Vienna University of Economics and Business). Furthermore, it also reflects on the experiences from the annual advanced transfer pricing courses and the conferences offered by the WU Transfer Pricing Center. The book is titled *Transfer Pricing and Financing*, and its objective is to capture the concepts of transfer pricing and present the fundamental principles applicable to intra-group financial transactions. Existing books and literature on this topic are observed to deal only with specific topics of international tax law and tax treaties which affords an opportunity for dedicated work that bridges both the conceptual framework and practical issues arising in this transfer pricing area. Therefore, this book aims to alleviate that knowledge deficiency by providing principle-based and practical knowledge on transfer pricing applied to financial transactions for both graduate and postgraduate studies as well as professionals working on transfer pricing matters on a daily basis. To achieve this, the book encompasses contributions from various authors including both practitioners and academics who have extensive experience in this field. Furthermore, it will also be used as a reference tool in the advanced transfer pricing courses organized by the WU Transfer Pricing Center.

This book benefits from the expertise of renowned academics and practitioners who have developed a beneficial instrument for individuals with different background knowledge. Each chapter contains a balanced mix of theoretical understanding and practical examples, i.e., case studies and references to key case law. Considering the importance and global influence of the OECD's and the UN's guidance on transfer pricing matters, each chapter takes into account their approach when analysing the related topics. Additionally, this book encapsulates selected country practices when this is relevant. The wide range of transfer pricing topics covered in this publication are divided into the following chapters:

(1) Introduction
(2) Loans
(3) Financial guarantees
(4) Cash pooling
(5) Hybrid financing
(6) Factoring
(7) Captive insurance
(8) Asset management.

Considering the evolving nature of transfer pricing in the specific topics mentioned above, this book will be periodically updated in order to provide up-to-date guidance to its first publication.

The editors would like to express their sincere gratitude to the contributors who made it possible to provide this ambitious work. Many thanks are forwarded to Kluwer Law International BV for supporting and cooperating with this publication project. Last, but not least, the editors would like to thank Raphael Holzinger, Marcelo H. B. Moura, Christina Sudrat, and Nina Klauß for their precious support during the publication process and Jenny Hill for providing linguistic support to the contributors during the publishing process.

Vienna, 28 February 2023
Dr Raffaele Petruzzi, LLM
Prof. Dr DDr h.c. Michael Lang

CHAPTER 1

Introduction

Raffaele Petruzzi

1 INTRODUCTION[1]

The current transfer pricing rules of most countries around the world are based on the utilization of the arm's length principle as the fundamental criterion for allocating the tax bases of Multinational Enterprises (MNEs) between different countries. This principle originated many years ago and requires that the nature of a transaction between related parties is in accordance with that of a comparable transaction between unrelated parties in similar circumstances.

In order to provide guidance for taxpayers and tax administrations on how the arm's length principle should be determined, international organizations such as the Organisation for Economic Cooperation and Development (OECD) and the United Nations (UN) began developing the OECD TPG in 1995[2] and the UN TPM in 2013, respectively.[3] However, notwithstanding the considerable amount of work in this area, the assessment of the arm's length principle is still characterized by a significant degree of complexity. This generates substantial uncertainty and numerous areas of concern in the application of the transfer pricing rules in all of the countries.

This situation is particularly evident in the case of intra-group financial transactions. Their terms and conditions between related parties should be in accordance with those actually agreed (or that would be agreed) upon by unrelated parties in similar circumstances. However, the considerable number of factors leading to their definition has generated an increasing prevalence of controversies between taxpayers and tax administrations.

This chapter introduces the topic of this book. Section 2 highlights the relevance of this topic, while section 3 provides an overview of the common types of financial transactions within MNEs. Section 4 subsequently describes the international guidance on the topic, while section 5 illustrates the application of the four-step analysis to financial transactions in general. Finally, section 6 provides a number of conclusions.

1. This chapter is based on Raffaele Petruzzi, *Transfer Pricing Aspects of Intra-Group Financing* (Wolters Kluwer 2016); Raffaele Petruzzi, *Transfer Pricing and Financial Transactions, in Fundamentals of Transfer Pricing: General Topics and Specific Transactions* 393–432, 393–432 (Raffaele Petruzzi et al. eds., Wolters Kluwer 2021).
2. OECD, *Transfer Pricing Guidelines for Multinational Enterprises and Tax Administrations* (OECD 1995); *OECD Transfer Pricing Guidelines for Multinational Enterprises and Tax Administrations* (OECD 1999); OECD, *OECD Transfer Pricing Guidelines for Multinational Enterprises and Tax Administrations 2010* (OECD Publishing 2010); *OECD Transfer Pricing Guidelines for Multinational Enterprises and Tax Administrations 2017* (OECD Publishing 2017); OECD, *OECD Transfer Pricing Guidelines for Multinational Enterprises and Tax Administrations 2022* (OECD Publishing 2022) (collectively 'OECD TPG').
3. United Nations, *United Nations Practical Manual on Transfer Pricing for Developing Countries* (2013); United Nations, *United Nations Practical Manual on Transfer Pricing for Developing Countries* (2017); United Nations, *Practical Manual on Transfer Pricing for Developing Countries 2021* (2021) (collectively 'UN Manual').

2 THE RELEVANCE OF THE TOPIC

Transfer pricing topics specifically related to intra-group financial transactions have considerably increased their relevance over the years and are currently the second topic most susceptible to review by tax administrations.[4]

Several factors are contributing to the intensification of this phenomenon. Foremost are the recent radical changes in the economic environment. In general, the risk of bankruptcy for many firms has significantly increased during the recent financial and economic crises (consequently inflating the remuneration required by external financing institutions for funding in terms of interest income, for example). On the contrary, the interest burden that multinationals are able to manage has decreased (in terms of financial expenses related to the funding they receive, for instance). These two elements substantially affect the value of compensations (i.e., market interest rates) that must be recompensed when borrowing and lending money on the market.[5]

In detail, the following aspects can be identified as just a few of the relevant causes generated by the recent financial and economic crises and the current market conditions:

- Changes in markets conditions: The supply of the liquidity of banks has been restricted (i.e., available third-party funding – especially bank financing – has been reduced), and risks have become more expensive (i.e., financing institutions require more substantial compensation in terms of interest income for the funding they provide).
- Need for enterprises' financial flexibility (especially cash): Firms must have greater reserves of cash at their disposal in order to be more competitive in the international market.
- Loss-status of many companies: The financial crises have generated losses in many corporations' businesses, as evidenced in their financial statements.
- Need for an increasing number of firms to refinance their individual businesses in a period when interest rates are more unstable.

The second factor contributing to the strengthening of the relevance of the topic is a legislative one. Numerous countries have indeed been frequently introducing measures in their domestic corporate tax laws that are aimed at either reducing the tax advantages of debt financing or increasing the tax advantages of equity financing. These measures, nevertheless, have often been designed in an arbitrary way and

4. EY, *2019 Transfer Pricing and International Tax Survey* 19 (EY 2019).
5. For transfer pricing purposes, this situation significantly affects discussions between taxpayers and tax administrations. For example, whenever the interest rate that is applied to an intra-group loan is too high because of the increased remuneration that external financing institutions require for their funding, the tax authorities of the borrower's country will attempt to reduce this interest rate by arguing that the borrower cannot manage such an interest rate. On the contrary, whenever the interest rate that is applied to an intra-group loan is too low because the borrower cannot manage a higher interest rate, the tax authorities of the lender's country will attempt to increase this interest rate by contending that an independent lender would require a higher interest rate.

disregard the financial reasoning that could possibly support an efficient corporate financing decision.

Additionally, the relative importance (also in terms of the amounts involved) of financial transactions, especially in MNEs, is another factor to consider. The significant degree of complexity that typically characterizes these types of transactions[6] are supplementary factors at the fundament of the increased importance of transfer pricing topics related to intra-group financing.

In this context, on the one hand, taxpayers must manage their transfer pricing policies related to these types of transactions in a situation of considerable uncertainty and scrutiny. On the other hand, tax administrations must address and justify their actions in an environment characterized by increasing complexity and unpredictability.

The crucial point of these policies and actions is the determination of the arm's length nature of financial transactions that are established between related parties. Otherwise stated, based on the arm's length principle, the terms and conditions of these transactions between related parties should be in accordance with those actually agreed (or that would be agreed) upon by unrelated parties in similar circumstances.

However, the current approaches and methodologies that have been implemented still appear to be unable to overcome all of the relevant issues despite the relevant work produced by the OECD,[7] the UN,[8] and other international organizations and associations[9] to provide guidance and certainty to the application of such principles.

3 COMMON TYPES OF FINANCIAL TRANSACTIONS WITHIN A GROUP

A 'financial asset' can be defined as 'any asset that is cash, an equity instrument, a contractual right or obligation to receive cash or another financial asset, to exchange financial assets or liabilities, or a derivative. Examples include bonds, bank deposits, stocks, shares, forward contracts, futures contracts, and swaps'.[10] The term therefore

6. Anuschka J. Bakker, *Transfer Pricing and Intra-Group Financing: Low-Hanging Fruit?*, 15 Derivatives & Financial Instruments, 27–33 (IBFD March–April 2013).
7. OECD, *Transfer Pricing Guidance on Financial Transactions: Inclusive Framework on BEPS: Actions 4, 8–10 – OECD*, https://www.oecd.org/tax/beps/transfer-pricing-guidance-on-financial-transactions-inclusive-framework-on-beps-actions-4-8-10.htm.
8. United Nations, *Chapter 9: Intragroup Financial Transactions*, in *United Nations – Practical Manual on Transfer Pricing for Developing Countries 2021* (2021).
9. *See*, for example, 42 *The Treatment of Capital Gains for Tax Purposes; The Interpretation of the Double Taxation Conventions; The Treatment of Debts and Interests Thereon in International Taxation* (IFA ed., Kluwer 1960); 67a *The Tax Treatment of Interest in International Economic Transactions* (IFA ed., Kluwer 1982); 79a *Deductibility of Interest and Other Financing Charges in Computing Income* (IFA ed., Kluwer 1994); 81b *International Aspects of Thin Capitalization* (IFA ed., Kluwer 1996); 93b *New Tendencies in Tax Treatment of Cross-Border Interest of Corporations* (IFA ed., Kluwer 2008); 97b *The Debt-Equity Conundrum* (IFA ed., Kluwer 2012).
10. OECD, *OECD Transfer Pricing Guidelines for Multinational Enterprises and Tax Administrations 2022, supra* note 2, para. 6.6.

includes an enormous variety of transactions and financial instruments. The following list exhibits the most commonly known:[11]

(1) Traditional financial instruments:
   - Equity instruments (e.g., bank deposits, common stocks, and funds).
   - Debt instruments (e.g., ordinary bank loans, ordinary bonds, debentures, government securities, and zero coupon bonds); and
(2) Financial derivatives:
   - Basic derivatives (e.g., stock options,[12] futures, forwards, and notional principal contacts).[13]
   - Hybrid derivatives (e.g., investment derivatives[14] and other hybrids).[15]

However, the following categories of financial transactions have been identified as being the most common and relevant in an intra-group context:[16]

- loans;[17]
- guarantees (financial guarantees and performance guarantees);
- cash pooling (or cash optimization structures);
- hybrid financing;
- derivatives; and
- other treasury services (e.g., foreign exchange risk management, factoring and forfeiting, commodity risk management, captive insurance, asset management, and carbon trading).

11. This classification is sourced in Antti Laukkanen, *Taxation of Investment Derivatives* 20 (IBFD 2007).
12. For example, call options and put options.
13. For example, swaps (such as interest rate swaps, currency rate swaps, and equity swaps), caps, floors, and collars.
14. For example, convertible bonds, warrant bonds, reverse convertible bonds, stock index bonds, interest index bonds, exchangeable bonds, and bull/bear bonds.
15. For example, subordinated loans, perpetual loans, jouissance shares, profit-participating loans, and silent participations.
16. United Nations, *supra* note 8 section 9.3; Antonio Russo & Omar Moerer, *Introduction, in Transfer Pricing and Intra-Group Financing: The Entangled Worlds of Financial Markets and Transfer Pricing* 5 (Anuschka J. Bakker & Marc M. Levey eds., IBFD 2012).
17. Intra-group loans may include 'lines of credit' (defined as a commitment by a lender 'to lend funds to a borrower up to a specified amount over a specified future period. Lines of credit are reviewed annually and do not require fees or compensating balances unless the line is guaranteed by the lender'. *See* Erik Banks, *The Palgrave Macmillan Dictionary of Finance, Investment and Banking* 275 (Palgrave Macmillan 2010)) and 'revolving facilities' (defined as 'a credit facility that is good for a stated period of time, but does not have a fixed repayment schedule. The borrower may draw down the line at any time, or repay it in full without penalty. The borrower usually pays a commitment fee that secures the line of credit when the application is taken by the lender' (*See Ibid.*, at 398.)). These credit facilities are used, for example, for businesses characterized by cyclical cash flows.

This book will specifically analyse the following intra-group financial transactions: loans,[18] financial guarantees,[19] cash pooling,[20] hybrid financing,[21] factoring,[22] captive insurance,[23] and asset management.[24]

4 THE INTERNATIONAL GUIDANCE ON THE TOPIC

4.1 The Historical Background

4.1.1 The Origins of Transfer Pricing Rules

The origins of transfer pricing rules date back to 1915 when the UK Commissioners were awarded the power to charge non-resident persons with further income taxes. These were based on the 'close connection' and 'substantial control' with resident persons, 'the course of business between those persons [could] be so arranged, and [was] so arranged, that the business done by the resident in pursuance of his connection with the non-resident [produced] to the resident either no profits or less than the ordinary profits which might [have been] expected to arise from that business'.[25] Two years later, the United States tax administration[26] was granted the authority to consolidate the accounts of two or more related trades or businesses 'whenever necessary to more equitably determine the invested capital or taxable income'.[27] These regulations subsequently led to the draft of the first transfer pricing rules that granted the United States Commissioner with the authorization to consolidate the accounts of affiliated corporations 'for the purpose of making an accurate distribution or apportionment of gains, profits, income, deductions, or capital between or among such related trades or business'[28] in order to avoid the international tax avoidance opportunities available to MNEs.[29]

In the meantime, the Committee of Technical Experts nominated in 1922 by the League of Nations to analyse issues related to double taxation and tax evasion produced the first Draft Model Convention for the Prevention of Double Taxation and

18. *See* Chapter 2 of this book.
19. *See* Chapter 3 of this book.
20. *See* Chapter 4 of this book.
21. *See* Chapter 5 of this book.
22. *See* Chapter 8 of this book.
23. *See* Chapter 9 of this book.
24. *See* Chapter 10 of this book.
25. *See* section 31 of the Finance (No. 2) Act of 1915 (quotation slightly amended by the author).
26. The Internal Revenue Service.
27. *See* Regulation 41, Articles 77–78, promulgated under the War Revenue Act of 1917.
28. Revenue Act of 1921, Ch. 136, section 240(d), 42 Stat. 260 (1921) (re-enacted in Revenue Act of 1924, Ch. 234, section 240(d), 43 Stat. 288 (1924), and Revenue Act of 1926, Ch. 27, section 240(f), 44 Stat. 46 (1926)).
29. Reuven S. Avi-Yonah, *The Rise and Fall of Arm's Length: A Study in the Evolution of U.S. International Taxation* 1 et seq. (Law & Economics Working Papers Law & Economics Working Papers Archive: 2003–2009 University of Michigan Law School Year 2007).

Evasion in 1927.[30] In this report, the concept of 'permanent establishment' was introduced in order to allocate taxing rights related to double taxation of business income. According to this concept, business income should have been taxed in the contracting state in which a permanent establishment including, among others, 'an affiliated company' was established. Consequently, such income should have been apportioned based on a separate accounting approach whenever an enterprise had permanent establishments in both contracting states. Nevertheless, no method of apportionment was identified when separate accounting was not available, and the determination of such an apportionment was left to the agreement between the contracting states' competent authorities.

The separate accounting approach was abandoned in the 1928 Model Convention for the Prevention of Double Taxation and Evasion,[31] and the method of apportionment of always being defined by an agreement between competent authorities was enacted. A decision on the method of apportionment was not made due to the committee's lack of time to more comprehensively address the issue.[32] Nonetheless, the general meeting unanimously suggested creating a standing fiscal committee dealing, *inter alia*, with the question of taxation of business income.[33] This was discussed in a first report by the American economist Thomas S. Adams;[34] however, the result of it was that the problem was characterized by more complexity than originally believed.[35]

In this context, the arm's length principle was suggested as being the most appropriate method in 1933 for allocating taxable rights related to business income between different countries. The American lawyer Mitchell B. Carroll was appointed by the fiscal committee to internationally analyse the rules adopted to allocate business income. He had referred to the arm's length principle introduced for the first time in the United States report to the League of Nations on income allocation in 1932.[36] This method was favoured by most countries at that time.[37]

Based on the Carroll Report, the arm's length principle was included in Articles 3 and 5 of the 1933 Draft Convention on the Allocation of Business Income between States for the Purpose of Taxation[38] as the preferred method for allocating income to permanent

30. League of Nations, *Report on Double Taxation and Tax Evasion, Presented by the Committee of Technical Experts on Double Taxation and Tax Evasion*, No. C.216.M.85 (April 1927).
31. League of Nations, *Report on Double Taxation and Tax Evasion, Presented by the Committee of Technical Experts on Double Taxation and Tax Evasion*, No. C.562.M.85 (October 1928).
32. Jens Wittendorff, *Transfer Pricing and the Arm's Length Principle in International Tax Law* 88 (Wolters Kluwer Law International 2010).
33. *Ibid.*
34. League of Nations, *Fiscal Committee: Report to the Council on the Work of the Committee – First Session*, No. C.340.M.140.1930.II (May 1930).
35. Wittendorff, *supra* note 34, at 89.
36. League of Nations, *Taxation of Foreign and National Enterprises: Vol. I*, No. C.73.M.38.1932.II.A (1932); Mitchell B. Carroll, *Global Perspectives of an International Tax Lawyer* 34 (Exposition Press 1978).
37. League of Nations, *Taxation of Foreign and National Enterprises: Vol. IV, Methods of Allocating Taxable Income*, C.425(b).M.217(b).1933.II.A, Geneva, 1933.
38. League of Nations, *Fiscal Committee: Report to the Council on the Work of thee Fourth Session of the Committee*, C.399.M.204.1933.II.A, Geneva, 26 Jun. 1933.

establishments and between associated companies. Since that moment,[39] it has been the preferred method for allocating business income between head offices and permanent establishments and also between related parties both in the OECD Model Convention (OECD Model) and in the UN Model Convention (UN Model). It is also the basic principle embedded in most transfer pricing rules around the world.

4.1.2 The Development of Transfer Pricing Issues Related to Intra-group Financing

Transfer pricing issues related to intra-group financing have been a critical topic for many years. Even in 1972, a note by the OECD Committee on Fiscal Affairs (CFA)[40] established that:

> 30. Two questions of interest to international companies are at present under consideration in Working Parties Nos. 4 and 5, viz. taxation of international loans and taxes on the issue and negotiation of securities.
>
> 31. It does not seem that there is need for further work in this area, at least not until these two Working Parties have completed their work.

The OECD continued working on issues related to intra-group financing notwithstanding the conclusions reached in that meeting. An OECD CFA report in 1973[41] emphasized the importance of tax issues related to the 'financial strategy' of MNEs. This work was initially aimed at addressing general tax issues related to financing and began focusing on transfer pricing aspects in 1974.[42] The OECD CFA issued a draft

---

39. The first tax treaty including the arm's length principle was the United States-France Tax Treaty negotiated in 1930 and signed in 1932.
40. OECD Committee on Fiscal Affairs, *Taxation Aspects of the Activities of International Companies* (Note by the Secretariat), CFA(72)7, Paris, 15 June 1972.
41. OECD Committee on Fiscal Affairs, *Report of Working Party No. 6 on Taxation of Multinational Enterprises* (Note by the Secretariat), CFA(73)4, Paris, 21 May 1973, paras 27–32.
42. OECD Committee on Fiscal Affairs, *Taxation of Multinational Enterprises: Transfer Prices* (Note by the Secretariat), DAF/CFA/WP6/74.1, Paris, 1 February 1974. At that time, it was indicated that:

> Finding an arm's length rate of interest appears to give rise to few problems since market rates for particular kinds of loans are readily available, although *Germany* refers to the difficulty that interest rates may differ between the two countries involved. *Germany* also notes that there is a connection between correct rates and companies' choice between equity and loan capital for their financing. In *Canada* and the *United States* a 5 per cent interest rate may be imputed in certain case, the latter country normally accepting deductions of between 4 per cent and 6 per cent. In *Switzerland* rates between 5½ per cent and 6¾ per cent are required according to the type of the loan. A number of countries are prepared to allow what are in fact less than arm's length rates where loans between related parties – not generally engaged in financial business – are concerned.

See also OECD Committee on Fiscal Affairs, *Summary of main conclusions at the first meeting on 14 May 1974*, DAF/CFA/WP6/74.4, Paris, 20 May 1974; OECD Committee on Fiscal Affairs, *U.S. Tax Treatment of Loans as a Problem in Transfer Pricing*, DAF/CFA/74.6, Paris, 26 June 1974; OECD Committee on Fiscal Affairs, *Summary of Discussions at the Second Meeting 17 June 1974*, DAF/CFA/74.7, Paris, 10 July 1974.

report for consideration one year later regarding the transfer pricing issues related to the treatment of loans.[43]

In 1979, this intensive work led the OECD to dedicate an entire chapter of its Transfer Pricing Report[44] to issues concerning loans.[45] It was clearly recognized that 'debt servicing can provide opportunities for profit shifting, for example, either from the subsidiary to the parent or vice versa depending on whether the lender charges an excessive rate of interest or the borrower pays less than normal interest'.[46] In that context, the term 'loan' was broadly defined and included 'loans or advances of money or other consideration, whether or not evidenced by a written instrument' as well as 'any form of indebtedness arising in the course of business out of sales, leases, the rendering of services or any other extension of credit'.[47]

The 1979 OECD Transfer Pricing Report suggested a two-step approach for dealing with intra-group loans:

(1) defining whether the transaction should be considered as a loan rather than an equity contribution;[48] and
(2) once it is established that an intra-group loan exists, measuring the interest rate that should be charged to it 'in similar circumstances in a transaction between unrelated parties'.[49]

The question of determining the arm's length interest rate was therefore to be answered by analysing two features of the loans, i.e., the amount of the principal and the amount of the interest that is charged.

Only a minimal number of guidelines were provided in regard to the first question. The OECD offered a brief overview of the possible options that could have been adopted by single countries in order to approach such an issue. It concluded that it was 'generally recommended' that a 'flexible approach' should have been adopted in which the 'special conditions of each individual case' would have been considered.[50]

Concerning the second question, the OECD provided a definition of the arm's length interest rate as 'the rate of interest which is charged or would have been charged at the

43. OECD Committee on Fiscal Affairs, *Transfer Prices: Treatment of Loans* (Note by the Secretariat), DAF/CFA/WP6/75.4, Paris, 28 February 1975. For previous drafts of this document, *see* OECD Committee on Fiscal Affairs, *Transfer Prices: Treatment of Loans* (Note by the Secretariat), DAF/CFA/74.12, Paris, 12 September 1974; OECD Committee on Fiscal Affairs, *Transfer Prices: Treatment of Loans* (Note by the Secretariat), DAF/CFA/74.17, Paris, 20 September 1974; OECD Committee on Fiscal Affairs, *Transfer Prices: Treatment of Loans* (Note by the Secretariat), DAF/CFA/74.21, Paris, 31 October 1974; OECD Committee on Fiscal Affairs, *Transfer Prices: Treatment of Loans* (Note by the Secretariat), DAF/CFA/74.26, Paris, 20 December 1974.
44. OECD, *Transfer Pricing and Multinational Enterprises* (Paris: OECD, 1979) ('Transfer Pricing Report').
45. OECD Committee on Fiscal Affairs, *The Determination of Transfer Prices Between Associated Enterprises* (Note by the Secretariat), CFA(79)1, Paris, 12 March 1979, Ch. V.
46. *Ibid.*, para. 181.
47. *Ibid.*, para. 182.
48. *Ibid*, paras 183–191.
49. *Ibid.*, paras 192–201.
50. *Ibid.*, para. 191.

time the indebtedness arose, in transactions with, or between, unrelated parties under similar circumstances'.[51] Therefore, the comparability analysis of all of the primary features of the loan would have been essential for answering such a question. This comparability analysis should have taken into account the following critical factors:[52]

- conditions of the financial markets;
- amounts and maturities;
- nature and purpose of the loan (trade credit, general purpose loan, real estate credit, etc.);
- currency or currencies involved (strong or weak currencies);
- the taxpayer's exchange risks of lending or borrowing in a particular currency; and
- security involved and credit-standing of the borrower.

After the OECD's initial intensive work on transfer pricing issues specifically dealing with intra-group financing, the focus of the CFA's efforts in this field focused on issues related to thin capitalization. The latter led to the issuance of the OECD Report on Thin Capitalization in 1986.[53]

However, a chapter specifically discussing transfer pricing issues related to intra-group loans was not included in the first version of the OECD TPG that was issued in 1995;[54] the reason for that omittance is ambiguous. The OECD began working on a global revision of the 1979 Transfer Pricing Report in 1992.[55] One of its objectives was a 'Revision of Chapter V of the 1979 report ("Loans") in light of the subsequent report on Thin Capitalisation'.[56] Indeed, issues related to thin capitalization were explicitly mentioned within the OECD CFA's planned future work in their 1994 Report.[57] Moreover, the concerns regarding loans were also considered in an OECD meeting a few months before providing the 1995 guidelines.[58] Nevertheless, on that occasion,

51. *Ibid.*, para. 198.
52. *Ibid.*, para. 199.
53. OECD, *OECD Report on Thin Capitalization*, adopted by the OECD Council on 26 November 1986. For an overview of the issues discussed in this report.
54. OECD, *Transfer Pricing Guidelines for Multinational Enterprises and Tax Administrations*, *supra* note 2.
55. OECD Committee on Fiscal Affairs, *Working Party No. 6 on the Taxation of Multinational Enterprises of the Committee on Fiscal Affairs: Revision of the 1979 Report on Transfer Pricing: Organisation of Future Work* (Note by the Secretariat), DAFFE/CFA/WP6(92)3, Paris, 18 March 1992.
56. OECD Committee on Fiscal Affairs, *Working Party No. 6 on the Taxation of Multinational Enterprises of the Committee on Fiscal Affairs: Revision of the 1979 Report on Transfer Pricing: Organisation of Future Work* (Note by the Secretariat), DAFFE/CFA/WP6(92)3, Paris, 18 March 1992, paras 2f.
57. OECD, *Report of the Committee of Fiscal Affairs on the OECD Transfer Pricing Guidelines for Multinational Enterprises and Tax Administrations: Part I – Principles and Methods* (Paris: OECD, 1994), p. 12.
58. OECD Committee on Fiscal Affairs, *Working Party No. 6 on the Taxation of Multinational Enterprises of the Committee on Fiscal Affairs: Summary Record of the Fourth-Seventh Meeting of the Working Party No. 6 Held on 26–27 April 1995*, DAFFE/CFA/WP6/M(95)1, Paris, 11 May 1995, para. 12.

those were also included and were to be addressed in the fiscal committee's future work.

More recently, the OECD drafted a discussion paper about thin capitalization legislation[59] aiming at:

- describing the meaning of 'thin capitalization';
- explaining the reason for many countries taking measures in their tax legislation to address thin capitalization;
- describing the legislative approaches frequently adopted by countries to these rules; and
- addressing a number of the issues frequently arising in this context.

However, this discussion paper has thus far not been approved.

The OECD TPG lacked a chapter specifically dealing with issues related to intra-group financing until recently.[60] However, the OECD finalized its new guidance on this topic in February 2020 in the framework of the work of Base Erosion and Profit Shifting Actions 4 and 8–10 mentioned above.[61]

The UN, on the other hand, has been providing its guidance on transfer pricing in its manual since 2013[62] and issued its final guidance on transfer pricing and intra-group financing in the 2021 update of the manual.[63]

4.2 The Current OECD Guidance

The OECD TPG did not extensively address the issue of intra-group financing until 2020. Only a minimal number of paragraphs of the guidelines had specific relevance for financial transactions. Therefore, transfer pricing issues related to intra-group financing should have been specifically dealt with by the general principles in the OECD TPG and by the guidelines provided in Chapter VII 'Special Considerations for Intra-Group Services'.

59. OECD, *Thin Capitalization Legislation: A Background Paper for Country Tax Administrations (Pilot Version for Comments)* (Paris: OECD, 2012).
60. However, the OECD has also provided other beneficial documents for interpreting the application of the arm's length principle to intra-group financial transactions. In addition to the OECD Report on Thin Capitalization mentioned above, the OECD Committee for Fiscal Affairs published its final Report on the Attribution of Profits to Permanent Establishments in 2010 (OECD, *2010 Report on the Attribution of Profits to Permanent Establishments* (Paris: OECD, 2010)). This report discusses intra-group financial transactions in various paragraphs; therefore, it can also be considered as a useful instrument for understanding the OECD framework on this topic.
61. OECD, *supra* note 7.
62. United Nations, *United Nations Practical Manual on Transfer Pricing for Developing Countries, supra* note 3; United Nations, *United Nations Practical Manual on Transfer Pricing for Developing Countries, supra* note 3.
63. United Nations, *Practical Manual on Transfer Pricing for Developing Countries 2021, supra* note 3, Ch. 9.

However, as mentioned before, the OECD finalized a new chapter completely dedicated to transfer pricing and financial transactions in February 2020[64] which became Chapter X of the OECD TPG. It is thus structured in the following sections:

A. Introduction
B. Interaction with the guidance in Section D.1 of Chapter I
  B.1. Determination of whether a purported loan should be regarded as a loan
  B.2. Identifying the commercial or financial relations
C. Treasury function
  C.1. Intra-group loans
  C.2. Cash pooling
  C.3. Hedging
D. Financial guarantees
  D.1. Accurate delineation of financial guarantees
  D.2. Determining the arm's length price of guarantees
  D.3. Examples
E. Captive insurance
  E.1. Definition and rationale for a captive insurance and reinsurance
  E.2. Accurate delineation of captive insurance and reinsurance
  E.3. Determining the arm's length price of captive insurance and reinsurance.

After a brief introduction, the guidance examines the interactions between this chapter and the general principles established in Chapter I, 'The Arm's Length Principle', with specific reference to the topics of: (a) determination of whether a purported loan should be regarded as a loan and (b) identification of the commercial and financial relations. The following sections explore issues referring to specific transactions, i.e., loans, cash pooling, hedging, financial guarantees, and captive insurances.

4.3 The Current UN Guidance

The UN TPM did not extensively address the issue of intra-group financing until 2021. Only a minimal number of paragraphs of the guidance had a specific relevance for financial transactions. Therefore, transfer pricing issues related to intra-group financing should have been specifically dealt with by the general principles in the UN TPM and by the guidance provided in Chapter B.4, 'Intra-Group Services'.

However, as mentioned previously, the UN finalized a new chapter completely dedicated to transfer pricing and financial transactions in April 2021.[65] Chapter 9, 'Intragroup Financial Transactions', is structured with the following sections:

9.1 Financing arrangements within MNEs
9.2 Corporate financing decisions
9.3 Common types of intragroup financial transactions
9.4 Common types of group financing departments / entities
9.5 Corporate income tax approaches addressing MNE financing decisions

64. OECD, *OECD Transfer Pricing Guidelines for Multinational Enterprises and Tax Administrations 2022*, *supra* note 2, Ch. X.
65. United Nations, *2021 UN TPM*, *supra* note 3, Ch. 9.

9.6 The application of the arm's length principle to financial transactions (in general)
9.7 The arm's length nature of intragroup financial transactions
9.8 Considering the creditworthiness of associated enterprises
9.9 Considering the risks embedded in the financial instrument
9.10 Potential Transfer Pricing Methods
9.11 The Use of Simplification Measures and Safe Harbours
9.12 The application of the arm's length principle to intragroup loans
9.13 The application of the arm's length principle to intra-group financial guarantees.

The chapter begins with an analysis of the issues related to intra-group financing from corporate finance and general tax perspectives. The guidance then provides clarifications over a number of key issues related to the application of the arm's length principle to all types of financial transactions. Finally, the chapter analyses the transfer pricing issues specifically referring to intra-group loans and intra-group financial guarantees.

5 THE FOUR-STEP ANALYSIS

Assessing the arm's length nature of an intra-group financial transaction would generally require that the conditions made or imposed between two related parties in their commercial or financial relations are similar to those that would have been made by independent parties in similar circumstances.

This would imply the performance of the following four-step analysis:[66]

- Step 1: The Identification of the Commercial or Financial Relations.
- Step 2: The Recognition of the Accurately Delineated Transaction.
- Step 3: The Selection of the Most Appropriate Transfer Pricing Method.
- Step 4: The Application of the Most Appropriate Transfer Pricing Method.

5.1 The Identification of the Commercial or Financial Relations

The process leading to the accurate delineation of the actual transaction undertaken begins with the identification of the commercial or financial relations between the related parties in a transaction. This process requires a preliminary understanding of the industry sector in which the MNE operates and the factors affecting the performance of any business operating in that sector.[67]

Subsequently, the role of each related party in the specific transaction should be defined, and the commercial or financial relations between them should be ascertained based on the understanding of the following key 'economically relevant characteristics' or 'comparability factors'.

66. *See* Raffaele Petruzzi, Giammarco Cottani, Stig Sollund & Sayee Prasanna, *Chapter 1: Introduction to Transfer Pricing, in Fundamentals of Transfer Pricing: General Topics and Specific Transactions* 3-37 (Raffaele Petruzzi et al. eds., Wolters Kluwer 2021).
67. OECD, *supra* note 2, paras 10.15–17.

5.1.1 *Contractual Terms of the Transaction*

Written contracts act as a commencement for understanding the intent behind the related parties entering into transactions. A typical contract captures the roles, responsibilities, functions, risks, assets, obligations, rights, and terms of the transactions. However, at times, the written contracts may not provide sufficient information, or the actual conduct of the parties to the transaction could vary significantly from the written agreement. In such cases, the substance of the transaction based on the actual conduct of the parties takes precedence over and above the written contract.

The most relevant contractual terms in the specific case of financial transactions are the following:[68]

- maturity or duration of the financing;
- schedule of repayment and repayment obligations;
- nature and purpose;
- level of seniority and subordination;
- geographical location of service provider and recipient;
- currency of the financing;
- existence of collaterals or guarantees;
- type of remuneration;
- costs related to the financing; and
- convertibility of the financing.

5.1.2 *Functional Analysis*

Under independent circumstances, the compensation for products transferred or services provided between related parties is commensurate with the functions undertaken, risks assumed, and assets deployed by the respective entities. Therefore, it is imperative to perform a detailed analysis of critical functions, key assets that are deployed, and the assumption of economically significant risks. Additionally, such an analysis should be 'including how those functions relate to the wider generation of value by the MNE group to which the parties belong, the circumstances surrounding the transaction, and industry practices'.[69] This will confirm the relevance of the performance of a comprehensive global value chain analysis of the MNE that should lead to the identification of the group's key value drivers.[70]

In the specific case of financial transactions, the functional analysis is considered a crucial element in determining the accurate delineation of the transactions and should be performed from the perspectives of both the service provider and the service recipient.[71] In this context, it is relevant to categorize how financial transactions are performed and organized within an MNE. They may simply be arranged by direct

68. *Ibid.*, paras 10.22 and 10.28.29; *2021 UN TPM*, *supra* note 3, para. 9.7.2.2.
69. OECD, *supra* note 2, para. 1.36.
70. *Ibid.*, para. 10.15.
71. *Ibid.*, paras 10.23–27; *2021 UN TPM*, *supra* note 3, para. 9.7.2.3.

agreements between single entities of the group. In such a case, a transaction-by-transaction approach could be easier to use,[72] and a simplified analysis of the specific transaction may be required to define the arm's length nature of the specific transaction.

Nevertheless, many MNEs organize these transactions through treasury entities or departments that will typically manage the financial arrangements of the group in order to centralize activities such as the following:

- management of the various financial risks;
- management of the cash and liquidity of the group;
- responsibility over debt and equity raising; and
- management of the relationship of the group with external banks and credit rating agencies.[73]

It is relevant to define the functions performed, assets used, and risks assumed by these entities or departments in all of these cases. The three following primary categories of treasury departments can generally be identified based on this functional analysis:[74]

(1) *Treasury entities or departments operating as cost centres*: The treasury entities or departments operate as service providers, assist group companies with routine services, and arrange transactions on their behalf but do not assume any risk of capital.
(2) *Treasury entities or departments operating as value-added centres*: The treasury entities or departments operate as cost-saving service providers, and they tolerate more risks and focus on achieving cost savings in addition to the activities performed by cost centres.
(3) *Treasury entities or departments operating as profit centres*: The treasury entities or departments operate as in-house banks, maximize the profits of their own operations, and assume the risk of capital.

5.1.2.1 Special Focus: The Risks Assumed

In the context of a functional analysis, the evaluation of the relevant risks that are undertaken by each transacting entity, the inherent risks in conducting the business activities by each of them, and the allocation of risks between all of these will be crucial. The financial capacity to assume the risks and the degree of control over those exercised by each entity ultimately play a role in determining their risk profile. The indicative steps established in the OECD TPG could be followed in determining this:

72. OECD, *supra* note 2, para. 3.9.
73. Russo & Moerer, *supra* note 16, at 10; OECD, *supra* note 2, paras 10.39–43; *2021 UN TPM*, *supra* note 3, para. 9.4.1.
74. Russo & Moerer, *supra* note 16, at 9; OECD, *supra* note 2, paras 10-44–49; *2021 UN TPM*, *supra* note 3, para. 9.4.2.

(i) Specific economically significant risks must be identified, which include strategic risks such as those emerging from changes in the external, technology, and political environments; operational risks that arise during the execution and conducting of business; financial risks due to an entity's ability to manage liquidity, cash flow, and creditworthiness; and hazard risks owing to external events such as natural disasters.[75]

(ii) An analysis must be performed of the contractual allocation of the economically significant risks by verifying how these specific risks have been contractually assumed between the parties to the transaction.[76]

(iii) A detailed functional analysis must be conducted in order to understand the conduct of parties, i.e., how the parties to the contract share the specific economically significant risks and identifying the parties assuming control over risk management functions. Additionally, observations must be made on the parties' roles in bearing the consequences of business outcomes that determine the financial capacity to assume the risks.[77]

(iv) An assessment must be made of whether the actual conduct of the transacting parties (Step 3) is in accordance with the contractual assumption of risks (Step 2).[78]

(v) If it is ascertained in Step 4 that the financial capacity to assume the risks and control over them (Step 3) adheres to the contractual assumption of risks (Step 2), Step 6 can be performed. If it is instead determined in Step 4 that the financial capacity to assume the risks and control over the risks (Step 3) does not accord with the contractual assumption of risks (Step 2), then the risks should be allocated between the parties based on their actual conduct (Step 3).[79]

(vi) The accurately delineated transaction is priced considering the financial consequences of the risks assumed and reallocated (whenever necessary), and appropriate compensation in accordance with the functions and risks assumed is warranted. Based on the above process, it is expected that the entity assuming greater risks would be entitled to higher returns.[80]

In the specific case of financial transactions, the following risks are of key relevance:[81]

- credit risk;
- interest rate risk;
- reinvestment risk;
- call/prepayment risk;

75. OECD, *supra* note 2, section D.1.2.1.1.
76. *Ibid.*, section D.1.2.1.2.
77. *Ibid.*, section D.1.2.1.3.
78. *Ibid.*, section D.1.2.1.4.
79. *Ibid.*, section D.1.2.1.5.
80. *Ibid.*, section D.1.2.1.6.
81. Ravi F. Dattatreya et al., *Risks Associated with Investing in Fixed Income Securities*, *in The Handbook of Fixed Income Securities* 21–22 (Frank J. Fabozzi ed., McGraw-Hill 8 ed. 2012).

- inflation (or purchasing power) risk;
- liquidity risk;
- exchange rate (or currency) risk;
- volatility risk;
- political or legal risk;
- event risk; and
- sector risk.

The service recipient's credit risk is the basic factor to be considered when financing decisions must be made. Credit risk can be measured with many different approaches and techniques that currently intend to make it more a matter of 'science' than of 'art'.[82]

Additionally, the use of several specific models can be suggested and agreed upon in advance between taxpayers and tax administration through the use of Advance Pricing Agreements and/or safe harbours. These can be advantageous for achieving a greater degree of simplification and certainty in the determination of the final result of the credit risk analysis. For example, in this context, the use of models developed by credit rating agencies[83] (such as Moody's RiskCalc®, S&P's CreditModel®, or CreditSights' BondScore®) can be beneficial and reliable tools that can be agreed upon with the tax administration.

Another method to define the borrower's credit risk in an even more simplified manner could be the analysis of its key financial ratios, for example, that are shown by credit rating agencies for specific sectors of business corresponding to a particular credit rating.[84] Such an oversimplified approach is not highly suggested; however, it might possibly provide an indication of the borrower's credit risk.

However, once the borrower's stand-alone credit risk is defined, for transfer pricing purposes, it should subsequently be: (a) assessed whether the implicit support deriving

82. These approaches and techniques have relevant advantages; however, they are not without error and therefore imply certain disadvantages. Indeed, the ultimate question of which model is more appropriate to use and how it is best to implement it in practice is not an easy one to answer. However, credit measurement should be performed effectively and taking into account all of the specific needs and factors. This should subsequently lead to coherent, consistent, and reliable results that are not overly incongruent depending on the model employed.
83. For more details on the rating assessment by S&P, *see* S&P, *On the Use of Models by Standard & Poor's Ratings Services* (21 December 2009); S&P, *Guide to Credit Ratings Criteria* (2010); S&P, *Understanding Standard & Poor's Rating Definitions* (3 June 2009); S&P, *Guide to Credit Rating Essentials* (2011); S&P, *Guide to Ratings Performance* (2011). For more details on the rating assessment by Moody's, *see* Moody's, *Rating Non-guaranteed Subsidiaries: Credit Considerations in Assigning Subsidiary Ratings in the Absence of Legally Binding Parent Support* (December 2003). For more details on the rating assessment by Fitch, *see* Fitch, *Corporate Rating Methodology: Including Short-Term Ratings and Parent and Subsidiary Linkage* (5 August 2013); Fitch, *Parent and Subsidiary Rating Linkage: Fitch's Approach to Rating Entities Within a Corporate Group Structure* (8 August 2012).
84. *See*, for example, Solomon B. Sanson & Scott Sprinzen, *Corporate Ratings Criteria, Standard & Poor's Financial Services LLC* 43 (Standard & Poor's in New York, NY, USA 2006), (Table 1: Key Industrial Financial Ratios, Long-Term Debt (three-year medians: 2002–2004)) (Copyright © 2006 Standard & Poor's Financial Services LLC. All rights reserved. Reproduced with the permission of the copyright owner).

from the borrower's group should be taken into account and (b) if yes, this implicit support should be quantified.

Regarding the first question, one of the most currently debated topics when considering transfer pricing aspects of intra-group financing is whether the borrower's credit risk should be assessed on a stand-alone basis (also known as 'stand-alone credit risk') or considering that the borrower belongs to a group (referred to as 'group credit risk'). When determining this, any 'implicit support' deriving from the group to which the borrower belongs should be taken into account. Both the OECD TPG and the UN TPM as well as some relevant case law suggest considering the 'implicit support' when establishing the borrower's credit risk.[85] The most important rating agencies (S&P,[86] Moody's,[87] and Fitch)[88] and some economic literature also encourage this approach.[89]

However, it is important to highlight that implicit support might also have a negative impact on the stand-alone credit risk in some cases. Indeed, when a subsidiary is owned by a weaker parent, the stronger subsidiary is generally rated no higher than the parent primarily because the parent will normally retain the ability to take assets from or burden the subsidiary with liabilities during financial duress. Additionally, the insolvency of the parent consequently causes bankruptcy for the subsidiary regardless of the latter's stand-alone strength.[90] The latter phenomenon that a subsidiary will unlikely have a better credit risk than its parent is known as the 'parent ceiling'.[91] Therefore, it can be deduced that the impact of any implicit support deriving from the group to which the borrower belongs should generally be taken into account.[92]

Once it has been established that implicit support should be considered when assessing the borrower's credit risk, the next question would be the quantification of this implicit support. In this aspect, rating agencies have developed beneficial methodologies that can plausibly be practically applied.

85. United Nations, *Practical Manual on Transfer Pricing for Developing Countries 2021*, *supra* note 3, paras 9.8.6–9; OECD, *supra* note 2, section C.1.1.3; *see also General Electric Capital Canada Inc v. Her Majesty The Queen* (2009) TCC 563; *Chevron Australia Holdings Pty Ltd v. Commissioner of Taxation* ([2015] FCA 1092).
86. S&P, *Corporate Ratings Criteria* (2006).
87. Moody's, *Rating Non-guaranteed Subsidiaries: Credit Considerations in Assigning Subsidiary Ratings in the Absence of Legally Binding Parent Support* (December 2003).
88. Fitch, *Parent and Subsidiary Rating Linkage: Fitch's Approach to Rating Entities Within a Corporate Group Structure* (8 August 2012).
89. *See* Joël Bessis, *Risk Management in Banking* 508–520 (Wiley 2 ed. 2002).
90. S&P, *Corporate Ratings Criteria* (2006), p. 85.
91. Exceptions to the parent ceiling can occur, for example, 'in the case of bankruptcy-remote special purpose vehicles for securitization, regulated entities, independent finance subsidiaries, and the rare instances that have extremely tight covenant protection' (S&P, *Corporate Ratings Criteria* (2006), p. 87). Besides the parent ceiling, what is known as the 'country ceiling' or 'sovereign ceiling' (e.g., the circumstance that a company will unlikely have a better credit risk than that of the country's government in which it is domiciled) is considered in some cases (indeed, in emerging market economies, for example, government defaults might be accompanied by a freeze on the foreign currency convertibility) (Moody's, *The Incorporation of Joint-Default Analysis into Moody's Corporate, Financial and Government Rating Methodologies* (February 2005), p. 5).
92. However, this question is still open to a different answer.

Based on S&P's analysis,[93] the quantification of the implicit support depends on various factors such as strategic importance, percentage of ownership, management control, shared name, domicile in the same country, common sources of capital, financial capacity for providing support, significance of the amount of investment, investment relative to the amount of debt for the venture or project, nature of other owners, management's stated posture, track record of parent company in similar circumstances, and nature of potential risks.

However, the S&P has introduced a methodology for quantifying implicit support that can also be fruitful for transfer pricing purposes.[94] Based on this methodology, the following six-step analysis should be employed to assess the borrower's overall credit risk considering the implicit support:

(1) The group's members must be identified. In this context, a definition of 'control' should be established.
(2) The group rating profile (GCP) should be determined. The S&P emphasizes that the GCP is not a rating but rather an opinion of a group's or subgroup's creditworthiness.
(3) The status of the borrower within the group should be assessed. This step identifies the borrower's strategic significance and therefore the resulting likelihood of group support.
(4) The borrower's stand-alone credit profile (SACP) should be evaluated, if required.[95]
(5) The borrower's overall credit profile (known as the issuer credit rating (ICR)) should be estimated. This step combines the borrower's SACP and the effects of group support by notching up or down from the SACP or from the GCP. Table 1.1 summarizes the five different levels of strategic importance and illustrates the notching process depending on the specific group status of the borrower.
(6) Any existing constraints to the potential borrower's overall credit profile should be applied depending on the relevant sovereign rating and/or transfer and convertibility risk assessments.

93. S&P, *Corporate Ratings Criteria* (2006), p. 87.
94. S&P, *General Criteria: Group Rating Methodology* (19 November 2013). This methodology can be applied to 'corporate or financial service group, including holding companies, and to U.S. public finance entities that utilize obligated groups/credit group structures to secure debt' (S&P, *General Criteria: Group Rating Methodology* (19 November 2013), p. 4). Specific guidelines are provided for financial service groups (S&P, *General Criteria: Group Rating Methodology* (19 November 2013), pp. 18–30), to United States public finance obligated groups (S&P, *General Criteria: Group Rating Methodology* (19 November 2013), pp. 30–32), and to corporate groups (S&P, *General Criteria: Group Rating Methodology* (19 November 2013), pp. 32–39).
95. This step can be undertaken by using the methodology explained in S&P, *General Criteria: Group Rating Methodology* (19 November 2013).

Table 1.1 Summary of Associating an Entity's Group Status with a Potential Long-Term ICR[96]

Potential Long-Term Group Status	*Brief Definition*	*ICR*
Core	Integral to the group's current identity and future strategy. The rest of the group is likely to support these entities under any foreseeable circumstance.	Generally at GCP
Highly strategic	Almost integral to the group's current identity and future strategy. The rest of the group is likely to support these subsidiaries under almost all foreseeable circumstances.	Generally one notch below GCP
Strategically important	Less integral to the group than highly strategic subsidiaries. The rest of the group is likely to provide additional liquidity, capital, or risk transfer in most foreseeable circumstances. However, some factors raise doubts about the extent of group support.	Generally three notches above SACP
Moderately strategic	Not important enough to warrant additional liquidity, capital, or risk transfer support from the rest of the group in some foreseeable circumstances. Nevertheless, there is potential for some above SACP.	Generally one notch above SACP
Non-strategic	No strategic importance to the group. These subsidiaries could be sold in the near to medium term.	Generally at SACP

Similarly, Fitch quantifies the implicit support and rating linkage between parent companies and subsidiaries by performing the following five-step analysis:[97]

(1) Whether a parent/subsidiary relationship exists should be ascertained. This step is primarily determined by analysing the level of ownership by the parent.
(2) Whether sector-specific criteria exist should be established. It would be necessary to check whether the parent and/or the subsidiary operate in some

96. *Source*: Michelle Brennan, 'General Criteria: Group Rating Methodology', *Standard & Poor's Financial Services LLC* (19 November 2013), p. 7 (Table 1, Summary of Associating an Entity's Group Status with a Potential Long-Term ICR) (Copyright © 2013 Standard & Poor's Financial Services LLC. All rights reserved. Reproduced with the permission of the copyright owner).
97. Fitch, *Parent and Subsidiary Rating Linkage: Fitch's Approach to Rating Entities Within a Corporate Group Structure* (8 August 2012).

specific sectors (e.g., insurance, financial, or public) characterized by specific regulations that could affect the rating linkage.

(3) The relative stand-alone credit strengths of the parent and the subsidiary should be verified.[98]

(4) The strength of the parent/subsidiary relationship should be analysed based on the legal ties (e.g., guarantees, dividends, and/or inter-company loan restrictions, cross-default clauses, operation in different jurisdictions), operational ties (e.g., level of control and commonality between management of the parent and of the subsidiary, centralized treasury, operational overlap, and/or integration), and strategic ties (e.g., strategic importance, tangible support).

(5) In regard to the formulation of conclusions and notching, Table 1.2 summarizes the relevant conclusions.

Table 1.2 Summary of the Conclusions of the Fitch Five-Step Analysis[99]

	Strength of Linkage	*Conclusions*
Parent weaker than subsidiary	Strong linkage	The stronger the linkage, the more that the parent's and subsidiary's credit rating will correspond.
	Weak linkage	The rating of the subsidiary will be higher than that of the parent.
Parent stronger than subsidiary	Strong linkage	The stronger the linkage, the more that the parent's and subsidiary's credit rating will be closely correlated with each other (but not necessarily identical).
	Weak linkage	The parent's and the subsidiary's credit rating will correspond to their respective stand-alone profiles.

Finally, Moody's methodology for quantifying the implicit support is based on the following two-step analysis:[100]

98. This step could be undertaken by using the methodology explained in Fitch, *Corporate Rating Methodology: Including Short-Term Ratings and Parent and Subsidiary Linkage* (5 August 2013).
99. *Source*: Fitch, *Parent and Subsidiary Rating Linkage: Fitch's Approach to Rating Entities Within a Corporate Group Structure* (8 August 2012), pp. 7-8 (Copyright © 2012 Fitch Ratings, Inc. All rights reserved. Reproduced with permission of the copyright owner).
100. Moody's, *Rating Non-guaranteed Subsidiaries: Credit Considerations in Assigning Subsidiary Ratings in the Absence of Legally Binding Parent Support* (December 2003). *See also* Moody's, *The Incorporation of Joint-Default Analysis into Moody's Corporate, Financial and Government Rating Methodologies* (February 2005).

(1) The stand-alone rating of the borrower is determined.
(2) The likelihood of support by the parent company even in the absence of any legally binding guarantees is established.

The assessment of this likelihood of support by the parent company is based on two factors. One is the parent's willingness to support (measured by the reference to factors such as reputation and confidence sensitivity, strategy, operational integration, marginal return on required prospective investment, and the role of financial regulators).[101] The second is the parent's ability to support (estimated based on the parent's own rating, the correlation between the parent's and subsidiary's financial condition, and the relative magnitude and timing of all expected investments).[102]

In conclusion, the following approaches may be used for establishing the credit risk of the service recipient:

- use the parent's credit risk;[103]
- begin with the parent's credit risk and notch it up or down in order to approximate the service recipient's credit risk;
- derive the service recipient's credit risk with an analysis of the financial ratios;[104] and
- use credit scoring tools.[105]

A mixture of the approaches listed above could also be adopted.

5.1.3 Characteristics of Property or Services

The characteristics of property transferred or services provided also play a relevant role. Criteria such as physical attributes, quality, volume, and reliability are essential in the case of tangible property. The form of transfers, type of intangible, duration, degree of legal protection, and the potential benefits of the intangible are ascertained for intangible transfers.

In the specific case of financial transactions, typical characteristics to be considered are those listed in section 5.1.1 above.

101. Moody's, *Rating Non-guaranteed Subsidiaries: Credit Considerations in Assigning Subsidiary Ratings in the Absence of Legally Binding Parent Support* (December 2003), p. 5.
102. Moody's, *Rating Non-guaranteed Subsidiaries: Credit Considerations in Assigning Subsidiary Ratings in the Absence of Legally Binding Parent Support* (December 2003), p. 5.
103. OECD, *OECD Transfer Pricing Guidelines for Multinational Enterprises and Tax Administrations 2022, supra* note 2, section C.1.1.4; United Nations, *Practical Manual on Transfer Pricing for Developing Countries 2021, supra* note 3, para. 9.11.2.
104. However, this approach does not take into account all of the qualitative analyses normally performed for defining the borrower's credit risk.
105. However, this approach is also not without flaws. For example, the nature of the model is quite simplistic; the approach relies on historical data, and it often lacks consideration for many quantitative and qualitative factors; and the key inputs to the model might be influenced by the controlled transaction.

5.1.4 *Economic Circumstances*

The markets in which the parties operate have relevant effects. For example, market forces, competitiveness, the business cycle of the industry vis-à-vis the parties to the transaction, and the geographical markets are relevant criteria to consider.

In the specific case of financial transactions, typical elements to take into account are the following:[106]

- currency differences;
- geographic locations;
- local regulations;
- business sectors;
- timing of the transaction; and
- macroeconomic trends.

5.1.5 *Business Strategies*

The business strategies pursued by the parties including the degree of innovation, product portfolio, and market penetration strategies that are adopted need to be ascertained. In the specific case of financial transactions, the financing policy and strategy of the MNE will be relevant.[107]

The above analysis will lead to the accurate delineation of the actual transaction undertaken by the related parties.

5.2 The Recognition of the Accurately Delineated Transaction

Step 1 above leads to the accurate delineation of the actual transaction undertaken by means of the identification of the commercial or financial relations. It will be subsequently necessary to determine whether independent enterprises under comparable circumstances would and could perform the accurately delineated transaction that is identified. The underlying principle in an arm's length analysis is that independent enterprises operate in a rational manner by considering options realistically available before concluding the transactions.

An accurately delineated transaction could be disregarded (and replaced by another transaction if appropriate) in specific and exceptional circumstances. This would occur if the intra-group arrangements when viewed in totality differ from those that would have been adopted by independent enterprises behaving in a commercially rational manner in comparable circumstances, thereby preventing determination of a mutually acceptable price by taking into account their options realistically available.[108]

This step is fundamental in order to reflect commercially rational arrangements under similar economic circumstances, i.e., the transaction being replaced by an

106. OECD, *supra* note 2, paras 10.30–33; United Nations, *2021 UN TPM*, *supra* note 3, para. 9.7.2.2.
107. OECD, *supra* note 2, paras 10.34–38; United Nations, *2021 UN TPM*, *supra* note 3, para. 9.7.2.2.
108. OECD, *supra* note 2, section D.2; United Nations, *2021 UN TPM*, *supra* note 3, para. 3.3.2.

alternative one that is determined to be rational or the possibility that the transaction could be negated based on an appropriate analysis that warrants it.

Moreover, MNEs could engage in transactions that are unique to their business circumstances and may not be common among independent enterprises. Failure to recognize a transaction merely due to the lack of comparable circumstances or due to the absence of a similar arrangement between independent parties does not provide valid grounds to disregard an otherwise valid transaction. A key point is to verify if the MNE in its entirety would be in the least favourable position if not for the tax benefits and had it not entered into the transaction which indicates a lack of rationality in entering into it.

It is worth underlining that, in the course of an audit, both the identification of the commercial or financial relations (i.e., Step 1) and the recognition of the accurately delineated transaction undertaken (i.e., Step 2) will not allow the tax administration to change the contractual arrangements between the related parties involved. Rather, it will permit an amendment to be made in the profitability of the intra-group transactions for transfer pricing purposes.

In the specific case of financial transactions, first and foremost, it should be established whether an independent provider of financial services (e.g., an independent commercial bank) under similar circumstances would provide a financial service comparable to the tested one. The answer to this question would require qualitative and quantitative analyses of the related parties' characteristics on a stand-alone basis. When the question is affirmatively answered, the assessment of the commercial rationality of the transaction requires the analysis of whether the service recipient would request and whether the service provider would have provided a similar financial service. Additionally, in this case, qualitative and quantitative analyses of the related parties' characteristics on a stand-alone basis would address these issues.

In practice, the answer to these two questions would most likely require a direct consideration of the market conditions from the perspective of both the service provider and the service recipient. Additionally, considerations would be required regarding the resulting arm's length nature of the service recipient's capital structure along with the more traditional debt servicing analysis. These would be based on the performance of an analysis concentrated on the following aspects:[109]

- *Business/businesses of the service provider and recipient*: This analysis will assess the impact of the service provider's and recipient's business or businesses on the tested transaction's probability of success.
- *Industry/industries in which the service provider and recipients operate*: This analysis will assess the impact of the industry or industries in which the service provider and recipient operate on the tested transaction's probability of success. It might be conducted, for example, by utilizing the Porter's Five Forces Model,[110] whereby the industry analysis will be based on the evaluation

109. Russo & Moerer, *supra* note 16, at 16.
110. Michael E. Porter, *How Competitive Forces Shape Strategy*, 57 Harvard Business Review 137 (Harvard Business Review March 1979); Michael E. Porter, *Competitive Strategy: Techniques*

of the following aspects: threat of new entrants; threat of substitute products or services; customers' (buyers') bargaining power; suppliers' bargaining power; and intensity of competitive rivalry.

- *Operational risk of the service provider and recipient*: The objective of this analysis is identifying the risks of the operations conducted by the service provider and recipient and to what extent these risks can influence the tested transaction's probability of success. It could be performed, for example, by using the 'SWOT analysis'. In this case, the following factors should be assessed: strengths of the service provider and recipient (characteristics that might afford a competitive advantage over other companies); service provider's and recipient's weaknesses (characteristics that might provide a competitive disadvantage compared to other companies); opportunities (elements that could be exploited to gain or improve a competitive advantage over other companies); and threats for the service provider and recipient (elements that should be avoided to decrease competitive disadvantages compared to other companies).
- *Financial situation of the service provider and recipient*: This analysis will be focused on the service provider's and recipient's financial statements (including the balance sheet, income statement, and statement of cash flows) and, based on those data, will assess the tested transaction's probability of success. Specifically, the critical aspects of this analysis will concentrate on assessing the service provider's and recipient's liquidity. It will also evaluate their ability to comply with the short-term obligations of the loan in regard to the payment of interest expenses, their solvency, and their ability to comply with the long-term obligations of the tested transaction. This analysis can be conducted using financial ratios including EBIT/interest, EBITDA/interest, cash flow from operations/interest, and free cash flow/interest to assess the service provider's and recipient's liquidity. Debt/EBITDA, debt/equity, and assets/equity can be used to estimate the service provider's and recipient's solvency.
- *Other relevant factors*: This analysis will consider if there are other factors that might be relevant for assessing the tested transaction's probability of success, such as the service provider's and recipient's reputation and their relationships with financial institutions.

Moreover, the OECD TPG lists the following indicators as advantageous for recognizing the actual transaction:[111]

for Analyzing Industries and Competitors (Free Press 1980); Michael E. Porter, *Competitive Advantage: Creating and Sustaining Superior Performance* (Free Press 1985); Michael E. Porter, *The Five Competitive Forces That Shape Strategy*, 86 Harvard Business Review 79–137 (January 2008); Nicholas Argyres & Anita M. McGahan, *An Interview with Michael Porter*, 16 The Academy of Management Executive 43–52 (Academy of Management May 2002).

111. OECD, *supra* note 2, para. 10.12.

- the presence or absence of a fixed repayment date;
- the obligation to pay interest;
- the right to enforce payment of principal and interest;
- the status of the funder in comparison to regular corporate creditors;
- the existence of financial covenants and security;
- the source of interest payments;
- the ability of the recipient of the funds to obtain loans from unrelated lending institutions;
- the extent to which the advance is used to acquire capital assets; and
- the failure of the purported debtor to repay on the due date or to seek a postponement.

However, some of the above factors might not be relevant for the correct recognition of the actual transaction.[112]

Finally, the UN TPM also provides some guidance on this topic.[113]

5.3 The Selection of the Most Appropriate Transfer Pricing Method

Once a transaction has been accurately delineated and recognized, it will be necessary to select the most appropriate transfer pricing method in order to determine the arm's length remuneration for the transaction. In this process, the following five methods that are commonly prescribed and which are categorized into: (a) traditional transaction methods and (b) transactional profit methods will be analysed:

Traditional Transaction Methods	*Transactional Profit Methods*
Comparable Uncontrolled Price (CUP) Method	Transactional Net Margin Method (TNMM)
Resale Price Method (RPM)	Transactional Profit Split Method (TPSM)
Cost-Plus Method (CPM)	

The typical process for selecting the most appropriate method takes the following factors into account:

- strengths and weaknesses of each method;
- appropriateness of the method that is considered in view of the nature of the controlled transaction based on the functional profile of the parties;
- availability of reliable information (particularly on uncontrolled comparable transactions) that is necessary for applying the selected method and/or other methods; and

112. Raffaele Petruzzi & Raphael Holzinger, *Accurate Delineation vs. Recognition of Intragroup Loans*, TNI 1111–1120 (Tax Analysts June 2020).
113. United Nations, *2021 UN TPM*, *supra* note 3, para. 9.7.1.

- the degree of comparability between controlled and uncontrolled transactions, including the reliability of comparability adjustments that may be required to eliminate material differences between them.[114]

All of the five methods mentioned above have the same degree of relevance. Therefore, the most appropriate method should be applied based on the specific circumstances of the case. However, traditional transaction methods are considered as being more direct for establishing the arm's length nature of transactions. It is generally suggested that the traditional transaction methods are preferred over the transactional profit methods when both are applicable with the same level of reliability. Additionally, the CUP method is to be given preference if more than one traditional transaction method is applicable with the same level of reliability to a specific situation. Nonetheless, the latter are inapplicable, and the transactional profit methods are considered more appropriate in the event of a non-availability of reliable information regarding uncontrolled transactions such as the details of gross margin that are essential for undertaking an analysis under the RPM or the CPM.

However, transactional profit methods cannot be applied merely due to the non-availability of information for the application of traditional transaction methods. Adequate consideration is to be given to traditional transaction methods before resorting to the use of transactional profit methods based on the criteria prescribed. It is worth accentuating that all methods (both traditional transaction methods and transactional profit methods) should be in accordance with Article 9 of the OECD and UN Models. In general, it will be better to apply the correct method using the wrong comparables than the wrong method using the right comparables.

Additionally, methods other than those prescribed above could be adopted for the purpose of the arm's length test. However, the reasons as to why these were inapplicable and why a method other than the prescribed methods is considered more appropriate need to be established.

In situations when the arm's length result could be derived by using more than one of the prescribed methods, it is suggested that the one that is considered to be more appropriate be used. However, the use of multiple ones could be provided as evidence for meeting the arm's length result when the situation warrants the same.

In the specific case of financial transactions, the CUP method is often used due to the nature of the 'commodity' of money.

However, various other methodologies could be employed to compensate for their activities at arm's length based on the functions performed, assets used, and risks assumed by the treasury departments. In the case of these operating as cost centres or value-added centres, the typical methods that are appropriate to achieve this objective would be the CUP method, the cost-plus method, or the TNMM based on costs.[115] In the case of treasury departments operating as profit centres, it may be appropriate to compensate for their activities by allocating most or all of the profits of the transaction to the department. Consequently, the 'spread' between the costs of funding and the

114. OECD, *supra* note 2, para. 2.2.
115. Russo & Moerer, *supra* note 16, at 9.

return on cash invested might be fully allocated to the treasury department.[116] Importantly, diligent attention should be paid to the 'substance' of these centralized activities whenever functions, assets, and risks are allocated to a treasury department.[117]

5.4 The Application of the Most Appropriate Transfer Pricing Method

A transfer pricing method will be applied after defining the most appropriate one based on the accurately delineated and recognized transaction. Considering that the principles to correctly apply this will be different depending on the specific financial transaction, this analysis will be presented in the following chapters of this book.

6 CONCLUSIONS

Transfer pricing aspects related to intra-group financial transactions are of key importance for both taxpayers and tax administrations. The relevance of this topic has been magnified by various elements such as the recent changes in the economic and financial environments, the legislative changes at both international and countries' levels as well as the prominent significance and complexity embedded in these types of transactions.

Notwithstanding the fact that transfer pricing rules have been implemented in the tax systems of most countries around the world and that the arm's length principle has been adopted as the relevant standard to be employed in this context, numerous issues related to the complexities of this principle continue to emerge. This is also valid concerning intra-group financial transactions.

The current guidance provided by the OECD TPG and the UN TPM on this topic does not completely eliminate these issues. Therefore, the topic of transfer pricing related to intra-group financing has led to a considerable increase over the past years in the number of controversies between taxpayers and tax administrations around the world.

The following chapters will present a more comprehensive analysis of the transfer pricing issues related to intra-group financing with a specific focus on loans,[118] financial guarantees,[119] cash pooling,[120] hybrid financing,[121] factoring,[122] captive insurance,[123] and asset management.[124]

116. *Ibid.*
117. *Ibid.* United Nations, *2021 UN TPM*, *supra* note 3, paras 9.4.3–4.
118. *See* Chapter 2 of this book.
119. *See* Chapter 3 of this book.
120. *See* Chapter 4 of this book.
121. *See* Chapter 5 of this book.
122. *See* Chapter 6 of this book.
123. *See* Chapter 7 of this book.
124. *See* Chapter 8 of this book.

CHAPTER 2
Loans

Antonio Russo, Andre Dekker & Tim Böhne

1 INTRODUCTION AND GENERAL CONSIDERATIONS

Intragroup finance transactions have emerged as one of the most significant forms of intercompany transactions in multinational groups. Within this large category of related party transactions, intercompany loans are one of the most common and often employed. This chapter describes their main features from both theoretical and economic perspectives.

An intercompany loan is the borrowing of financial resources from one related party by another that must be repaid at a later time. They come in many forms and are typically adapted to the needs and requirements of both the borrower and lender. The latter assumes the relevant risks in the transaction, for example, regarding the borrower's failure to (re)pay the loan and its interest.

These types of loans are often considered in relation to tax optimization because of the treatment of interest (generally tax deductible, although with some limitations and exceptions) under the tax laws of most countries. Bearing in mind the fact that capital is highly mobile, the impact of intercompany loans on the effective tax rate of a multinational enterprise (MNE) group can be further modified to achieve the maximum advantages by certain deliberate tax features.

While tax optimization can be one of the motives behind MNEs financing their entities through debt capital, other non-tax factors can also exist. For instance, the OECD acknowledged the phenomenon of MNEs using excessive leverage as a deliberate strategy to achieve tax optimization as early as 1986 in its report on thin capitalization (also known as hidden equity capitalization). However, it also noted that non-tax, commercial reasons could be the explanation for MNEs employing debt rather than equity capital for corporate financing needs.[1]

Thin capitalization has assumed increased significance in the application of the arm's length principle. The (ideal and sustainable) financial structure of a corporation is essentially one of the foundational aspects of corporate finance theory. Modigliani and Miller reached a seminal conclusion in their incisive papers published in 1958 and 1961:[2] Under certain conditions, the total value of a firm is independent of its financial structure. Therefore, it could be inferred that there are no genuine economic incentives to choose debt over equity. However, even presenting the current knowledge of corporate finance in the form of stylized facts, the internal factors of a company (such as management's behavioural issues and moral hazard), those that are external (such as clientele effects in the supply side of debt financing), and tax considerations may provide strong incentives to prefer debt over equity.[3]

Increasing Scrutiny on Intercompany Debt

Intercompany loans and the arm's length treatment of these transactions have been under closer scrutiny by the tax authorities in recent years. This phenomenon results primarily due to the following predominant reasons:

- the comparative significance and materiality that intercompany loans have acquired in MNEs;

1. In para. 10 of the OECD *Thin Capitalisation Report*, the OECD notes that, while there can be non-tax reasons for multinational enterprises to use loan capital rather than equity capital in any particular case (e.g., ease of repayment, allowing capital to be geographically mobile, etc.), tax advantages might still be the most important motive, and tax authorities should take this into account; *see* OECD, *Thin Capitalisation: Taxation of Entertainers, Artistes and Sportsmen* (OECD Publishing 1987), adopted by the OECD Council on 26 November 1986.
2. Franco Modigliani & Merton H. Miller, *The Cost of Capital, Corporation Finance and the Theory of Investment*, 48 The American Economic Review 261–297 (American Economic Association 1958); Merton H. Miller & Franco Modigliani, *Dividend Policy, Growth, and the Valuation of Shares*, 34 The Journal of Business 411–433 (University of Chicago Press 1961).
3. However, at a certain point, debt becomes too expensive. For a general analysis of modern corporate finance theory, the authors refer to Jean Tirole, *The Theory of Corporate Finance* (Princeton University Press 2006).

- tax authorities' enhanced awareness and attention regarding intercompany loans, including a more comprehensive understanding of the technical aspects involving these transactions;
- an increasing amount of guidance available on the market, including a separate chapter (i.e., Chapter X) of the OECD Transfer Pricing Guidelines for MNEs and Tax Administrations 2022[4] (*OECD TPG*).

Further attention and scrutiny with respect to intercompany loans have been caused by general market developments, including movements of interest rates over time. For instance, the leading market interest rates (e.g., interbank offering rates, such as LIBOR and EURIBOR) have been negative over the past few years and have consequently directly affected data used as comparables to set or test the arm's length price of intercompany loans. Furthermore, the developments around the COVID-19 crisis have heavily affected the credit spreads on the market which, in turn, have directly impacted arm's length rates applicable to them.

Due to the direct effects of market developments on the treatment and pricing of intercompany loans, the number of questions raised by the global taxing authorities has further increased. Key topics include the pricing of intercompany debt positions, the arm's length character of terms and conditions applied, and the options realistically available to both the borrower and lender.

Following the latest OECD TPG, it is expected that the attention placed by tax authorities on intercompany debt could further increase. Therefore, it is important for multinational groups to be aware of the latest developments, guidance, and best practices regarding transfer pricing.

2 IDENTIFICATION OF THE COMMERCIAL OR FINANCIAL RELATIONS BETWEEN THE RELATED PARTIES AND THE ACCURATE DELINEATION OF THE LOAN TRANSACTION

A comparability analysis is fundamental for the application of the arm's length principle to an intragroup transaction, i.e., the exercise in which the terms and circumstances that exist in a related party transaction are compared with those that would have been made had the parties been unrelated and were entering into a comparable transaction in a comparable situation.[5]

The comparability analysis comprises two primary stages:

(1) The first is identifying the commercial or financial relations between the related parties as well as the conditions and economically relevant circumstances attached to those relations so that the intercompany transaction may be accurately delineated.

4. OECD, *OECD Transfer Pricing Guidelines for Multinational Enterprises and Tax Administrations 2022* (OECD Publishing 2022).
5. *Ibid.*, para. 1.33; United Nations, *Practical Manual on Transfer Pricing for Developing Countries 2021* (2021), paras 3.1.1–2.

(2) The second is comparing the conditions and the economically relevant circumstances of the accurately delineated intercompany transaction with those of comparable transactions between independent enterprises.

Establishing the economically relevant characteristics or comparability factors of the commercial or financial relations between the related parties is necessary for accurately delineating the intragroup transaction. These include:[6]

- contractual terms of the transaction;
- functions performed, assets used, and risks assumed by the related parties;
- nature and characteristics of the products transferred or services provided;
- economic circumstances of the related parties and the market in which they operate; and
- the parties' business strategies.

As described above, the determination of the contractual terms between the related parties in an intragroup transaction remains the point of departure of the analysis. However, the tax authorities would respect the contractual allocation of functions, assets, and risks as well as the resulting allocation of profits and remuneration if the contractual allocation corresponds to the actual behaviour of the related parties in the transaction.

Through this process of accurately delineating the transaction, the arm's length price of the 'real' intragroup transaction is determined instead of the arm's length price of a contract-based transaction that may not be in accordance with the associated enterprises' actual contributions to the value created.

The approach for allocating risks is another important element introduced in the guidance on the accurate delineation of intragroup transactions. To allocate economically material risks in the context of an intragroup transaction, a two-pronged test must be performed under which a risk can only be allocated to an entity if the entity has both of the following characteristics:[7]

- if it has the financial capacity to assume the risk, i.e., if the entity has access to funding to bear the risk and its consequences should the risk materialize;
- if it 'controls' the risk, i.e., if the entity has the capability and actually performs decision-making relating to taking on or laying off the risk, including its management and mitigation.

The above guidance on the accurate delineation of intragroup transactions and the framework for the allocation of risk are general in nature and apply to all intragroup financing transactions (including intercompany loans).

6. OECD, *supra* note 4, para. 1.36; United Nations, *supra* note 5, para. 3.2.4.
7. OECD, *supra* note 4, para. 1.60; United Nations, *supra* note 5, para. 3.4.4.30.

2.1 OECD and UN Guidance on Financial Transactions

The OECD TPG, Chapter X, section B includes multiple references to the guidance in its Chapter 1, sections D.1. and D.2. regarding the identification of commercial and financial relations and the recognition of the accurately delineated transaction. In the accurate delineation of the provision of funding (e.g., intercompany loans), the OECD TPG's Chapter X and the UN TPM's Chapter 9 focus on the characteristics of the transaction and related contractual documentation:[8]

- presence or absence of a fixed repayment date;
- obligation to pay interest;
- right to enforce the payment of principal and interest; and
- existence of financial covenants and security.

In addition, the accurate delineation of intercompany loans takes into account the commercial and financial context within which the funds were lent. Examples include the lender's status, the ability of the borrower of the funds to obtain financing from independent lenders that is used to acquire capital assets, and the risk of the debtor's failure to repay the loan.[9]

The following example[10] illustrates the concept of accurate delineation relating to lending funds:

Example

Company B is a member of an MNE group. The former requires additional funding for its business operations and receives an advance of funds from Company C that is a related party. This occurs through a fixed-term loan; however, Company B's financial projections show that it will be unable to repay the loan at the end of the term. It could be concluded from that information that an independent party would be unwilling to provide such a loan. Therefore, the amount of the loan for transfer pricing purposes must be a function of the maximum amount that an independent lender would be willing to advance to Company B and the maximum amount that an independent borrower would be willing to borrow. The loan amount in excess is thus disregarded for the purposes of determining the amount of interest that Company B would have paid at arm's length.

The OECD TPG, paragraphs 10.8 and 10.9 and the UN TPM, Chapter 9, section 9.5 further indicate that the accurate delineation of the intercompany transaction is not the only approach to address the balance of the capital structure and interest deductibility. Accordingly, they also mention domestic interest deduction limitations and

8. OECD, *supra* note 4, para. 10.12; United Nations, *supra* note 5, para. 9.7.2.2.
9. OECD, *supra* note 4, para. 10.12.
10. Example from para. 10.13 of the OECD TPG.

debt/equity requirement rules (e.g., the 30% EBITDA rule and thin capitalization rules) as approaches to be considered.

Domestic interest deduction limitation rules (affecting the level of interest) and capital structure requirements (impacting the principal amount) could result in situations that are significantly different from the outcomes of a transfer pricing analysis. Thus, the latter could be below or in excess of the outcome achieved by applying domestic rules. If these and the guidance contained in the OECD TPG, Chapter X are applied in combination, domestic rules should only be relevant for the interest still recognized under the arm's length principle. However, it could be argued that specific rules based on an economic rationale rule out any further interest disallowance.

An analysis of all of the factors affecting the performance of businesses in the relevant industry sector must be performed when accurately delineating an intragroup financing transaction. MNEs operating in different sectors, for example, may require different amounts of financing or different levels of short-term cash balances.[11]

Control over risk

The OECD TPG, Chapter X applies the concepts of 'control over risks' and 'financial capacity to assume risks' as introduced in the OECD TPG, Chapter I (paragraph 1.98) to financial transactions. In the event that a lender is not exercising control over the risks associated with the advance of funds or does not have the financial capacity to absorb those risks, they should subsequently be allocated to the entity actually exercising control and with the financial capacity to assume them.[12]

Options realistically available

The OECD TPG, Chapter X and the UN TPM, Chapter 9 further incorporate the concept of 'options realistically available' as contained in the OECD TPG, paragraph 1.38 and the UN TPM paragraph 3.3.2.2. to financial transactions. Specifically, they note that independent enterprises would consider all other options realistically available to them before entering into a financial transaction, and they will only enter into the transaction if no alternative affords a more attractive opportunity.[13] In this respect, both parties' perspectives of the transaction must be considered, i.e., a two-sided approach. While a lender may contemplate other investment opportunities, a borrower may assess its need for additional funds for meeting operational requirements.

2.2 A Two-Sided Analysis of Intercompany Loans

A transfer pricing analysis of intercompany loans generally requires performing a two-sided analysis. First, the characteristics of the borrower, including the loan

11. *See also* OECD, *supra* note 4, Ch. X section B.3.4–5; United Nations, *supra* note 5, para. 9.7.2.2, providing detailed information on the accurate delineation of intragroup financing transactions.
12. OECD, *supra* note 4, para. 10.25.
13. *Ibid.*, para. 10.19; United Nations, *supra* note 5, para. 9.12.2.7.

amount and overall terms and conditions of the loan, must be analysed. This part of the analysis addresses the following questions:

(1) *Could* the borrower obtain access to a similar level of debt from a third-party lender?
(2) *Would* the borrower actually borrow such or a similar amount (with similar features) at arm's length even if funds at that level could be borrowed given the features of its business and notional shareholders? Stated differently, is there a commercial rationale for this transaction?[14]

There are multiple parts to this analysis that should include a business and industry analysis, financial modelling to stress-test the borrower's financials, an analysis of the borrower's creditworthiness, and a test to confirm that the overall terms and conditions of the loan are market-conforming.

Following the analysis of the 'fundamentals' as outlined above, an arm's length price for the loan transaction can then be established. In an arm's length situation, several factors will influence the spread or margin to be added to the base rate (e.g., the opportunity cost or time value of money). These factors include the borrowing entity's creditworthiness, the time of the transaction (e.g., the 2008 credit crunch caused an increased cost in lending or quantitative easing resulted in a decreased cost in lending), term/tenor, covenants, seniority, embedded options, or other features underlying the loan agreement.

The arm's length interest rate is often determined by using the comparable uncontrolled price (CUP) method or by adopting other methods such as the build-up approach (discussed in more detail in section 4 of this chapter). This approach entails the use of a specific base rate adding an arm's length spread which comprises transaction-specific relevant risk factors. Relevant risk factors such as credit risk relate to the creditor, but they can also be identified in the indenture of the loan or note. The commencement for evaluating a loan transaction between related parties would be an analysis of the debtor's creditworthiness followed by an analysis of the contractual terms. Therefore, well-drafted and detailed intercompany agreements are essential for preparing and establishing arm's length terms and conditions.

Testing whether the borrowed amount of debt in an intragroup setting is considered at arm's length, i.e., whether the borrower could obtain similar funding from an independent lender, is done in accordance with the process followed by commercial independent banks. To determine whether a borrower has the capacity to meet its obligations under a loan, commercial independent banks consider several financial, operational, market, and economic factors affecting the borrower. A bank will establish the level of credit risk related to the transaction in question by using analytical methods and decide whether it will lend the requested amount to the borrower.

For transfer pricing purposes, replicating the screening process applied by commercial banks for concluding to a feasible extent whether a loan could be issued in an

14. OECD, *supra* note 4, para. 1.144.

intragroup context is preferable. Establishing whether a group entity could have obtained a certain amount of debt on a stand-alone basis from an external creditor is a multipronged analysis involving the following steps:

- business/industry analysis;
- operational risk assessment;
- financial statement analysis;
- cash flow analysis;
- forecast and probability measurement;
- credit scoring analysis; and
- comparables analysis.

The business analysis assists in understanding the relevant aspects of the company that could potentially affect its operating results and thus its capacity to repay the debt. One of the ways in which this analysis can be undertaken is through the top-down approach.

The first step begins with a macroeconomic perspective that concentrates on the economy (or economies) in which the company operates, foreign exchange market expectations, capital markets, the forecasted developments, and their impact on the corporation being analysed.

The second step focuses on the industry in which the company operates. Several aspects could affect the profitability of companies within a particular industry and whether such profit margins will continue to be earned or will vary in the future. Porter's five forces model is a basic tool for performing an industry analysis and is useful for this purpose.[15]

The third step of the top-down approach involves analysing the company itself, its business strategy, and whether it operates efficiently and productively; this should be reflected in the company's financials and forecasts. This could be performed, for example, with a SWOT[16] analysis.

Moreover, a financial analysis and modelling are required as part of the analysis. When methodically examining the company's financials, the process typically begins with the information recorded in the company's annual report, i.e., its balance sheet, income statement, and statement of cash flow. This should concentrate on the borrower's capacity to discharge its obligations under the loan agreement. These obligations are both short term (i.e., interest obligations) and long term in nature (i.e., principal repayment). Hence, the financial analysis should involve a comprehensive consideration of whether the borrower has the capacity to pay interest and is able to generate sufficient cash flow to repay the principal amount of the loan at maturity.

15. Michael E. Porter, *The Five Competitive Forces That Shape Strategy*, 86 Harvard Business Review 79–137 (January 2008).
16. Strengths, weaknesses, opportunities, and threats. *See* Mostafa Benzaghta et al., *SWOT Analysis Applications: An Integrative Literature Review*, 6 Journal of Global Business Insights 55–73 (March 2021).

2.3 Analysing the Creditworthiness of the Borrower

Considering the principles of rational loan pricing, there are generally two elements to an interest rate: (i) a base rate (e.g., the opportunity cost, often a risk-free rate such as the yield on high-rated government bonds in the market); and (ii) the credit spread or credit margin that remunerates the lender for the credit risk assumed. An important element of determining the relevant credit risk in a transaction is the borrower's credit rating.

Credit ratings are determined by means of qualitative measures, for example, the strategy of the company and the quality of its management, and quantitative measures, such as the liquidity and solvency ratios mentioned previously. The company's financials should be modelled to reflect the financial situation before and after the company enters into the loan transaction; i.e., the impact of the loan and related interest payments should be modelled. The primary advantage of determining credit ratings is the ease of comparing companies in the same industry with a similar credit standing.

The measure of creditworthiness (as represented by a qualitative credit rating to which a probability of default is attached based on the quantitative model used for the determination) is typically the most significant single determinant of the credit spread.

Traditionally, the usual approach for conducting a credit risk assessment in the context of the application of the arm's length principle was to assume that the borrower is a wholly independent enterprise. However, *General Electric Capital Canada Inc. v. Her Majesty The Queen*[17] (the *GE Capital* case) introduced a new facet to the analysis by de facto challenging this assumption. The argument proposed by the Canadian tax authorities (and partially accepted by the Tax Court of Canada) was that the default risk in a group is reduced as a parent would not allow a strategically important subsidiary to fail. Thus, this implies that the borrower's credit rating should be approximate to that of the parent instead of its rating on a stand-alone basis and inferring the existence of implicit support.

Should implicit support be considered?

Is taking into account implicit support consistent with the arm's length principle? The OECD TPG and the UN TPM appear to be clear (in both the OECD TPG, paragraphs 1.178 and 7.13 and the UN TPM, paragraph 2.5.5.3) in stating that incidental benefits from the passive association of integration should not hinder the application of the arm's length principle. In fact, benefits from such passive association without a deliberate concerted action of group members do not need to be separately compensated. Specific examples are also presented in the OECD TPG, paragraphs 1.184–1.187 and the UN TPM, paragraphs 2.5.5.5–2.5.5.8 that deal with group synergies in the context of intragroup loans. They explicitly address the concept of implicit support when assessing the credit ratings of borrowing entities within an MNE and the effect on the arm's length pricing of such intercompany loans.

---

17. *General Electric Capital Canada Inc v. Her Majesty The Queen*, para. 24.

The OECD and the UN provide additional guidance with respect to the notion of implicit support in the OECD TPG, Chapter X and the UN TPM, Chapter 9, respectively. The OECD's Chapter X, section C.1.1.3. and paragraphs 9.8.6–9.8.8. again highlight that an independent borrower would take into account the effect of group membership when considering the terms and conditions of an intercompany loan. Specifically, the OECD states in paragraph 10.78 that group support can have an impact on the credit rating of the borrowing entity. Additionally, the borrower's comparative status within the group may assist in assessing the amount of influence that the group support has on the borrower's credit rating. The likelihood of the borrower receiving group support depends on how important the borrower is to the group and how linked it is to its related parties.

Court Case

In the *GE Capital* case, GE Capital US (GECUS) provided its wholly owned subsidiary, GE Capital Canada (GECC), explicit guarantees for GECC's debt issuances. GECUS annually charged GECC a fee worth 1 % of the debt issuances' face amount. The dispute revolved around the question of whether the guarantee fee was at arm's length. The tax court judge, based on expert opinion, found that GECC's credit rating without the explicit guarantee would be, at most, 'BBB-' due to GECUS' implicit support. However, GECUS' credit rating of 'AAA' improved GECC's credit rating to 'AAA' through the extended guarantee. Therefore, the 1 % guarantee fee was found to be at arm's length. The federal court confirmed that implicit support is a significant factor for estimating arm's length compensation of guarantee fees. Comparing prices of loans without considering implicit support would fail to recognize all of the relevant economic circumstances of a controlled transaction.

On the one hand and following the *GE Capital* case, the concept of implicit support is a key element that is part of the transfer pricing analysis. On the other hand, following the *Chevron* case,[18] it has been evaluated as having little impact on market prices.

Court Case

In the *Chevron* case, a credit facility of USD 2.5 billion that Chevron Australia Holdings Pty Ltd (CAPHL) borrowed from its US-based affiliate, Chevron Texaco Funding Corporation (CTFC), comes to attention. This credit facility was unsecured, and CTFC borrowed money in USD at a rate of 1.2 %–2 % per annum from

18. *Chevron Australia Holdings Pty Ltd v. Commissioner of Taxation* (No. 4) [2015] FCA 1092 (23 October 2015).

independent parties. These rates were influenced by a credit guarantee provided by the parent company, Chevron Inc. Subsequently, CTFC loaned the borrowed funds to CAPHL at a 9% per annum rate. Chevron argued that the interest rate accounts for the exchange rate risk between the USD and AUD. The dispute revolved around the question of whether the interest paid by CTFC to CAPHL exceeded the arm's length price. The court disallowed the substantial deductions by CAPHL. A broad range of conditions should be considered for the assessment of arm's length pricing so that a lower arm's length interest rate would be accepted under similar circumstances. Chevron had not sufficiently substantiated the intragroup interest paid. Contrary to the *GE Capital* case, the parent's support without a legally binding explicit guarantee, also known as implicit support, had little impact on the price in this case.

The June 2022 Dutch Transfer Pricing Decree[19] stipulates that implicit support adjustments are to be taken into account for transfer pricing purposes particularly for intercompany guarantees. It is reasoned that affiliation is taken into account when establishing interest rates on loans or performing a credit rating assessment of a subsidiary by independent banks, financial service providers, and rating agencies. For instance, Standard & Poor's (S&P) distinguishes subsidiaries between core, highly strategic, strategically important, moderately strategic, and non-strategic;[20] thus, it should also be taken into account for transfer pricing purposes.

It is important to realize that it should not be assumed that a parent company would intervene and support a financially distressed subsidiary in the absence of a legally binding obligation to do so when considering an affiliation for determining a subsidiary's credit rating for transfer pricing purposes.

As stated by Moody's, it is possible that group support is not forthcoming even in situations when a borrowing subsidiary is strategically important to the parent unless it can be justified by convincing returns on incremental parental investments. This pattern can be observed in many big-ticket credit defaults that were backed only by comfort letters and verbal statements.[21]

Therefore, implicit support, i.e., support in the absence of legally enforceable support, should not be assumed; instead, its possibility should be evaluated by means of the parent's willingness and ability to support its subsidiary. The former might depend upon the commercial relationships between the parent and the subsidiary or the strategic ties between the two entities, the extent of management control, and the

19. Directoraat-generaal Fiscale Zaken, Directie Verbruiksbelastingen, Douane en Internationale Aangelegenheden, *Internationaal Belastingrecht. Verrekenprijzen, toepassing van het arm's-lengthbeginsel en de Transfer Pricing Guidelines for Multinational Enterprises and Tax Administrations (OESO-richtlijnen)*, nr. 2022-0000139020, Staatscourant 2022, nr. 16685 (June 2022).
20. S&P Global, *General Criteria: Group Rating Methodology* (December 2021).
21. Moody's Investor Service, *Rating Non-guaranteed Subsidiaries: Credit Considerations in Assigning Subsidiary Ratings in the Absence of Legally Binding Parent Support* 1 (December 2003).

business correlations, e.g., whether the subsidiary's success is important for the parent's performance.[22]

Evidence of a parent's support for its subsidiary should be taken into account, such as historic capital contributions. An instance of this can be seen in a 2009 rating action of Moody's in which the ratings of the subsidiaries of General Electric Capital Corporation (GECC) were set at par with the rating of GECC and General Electric (GE).[23] In the rating action, Moody's stated that its action was informed by its belief that the GE parent entity would continue providing unflinching support to GECC which could be inferred from GE's implicit and explicit actions, including equity infusions of USD 15 billion in the previous two quarters.

The question of whether implicit support should be taken into account for transfer pricing purposes or if it is in accordance with the arm's length principle will now be temporarily disregarded. If implicit support is indeed considered in a transfer pricing analysis, it can be concluded from the above discussion that any reference to implicit support being present within an MNE must be supported by a thorough assessment of the actual facts and circumstances of each particular case. Moreover, significantly, no specific guidance exists on how the above analysis on the parent's ability and willingness to support its subsidiary should be converted into an accurate adjustment of the subsidiary's stand-alone credit rating,[24] as a '[...] rating assignment is as much an art as it is a science'.[25]

An illustration and pragmatic approach to this statement is the notching process whereby the rating is notched up (or down) to account for qualitative factors, such as affiliation, beginning with an entity's stand-alone credit rating. It is a phenomenon in which a credit rating agency bumps the credit rating up or down on a borrower's specific debts or obligations. For instance, the benefit from affiliation could lead to a one- to three-notch adjustment. An extract of the group rating methodology as published by S&P for notching up (or down) the stand-alone credit rating of a borrower based on its strategic importance is provided in Table 2.1.

22. Additional considerations are provided in *supra* note 21; Fitch Ratings, *Parent and Subsidiary Linkage Rating Criteria* (December 2021).
23. Moody's Investor Service, *Rating Action: Moody's Downgrades GE and GECC to Aa2, Outlook Stable* (March 2009).
24. A. Tarassov and T. Tsiopoulos proposed a potential approach for making such an adjustment, at least for transfer pricing purposes, which was based on organizing the relevant considerations in 'scorecards' that would subsequently be employed to cluster the affiliates and attribute a score. *See* Andrei Tarassov & Thomas Tsiopoulos, *Transfer Pricing and the Halo Effect in Practice*, 20 Tax Management Transfer Pricing Report 846–852 (Bureau of National Affairs 2012).
25. Standard & Poor's, *Corporate Ratings Criteria* 1 (April 2008).

Table 2.1 Summary of Guidance Contained in the S&P Group Rating Methodology Paper

Group Status	*Brief Definition*	*Potential Issuer Credit Rating (ICR)*[26]
Core	Integral to the group's current identity and future strategy. The rest of the group is likely to support these entities under any foreseeable circumstances.	Group Credit Profile (GCP).
Highly strategic	Almost integral to the group's current identity and future strategy. The rest of the group is likely to support these group members under almost all foreseeable circumstances.	One notch lower than the GCP, unless the SACP on that entity is equal to, or higher than, the GCP. In such a case, the potential ICR is equal to the GCP.
Strategically important	Less integral to the group than 'highly strategic' group members. The rest of the group is likely to provide support in most foreseeable circumstances. However, some factors raise doubts about the extent of group support.	Three notches above SACP. This is subject to a cap of one notch below the GCP, unless the SACP is at least equal to the GCP, in which case the potential ICR is equal to the GCP.
Moderately strategic	Not important enough to warrant support from the rest of the group in some foreseeable circumstances. Nevertheless, there is potential for some support from the group.	One notch above SACP. This is subject to a cap of one notch below the GCP, unless the SACP is at least equal to the GCP, in which case, the potential ICR is equal to the GCP.
Non-strategic	No strategic importance to the group.	SACP, subject to a cap defined by the GCP.

Source: S&P, General Criteria: Group Rating Methodology, 14 December 2021.[27]

Risk and loan characteristics

Risk plays a significant role in debt contracting, and it must be determined whether the risk assumed in the intercompany transaction would be acceptable from an independent lender's perspective. Measures for risk control are applied by banks and can be

26. Which distinguishes it from the stand-alone credit profile (SACP).
27. Available at https://disclosure.spglobal.com/ratings/en/regulatory/article/-/view/sourceId/10999747.

observed directly in loan indentures, such as financial covenants, making them candidates to benchmark risk factors when observing transactions between unrelated parties in public financial transaction databases. Financial covenants indicate the maximum level of risk that the lending party is willing to assume in relation to the transaction. Financial covenants are generally identified as two types:

(1) *Negative covenants* impose limitations on the borrower, such as restrictions on asset sales, additional borrowing, or any loan that ranks senior to the current debt issuance.
(2) *Affirmative covenants* mandate that the borrower maintains certain financial ratios such as liquidity and solvency ratios in order to provide some form of assurance that it can fulfil its short-term and long-term obligations under the loan.

Failing to discharge its obligations under the covenants included in the loan agreements might effectuate a default and allow the lender to file for bankruptcy proceedings against the borrower.

It can be ascertained whether the amount of risk assumed in the intercompany transaction would be accepted in an unrelated setting by comparing the covenants included in the loan transactions between independent parties with those included in the intercompany loan agreement and the financial ratio of the company under review.

The price of the transaction must be determined following the positive assessment that an intercompany loan transaction would have been entered into at arm's length. To do so, it is essential to address how different risk factors such as credit risk, maturity, and seniority could affect the interest rate of the loan and to indicate the extent by which the risk factors influence the interest rate. Credit risk, for example, is a key element in determining the arm's length price. The borrower's default risk or probability of default is one of the three components embedded in credit risk; the other two are the credit spread risk and downgrade risk. An interest premium or spread that is connected to the debtor's probability of default is usually included in the interest rate in order to remunerate the lender for the assumed credit or default risk.

The creditworthiness of the debtor, which is often expressed with a credit rating, is quantified by the probability of default. Credit ratings are opinions issued by credit rating agencies on the creditworthiness of a company based on qualitative and quantitative analyses, and they are generally accepted as convenient tools for differentiating the companies' credit quality. Examples of prominent credit rating agencies include S&P, Moody's, and Fitch. Table 2.2 lists the various rating categories used by these agencies to express their opinion of a company's creditworthiness.

Table 2.2 Rating Categories of Credit Rating Agencies (Decrescent)

Investment grade	S&P	AAA	AA+	AA	AA–	A+	A	A–	BBB+	BBB	BBB–		
	Moody's	Aaa	Aa1	Aa2	Aa3	A1	A2	A3	Baa1	Baa2	Baa3		
	Fitch	AAA	AA+	AA	AA–	A+	A	A–	BBB+	BBB	BBB–		
Non-investment grade	S&P	BB+	BB	BB–	B+	B	B–	CCC+	CCC	CCC–	CC	C	D
	Moody's	Ba1	Ba2	Ba3	B1	B2	B3	Caa1	Caa2	Caa3	Ca	C	D
	Fitch	BB+	BB	BB–	B+	B	B–	CCC+	CCC	CCC–	CC	C	D

Source: S&P, *Guide to Credit Rating Essentials*, 2019;[28] Fitch Ratings, *Rating Definitions*, 2022;[29] and Moody's, *Rating Symbols and Definitions, 2022.*[30]

The highest rating of AAA (triple A) is the best one obtainable for which an entity is considered risk-free; i.e., the probability of default for securities with an AAA rating is almost zero. The risk of default increases; i.e., the creditworthiness depreciates, as an entity proceeds further down the credit rating scale.

Credit ratings can generally be clustered into three main categories:[31]

(1) investment grade: limited risk that includes rating categories from AAA to BBB–;
(2) speculative grade: risky that includes rating categories ranging from BB+ to B–;[32] and
(3) junk grade: very risky and includes all categories below B–.

The borrower's credit rating is a generally accepted indicator for its creditworthiness and therefore for the credit risk assumed by the lender. Official credit ratings are generally only available for MNE groups' parent companies. In practice, one of the parent's subsidiaries, not the parent itself, is the borrower in an intercompany loan agreement for which a stand-alone credit rating should ideally be established.[33] This

28. Available at https://www.spglobal.com/ratings/_division-assets/pdfs/guide_to_credit_rating_essentials_digital.pdf.
29. Available at https://www.fitchratings.com/research/structured-finance/rating-definitions-21-03-2022.
30. Available at https://www.moodys.com/researchdocumentcontentpage.aspx?docid=pbc_79004.
31. S&P, *Intro to Credit Ratings*, https://www.spglobal.com/ratings/en/about/intro-to-credit-ratings.
32. Some practitioners refer to the speculative grade as the non-investment grade.
33. In establishing the credit risk related to a specific debt instrument, any potential credit enhancement procedures that have occurred in relation to the loan, for example, by means of a parental guarantee or any collateral pledged, should also be considered.

could be determined, for example, by conducting a z-score analysis by using proprietary econometric credit scoring models licensed by the previously mentioned credit rating agencies or by employing scoring models established internally.[34]

Interplay of intercompany loans with other intragroup transactions

The UN TPM provides beneficial examples that stress the significance of taking into account the interaction between intercompany loans and other intragroup transactions.[35] According to it, financing arrangements and the commercial purposes of funding can be an indicator for identifying the functions and economic circumstances of an MNE. Additionally, other intragroup transactions for the transfer of property or services that may be supported by the financing arrangements can be delineated.

Even though the intragroup financial transaction under review may have been accurately distinguished and the interest rate for that transaction may have been determined to be at arm's length, that same transaction may reveal certain economically significant characteristics of the related parties. This can be useful for improving the comparability analysis for the purposes of assessing other intragroup transactions.

3 RECOGNITION OF THE ACCURATELY DELINEATED TRANSACTION

One of the most significant recent changes incorporated in the OECD TPG and the UN TPM is the introduction of the concept of the 'accurate delineation' of intragroup transactions. This concept was introduced in the OECD TPG' Chapter I and the UN TPM's Chapter 3 and essentially consists of a thorough analysis of the economic substance in an intragroup transaction. This process of recognizing the accurately delineated transaction goes beyond the contractual allocation of functions, assets, and risks between related parties by also examining their actual conduct in relation to the covered transaction.

With this process of accurate delineation, the intention is to arrive at the arm's length price of the actual substance of the intragroup transaction rather than engaging in an exercise in which the transfer price is based on the contractual terms of the intragroup transaction that may not be in accordance with the actual contributions of the related parties in the value creation.

Another important element introduced in the guidance on the accurate delineation of intragroup transactions is the approach for the allocation of risks. To allocate economically material risks to an entity in the context of an intragroup transaction, it should be assessed whether the respective party meets the following two thresholds:

34. A common approach to establishing a credit rating for a related party borrower is to use a credit rating agency's (probability of default) econometric models such as Moody's RiskCalc™ or S&P's equivalent CreditModel,™ based on the borrower's stand-alone historical (or modelled) financial data. The resulting credit rating is then used to identify spreads charged on market transactions involving similarly rated debt.
35. United Nations, *supra* note 5, para. 9.12.3.

(1) if it has the financial capacity to assume the risk which can be described as having access to funding to take on the risk and bear its consequences should the risk materialize; and
(2) if it 'controls' the risk which can be described as having the capability to perform and actually performs decision-making in relation to taking on or not assuming the risk, its management, and its mitigation.

The guidance found in the OECD TPG' Chapter I in relation to the accurate delineation of intragroup transactions is general and applied to intragroup financing transactions. The guidance for these as included in the OECD TPG further tailors this concept specifically in the context of intragroup financing transactions.

3.1 Specific Guidance on the Accurate Delineation of Intragroup Financing Transactions

The OECD TPG Chapter X, section B.1. and the UN TPM paragraph 9.7 deal with determining whether an intragroup financing transaction characterized by the taxpayer as a loan should be regarded as a loan and the circumstances in which intragroup financing transactions may be recharacterized. Section B.1. begins by noting that it is possible that a borrower's debt-equity mix that belongs to an MNE group is different from that of an independent entity in the same or similar situation. This may consequently have an impact on the amount of interest to be paid by the borrower and its tax base in a certain tax jurisdiction.[36]

It is notable that the Commentary on Article 9 of the OECD Model Tax Convention (which enshrines the arm's length principle) states that the provisions of Article 9 are relevant not only for determining if the interest rate in an intragroup loan is at arm's length. They are also pertinent for ascertaining whether it is apparent that such a transaction's characterization as a loan should be respected in the first place or if it should be distinguished as some other type of payment (like an infusion of equity).[37]

However, the proposed change to the Commentary on Article 9 of the OECD Model Tax Convention (as included in the discussion draft released by the OECD as a public consultation document)[38] replaces this guidance and instead indicates that a state may need to examine if the characterization of a loan should be accepted as such. Alternatively, it questions if it should be recharacterized as some other type of payment, taking into account not only the OECD TPG but also factors discussed in its domestic laws (including doctrines developed through case law).

Thus, it can be inferred from the above that the accurate delineation of the transaction might indicate that a portion (or all) of the loan transaction may need to be recharacterized (e.g., as an infusion of equity capital) prior to applying the arm's length

36. OECD, *supra* note 4, para. 10.4.
37. OECD, *Model Tax Convention on Income and on Capital 2017* (OECD Publishing 2019), Article 9(3)(b).
38. *See* OECD, *Proposed Changes to Commentaries in the OECD Model Tax Convention on Article 9 and on Related Articles: Public Consultation Document* (March 2021).

principle for determining the appropriate rate of interest in an intragroup loan transaction.

This is also in accordance with the general discussion on disregarding an intercompany transaction by the tax authorities under the OECD TPG, Chapter I, section D.2. which stipulates that the tax authorities would be empowered to disregard an intercompany transaction in the form entered into by related parties. This requires a set of circumstances in which the arrangements made in relation to the transaction that are viewed in their totality differ from those that would have been adopted by independent enterprises behaving in a commercially rational manner in comparable circumstances.

The OECD TPG provide specific guidance on the set of circumstances in which an advance of funds may be recharacterized.[39] Furthermore, the UN TPM, paragraph 9.7.2 provides a few hypothetical examples of when an intercompany advance of funds may be made. Additionally, it illustrates when a transaction may end up being disregarded or recharacterized after evaluating features such as the contractual terms of the transaction, the price for obtaining the financing, repayment obligations or the presence of collateral or other security. The analytical process would begin with an accurate delineation of the intragroup financing transaction and, depending on the facts and circumstances, the following economically relevant characteristics may be useful indicators for concluding whether recharacterization is warranted:[40]

- presence or absence of a fixed repayment date;
- obligation to pay interest;
- right to enforce the payment of principal and interest;
- the funder's status in comparison to regular corporate creditors;
- existence of financial covenants and security;
- source of interest payments;
- ability of the recipient of the funds to obtain loans from unrelated lending institutions;
- extent to which the advance is used to acquire capital assets; and
- failure of the purported debtor to repay on the due date or seek a postponement.

Example

An entity (Company A) receives funding from a related party (Company B) that is contractually termed as a loan. An examination of the facts and economically relevant circumstances, however, indicates the following:

- No penalties are attached to the late payment/non-payment of interest by Company A.

39. OECD, *supra* note 4, Ch. X section B.1.
40. *Ibid.*, para. 10.12.

- Company A does not provide any financial covenant or security within the terms of the loan agreement.
- Company A receives multiple postponements granted by Company B with regard to the due date of the repayment.

Based on the above, a sufficient number of elements may be present to conclude that the entire (or part of the) loan transaction may actually be recharacterized as an infusion of equity capital.

However, while providing this particular guidance on the circumstances in which a loan transaction may be characterized as something else by following the approach of the accurate delineation of the transaction, the OECD TPG also promptly note that it is the individual tax jurisdictions' responsibility to determine alternative approaches to the recharacterization of intragroup financing transactions. An example would be a thin capitalization regime that employs a fixed debt-to-equity ratio.

3.2 Case Study on the Recharacterization of an Intercompany Loan Transaction

To put the theoretical guidance into perspective, a case study is presented in the section below that provides an example of the potential recharacterization of financing transactions.

Example

Company A provides funds to an affiliated party, Company B, in the form of a EUR 2.5 billion revolving credit facility (RCF) arrangement. The RCF, with a total amount of EUR 2.5 billion and a maturity of five years, yields an interest margin of 250 basis points (or bps). After five years, the amount drawn under the RCF sums up to EUR 2.2 billion. It is being renewed due to an inability to repay it and now has a maturity of three years and a maximum amount of EUR 3 billion. At the beginning of the sixth year, the amount drawn under the RCF increased to EUR 2.7 billion.

The RCF under review may instigate a dispute with the tax authorities as the adjustments made to the RCF might not be in accordance with the arm's length principle. Specifically, the tax authorities could challenge the following:

(1) The actual tenor of the RCF: Notwithstanding the contractual three-year maturity of the RCF and the subsequently renewed RCF, the actual maturity of the transaction is eight years.

(2) The pricing of the loan: In accordance with the extension of the maturity, a corresponding increase in the pricing of the RCF should be made.

(3) In the case at hand, the amounts borrowed under the RCF never went below a base amount of EUR 2.2 billion which implies that the transaction was never (fully) repaid and could be regarded as support for the conclusions outlined above.

4 SELECTION OF THE MOST APPROPRIATE TRANSFER PRICING METHOD

Once the commercial and financial relations between the parties to the intercompany loan have been identified and the loan transaction has been accurately delineated and recognized, the next step in the process of pricing an intercompany loan transaction at an arm's length basis is the selection of the most appropriate transfer pricing method. In practice, these are often considered in the context of intragroup financing arrangements and are discussed in the following.[41]

CUP method

The CUP method is often used in the context of intragroup financing transactions due to the widespread existence of financial markets for borrowing and lending, the frequent occurrence of such transactions between independent parties, and the widespread availability of information on the loan market. A number of financial databases such as Bloomberg and Refinitiv's Loan Connector provide a wealth of information on the various terms and conditions being applied in loan transactions occurring on the market.

The CUP method utilizes comparable market prices for the tested intercompany loan based on internal comparables. It will make reference to similar transactions between one of the parties to the controlled transaction and an unrelated party. Adversely, it will analyse similar transactions between a company of the same MNE and unrelated companies engaging in similar transactions under similar circumstances. To apply the CUP method, the availability of both internal and external CUPs should be investigated (as discussed in more detail in section 5 of this chapter).

Cost of funds approach

As an alternative to comparable uncontrolled loan transactions, data based on spreads on corporate bonds with similar credit ratings are often used. Here, characteristics apart from credit risk and maturity need to be priced independently. This is often referred to as the build-up approach.

As a drawback, as typical analyses using bond data are conducted based on indices and not individual bonds, they are often imprecise or insufficiently accurate regarding

41. For a comprehensive overview of the various transfer pricing methods that can be considered for intragroup financing arrangements, *see Ibid.*, Ch. X section C.1.2; United Nations, *supra* note 5, Ch. 9 section 9.10.

the date of the transactions, amount, seniority, additional fees, covenants, penalties, embedded options (such as call, put, and conversion), securities, and collaterals, among others.

Apart from employing the CUP method and in a situation in which comparable uncontrolled transactions cannot be identified (thus resulting in an inability to reliably apply the CUP method), another approach to determine the arm's length interest for the intercompany loan transaction is the cost of funds for the creditor with a proper mark-up/interest spread. Essentially, the cost of funds relates to the borrowing costs that the creditor incurs (either externally or internally borrowed) in raising money which is thereafter lent onward within the MNE as an intercompany loan. The cost base would also include other related expenses incurred in the process of securing the loan (e.g., up-front fee, commitment fee, success fee, annual fee) to which a mark-up is to be added that is usually based on a return on equity approach.

Other components (or building blocks) may need to be considered in pricing an interest rate such as:

- a premium for (il)liquidity (bonds versus loans);
- a country risk premium;
- a premium or discount for security/collateral;
- convertibility;
- embedded options;
- term of the loan;
- fixed versus floating interest rate type;
- revolving versus term loan; and
- other fees charged by lenders at arm's length.

Furthermore, adjustments may be required, for example, for currency risk, especially considering that most publicly available information refers to EUR- or USD-denominated markets.

Economic modelling

In other cases, it may be appropriate to rely on economic models to construct an arm's length interest rate applicable to intragroup loans. Typically, these calculate the arm's length interest rate by considering the applicable risk-free rate (i.e., currency-specific) combined with certain premiums for identified risk components (e.g., credit risk, maturity, and subordination) of the intragroup loan under review.

Court Case

In the *Lender Société*[42] case, the taxpayer required financing EUR 26 million for the acquisition of real estate. The acquisition was financed through a shareholder loan of EUR 6 million at 12% interest per annum and a bank loan of EUR 20

42. *Luxembourg v. Lender Société*, No. 42043C (Administrative Court 17 July 2019).

million. The dispute revolved around the arm's length price of the shareholder loan as tax authorities in Luxembourg considered 12% per annum as excessive. The shareholder loan was unsecured and was not guaranteed with collateral. The shareholder loan that had been provided by a sole shareholder was justified by two transfer pricing reports. One report used the CUP method, while the other used the capital asset pricing model. Tax authorities, however, conducted their own analysis which produced an arm's length price of 3%. The court confirmed this number and classified the excessive 9% interest as a hidden profit distribution.

Safe harbours

The UN TPM acknowledges that certain jurisdictions have introduced transfer pricing safe harbours of which the majority are concerning interest rates for intercompany loans.[43] Some jurisdictions issue official interest rates every year that apply to intercompany loans that eliminate the taxpayers' obligation to prove that the remuneration for such transactions is at arm's length. At the same time, they provide some comfort that the intercompany rate will not pose a risk of base erosion. Similar simplifications for the purposes of the credit rating are stipulated and seek to rely on the group rating under certain conditions.[44]

Court Case

In a Finnish case,[45] a loan from a third party with interest equalling approximately 3% per annum came to the court's attention. However, the interest that the concerned parties had set for this intragroup loans was set at 9.5%. This figure was based on the calculated average group interest rate of all of the loans taken by all of the companies within the group, from third parties, and the concerned shareholders. The supreme administrative court established that this practice is not acceptable because financing can be obtained from a non-related party at a substantially lower rate. As a result, the excess interest above 3% was considered hidden profit distribution, and it was declared non-deductible.

In the following section, the focus is on the practical application of the CUP method for determining the arm's length pricing of intercompany loan transactions.

5 APPLICATION OF THE SELECTED TRANSFER PRICING METHOD

As discussed in the previous sections, the analysis of the facts and circumstances of a typical intercompany loan transaction generally leads to selecting the CUP method as the most appropriate transfer pricing method for determining the arm's length interest

43. United Nations, *supra* note 5, para. 9.11.1.
44. *Ibid.*, para. 9.11.2.
45. Supreme Administrative Court KHO:2010:73 (Finland).

rate of an intercompany loan transaction. Market data on a transactional basis is scarce, which is unlike other types of commonly occurring intercompany transactions (such as the provision of services or the sale of tangible goods). However, the widespread occurrence of borrowing and lending transactions in the global financial markets together with the information collected therefrom facilitates the application of the CUP method to financial transactions.

In most cases, this consists of a comparability analysis followed by evaluating and identifying potential internal comparable transactions. If those that are ascertained are not sufficiently comparable to the tested controlled transaction, economically reliable comparability adjustments might be required. In the event that no internal comparable transactions can be identified or when it is not possible to apply reliable economic adjustments to address differences in comparability, external comparable loan transactions should be identified using appropriate databases and applying reliable comparability adjustments when necessary.

The application of the CUP method will be discussed and illustrated with a case study that follows the typical steps in the analysis of intercompany loans. Although the names, jurisdictions, and the case itself are fictitious examples, the factual pattern and considerations below are a realistic representation of a typical MNE dealing with intercompany financing transactions.

5.1 Case Study: Intercompany Loans

Example

Cargo N.V. (CNV NL) is the parent company of a Dutch multinational group (*Group*) that is a prominent player in the car manufacturing industry. CNV NL is a publicly listed company, and it has been rated 'A' by a globally recognized credit rating agency. Apart from being the parent entity, CNV NL also serves as the treasury centre of the Group for which it ensures that its entities are sufficiently liquid.

One of the subsidiaries of CNV NL is Cargo Deutschland Manufacturing GmbH (CDM) based in Germany. It operates a small production facility (under a contract manufacturing basis), and it is one of the manufacturers of an incipient line of automobiles launched by the Group to fulfil a long-term market penetration strategy. CDM requires working capital funding for its operational activities. On 1 January 2022, CNV NL agreed to provide an intercompany subordinated unsecured loan to CDM for EUR 500 million for a fixed period of five years. Throughout the loan, CNV NL will charge a floating interest rate indexed to the three-month Euro Overnight Index Average (EONIA) plus an arm's length margin based on a transfer pricing analysis.

It is determined that CDM would be rated BBB for this transaction based on the analysis of CDM's historic and recent financial performance as well as CDM's relative strategic importance within the Group.

In addition, after evaluating CDM's business plans and financial forecasts, it is expected that it has sufficient financial capacity to: (i) continue serving all pre-existing liabilities and (ii) be able to repay the loan granted by CNV NL. Furthermore, the Group has confirmed with external banks that third parties would be willing to offer CDM funding for working capital requirements under broadly similar terms and conditions as these are considered standard for the industry. It was thus concluded by CNV NL that the intended intercompany transaction could be accurately delineated as a loan based on all of the above.

CNV NL has identified a potentially comparable transaction that could be used in the transfer pricing analysis of the intercompany loan provided to CDM. On 30 November 2021, CDM borrowed a sum of EUR 800 million from a third-party bank for general corporate purposes (including working capital). It was granted the loan for a period of seven years with a floating interest rate indexed to the three-month EONIA plus a margin of 150 bps; it had a senior rank, and no collateral secured it.

Step 1: Identify the key terms and conditions of the analysed intercompany transaction

As indicated in previous sections of this chapter, the first step in applying the comparability analysis involves establishing the economically relevant characteristics or comparability factors of the financial transactions. For that purpose, it is useful to identify the key terms and conditions of the analysed intercompany transaction as these provide relevant information for selecting comparable transactions. In that context, Table 2.3 summarizes the key terms and conditions of the intercompany loan between CNV NL and CDM.

Table 2.3 Key Terms and Conditions of the Intercompany Loan Between CNV NL and CDM

Concept	*Terms and Conditions*
Effective date:	1 January 2022
Creditor:	CNV NL
Debtor:	CDM
Principal amount:	500 million
Currency:	EUR
Maturity of the loan:	1 January 2027
Purpose:	General corporate purpose (working capital)
Ranking:	Subordinated unsecured
Interest rate:	Floating, 3M EONIA plus arm's length spread

In an arm's length situation, interest rates are dependent on a number of different factors. The risk-return trade-off concept in economics describes the relationship between the expected return and the assumption of risk. In the context of loan transactions, the features of a loan that increase the lender's exposure to risk (such as a financially disadvantaged borrower's creditworthiness, long-maturity debt instruments, or the lack of collateral and guarantees) tend to increase the expected return that the investor would require to enter into the transaction and, therefore, the interest rate charged in a loan transaction. Conversely, features that limit the lender's risk (including the existence of collateral or restrictions on the borrower's future behaviour) tend to result in a lower interest rate.

Ceteris paribus, the impact on risk exposure and interest rates upon changes in the characteristics of a loan is not equal across the different features of a loan. For example, those such as the borrower's credit rating or the purpose, maturity, and ranking of the loan tend to have a greater influence on the level of interest rate than (for example) the principal amount, the frequency at which interest payments are made, or the amortization schedule.

Court Case

In the *Diligentia* case,[46] a parent company of a firm that operates in the real estate industry. After a takeover of the enterprise by another group, external loans in Diligentia were replaced with intragroup loans from the new parent, Skandia Liv. Before this, the average interest rate of the loans was 4.5%; however, the new loans were set at an interest rate of 9.5% per annum. The dispute revolves around the arm's length interest levels as Swedish tax authorities opined that 9.5% was excessive and regarded the additional interest as dividends. The supreme administrative court stated that different conditions apply when a parent grants a loan to its subsidiary. In contrast to a parent, an external lender has limited insight into the borrower. The loan, in this case, has an arm's length interest that is lower than would be the case for the same agreement between independent parties. The credit risk for a parent is less than that of an external lender. Therefore, the 9.5% charged by the parent was deemed excessive, and the interest rate was set at 6.5%.

Court Case

In the recent *A Oyj* case,[47] the parent of A-group, A Oyj, borrowed an amount from a third independent party. The funds from this loan were subsequently borrowed by B Oy from its parent, A Oyj. After the second loan, the funds were

46. *Sweden v. Diligentia AB*, No. 2483-2485-09 (Regeringsrätten 28 June 2010).
47. Korkein hallinto-oikeus [KHO] 21.5.2021 KHO:2021:66 (Finland).

again lent out from D Oyj to its own subsidiary in Russia, ZAO C. The interest rate that B Oy charged its daughter company was based on A Oyj's average margin of external financing plus 10%. Finnish tax authorities disagreed with the charged interest. The authorities proposed to take the separate entity principle and ZAO C's credit rating into account. The resulting interest was higher than what was charged in the case after which the difference was added to B Oy's taxable income. The Supreme Court overturned an earlier decision handed down by the administrative court and ruled in favour of A Oyj. It stated that ZAO C had received intragroup services in the form of financing from A Oyj through B Oy. The arm's length interest was based on the cost-plus pricing method and was considered as the most appropriate transfer pricing method that could be derived by taking the costs incurred by the Finnish companies in obtaining the financing. ZAO C benefitted from the creditworthiness of the group. The tax adjustments by the tax authorities were annulled.

While some of the comparability factors have an appreciable effect on the price, transfer pricing analysts usually rely on financial theory to devise techniques to adjust comparability differences that might have a substantial influence on the price of a transaction. The following section illustrates the typical process of the comparability analysis and how financial theory is applied as the analytical framework for devising adjustments as part of the application of the CUP method once potentially comparable transactions have been identified.

Step 2: Identify internal potentially comparable transactions and apply reliable economic adjustments to address the differences in comparability

This step consists of identifying potentially comparable transactions and applying reliable economic adjustments. For the application of the CUP method, the availability of both internal and external CUPs should be investigated. The CUP method is based on internal comparables and utilizes comparable market prices for a tested intercompany loan. It considers similar transactions between one of the parties to the controlled transaction and an unrelated party or those between a company of the same MNE and unrelated companies engaging in them under similar circumstances.

Commonly, the availability of internal comparables is first investigated in the application of the CUP method to intercompany loans as this information is usually readily available to the MNE group. In some instances, internal comparables may provide information that is more complete and reliable than external comparables for assessing comparability in relation to the transaction under review.

The main terms and conditions of: (i) the analysed intercompany loan between CNV NL and CDM and (ii) the third-party bank loan identified by the Group as a potential internal comparable are summarized in Table 2.4.

Table 2.4 Comparison of the Terms and Conditions Between the Loan and a Comparable Transaction

Concept	*Terms and Conditions of the Intercompany Loan*	*Terms and Conditions of the Third-Party Bank Loan*
Effective date	1 January 2022	30 November 2021
Creditor	CNV NL	Third-party bank
Debtor	CDM	CDM
Principal amount	500 million	800 million
Currency	EUR	EUR
Maturity of the loan	1 January 2027 (five years)	30 November 2028 (seven years)
Purpose	General corporate purpose (working capital)	General corporate purpose (working capital)
Ranking	Subordinated unsecured	Senior unsecured
Interest rate	Floating, 3M EONIA plus arm's length spread	Floating, 3M EONIA plus 150 bps

The comparability analysis of these loans can be summarized as follows.

Effective Date

The analysed intercompany loan and the identified potentially comparable uncontrolled transaction were both entered into around the same period, i.e., between the end of the calendar year 2021 and the beginning of the calendar year 2022. CNV NL and CDM have concluded that no material macroeconomic volatility in the region or the financial markets was observed between 30 November 2021 and 1 January 2022. This would include things that could have had a material effect on the prevailing market interest rates at the time the third-party bank loan was granted and the time the intercompany loan was activated. In the case at hand, it can be considered that, although minor differences are observed in the effective date of the analysed transaction and the identified potential comparable transaction, these minor differences do not exert a material difference in pricing. Thus, no economic adjustments are required.

In practice, transfer pricing analysts assess whether the macroeconomic circumstances at the time the analysed intercompany transaction was put in place are not materially different from those prevailing at the time that the identification of the potential comparable was performed. In this context, it is generally considered that comparable transactions that occurred closer to the time of the analysed intercompany loan are more reliable comparables.

Principal Amount

The principal amount of the identified potentially comparable uncontrolled transaction is higher than the amount borrowed by CNV NL from the intercompany loan.

The tolerance range of principal amounts that can be reasonably considered comparable for the purposes of the application of the CUP method is not a standard metric but is subject to a prudent assessment of the facts and circumstances of the transaction. The analysis will primarily depend on the sensitivity of the level of the interest rate of the loan upon the changes in the principal amount, the availability of comparable data, and the availability of sufficient data to apply reliable economic adjustments.

Because of this, for the application of the CUP method, transfer pricing analysts are generally willing to accept reasonable differences in the principal amount in potentially comparable transactions without applying further adjustments.

In the case at hand, it is considered that the variance in the principal amount between the internal comparable and the analysed transaction does not lead to a material difference in the pricing of the transaction; thus, no economic adjustments are required.

Maturity or Tenor

There are differences between the maturity of the identified potentially comparable uncontrolled transaction and the maturity of the loan between CDM and CNV NL.

The maturity or tenor of a loan has an appreciable effect on the price. To analyse the effect of maturity on the arm's length interest rate, yield curves can be referenced which are indicative of the required yield on a debt instrument for different maturities. Usually, the required yield is positively correlated with maturity. Thus, it increases when the maturity of the debt instrument does the same. Figure 2.1 represents the yield curve observed for the EUR Corporate Bond BBB Index and outlines the simultaneous rise in required return and the tenor of the debt security.

Figure 2.1 Yield on EUR-Denominated Industrial Bonds Rated BBB

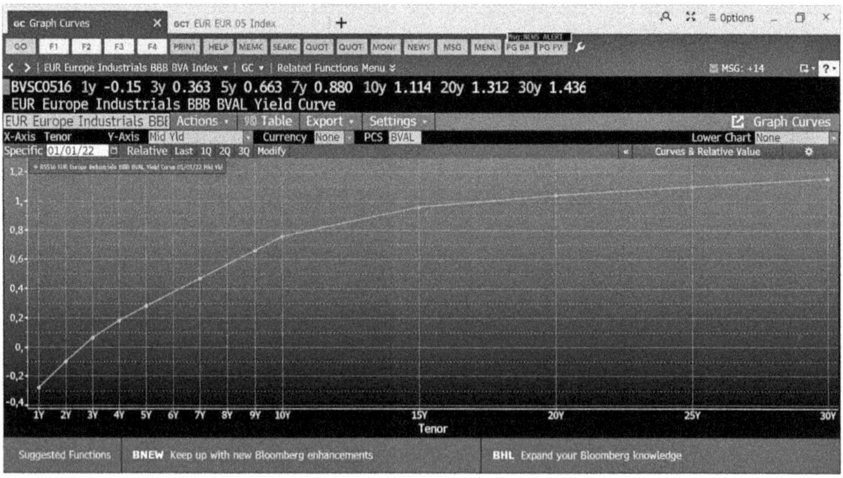

Source: Screenshot of Bloomberg Professional Services database.

According to the liquidity preference theory, the slope of the above yield curve is understood as the premium demanded by investors to allocated resources in long-term instruments as the risk increases when doing so. Hence, a risk-averse investor would require a higher return on long-term investments in order to compensate for the additional risks assumed in the transaction. The maturity premium, however, should also remunerate the investor for the resulting illiquidity by entering into investments, such as loans, with a longer tenor.

Practitioners rely on this financial theory for the application of comparability adjustments in the context of the CUP method. In this circumstance, maturity adjustments are often performed using the spread between yields observed in bond issuances with maturities equal to those agreed in the potentially comparable loans and the yield of bonds issued with a maturity equivalent to that of the analysed intercompany transaction. For the purposes of the example in this chapter, following standard practices, a EUR-denominated industrial bond index comprising issuances rated BBB has been selected that matches the characteristics of the analysed intercompany loan. The term structure of this index is shown in Figure 2.2.

Figure 2.2 Term Structure of EUR-Denominated Industrial Bonds Rated BBB as of 1 January 2022

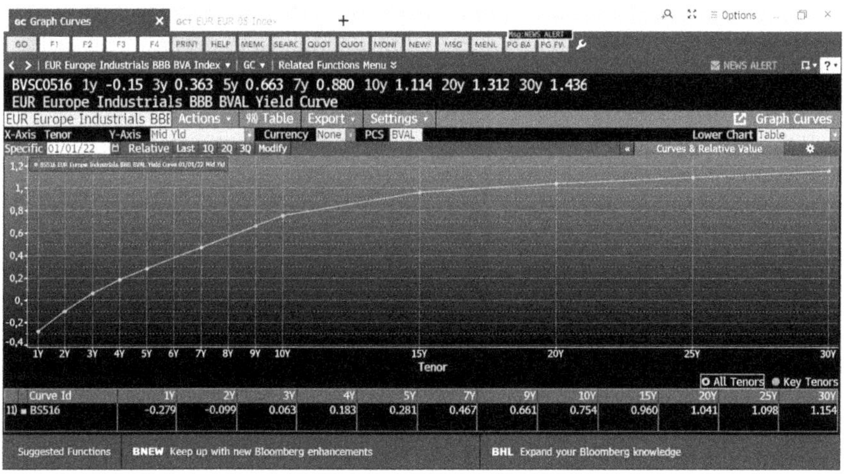

Source: Screenshot of Bloomberg Professional Services database.

The identified yield spread, i.e., the difference between the five-year and seven-year term rates of the yield curves, is considered the additional spread required by investors for allocating resources to a security with a seven-year maturity compared to the analysed intercompany transaction that has a maturity of five years. It is therefore considered that, based on data as of 1 January 2022, the identified comparable transaction embeds a premium of 18.6 bps (i.e., 28.1 bps to 46.7 bps) which should be deducted from the unadjusted rate to neutralize the effect on pricing due to differences in maturity.[48]

After applying this comparability adjustment, the modified arm's length rate of the comparable loan is 3M EONIA plus 131.4 bps (i.e., original unadjusted rate of 3M EONIA, plus 150 bps, minus the maturity premium of 18.6 bps).

Ranking

As identified earlier, the ranking of the analysed transactions is different. The intercompany loan was issued with a subordinated ranking, while the identified comparable transaction has a senior ranking. Both transactions are unsecured. The applied seniority or ranking of a loan or note, i.e., whether it is subordinated or a senior instrument, has a noticeable effect on the required rate of return demanded by the lender.

Seniority refers to the order of repayment of the different debt instruments in the event of the bankruptcy of the debtor. Typically, secured and senior debt must be repaid before subordinated debt (which is repaid prior to the equity owners). Thus, the level of credit risk assumed (and, correspondingly, the required return) in relation to subordinated debt instruments is higher.

Thus, it is essential to set a specific rating for the debt instrument under review by reference to the credit rating assigned to the borrower and subsequent adjustments for different default frequencies that are witnessed between various debt instruments to properly reflect the credit risk assumed by the creditor. Debt default frequencies are usually assumed equally across all of the borrower's debt instruments, i.e., reflecting the company's overall credit rating. However, if the company's debt instruments have different default frequencies, then these should also be taken into account in estimating the rating to be assigned to a specific debt instrument.

To quantify this risk differential among debt seniority classes, assessing differences in expected default frequencies and loss severities among debt seniority classes of companies in different credit rating categories is useful. The comparative differences in expected loss severities of specific debt instruments might require a different rating to be assigned to such instrument depending on the magnitude to appropriately reflect the credit risk (expected loss rate) assumed in relation thereto.

To determine a debt-specific rating, the difference in loss severity of the different seniority classes is compared with that of a benchmark rating, e.g., senior unsecured instruments carrying a rating equal to that of the debtor. This analysis justifies either an upward or downward rating notch.

For instance, on average, subordinated bonds recover less than senior unsecured bonds. Thus, to evaluate the proper level of credit risk assumed, a downward adjustment of the credit rating is justified. In practice, based on general guidance issued

48. For the purposes of this example and for illustrative purposes, the authors have used a single market data point applicable to the date of the transaction to determine the arm's length maturity risk premium. In practice, it is common to apply time series and statistical analyses to arrive at a range of market premiums based on historical data available around the period of time of the analysed transaction.

by renowned credit rating agencies, these types of adjustments consist of a downward one-notch adjustment of the credit rating of the instrument to account for the additional risk assumed in a subordinated loan compared to a senior loan. The downward notching adjustment might be larger for deeply subordinated instruments (i.e., up to two notches).

To quantify the effect on the interest rate of the loan due to differences in ranking, transfer pricing analysts usually rely on bond yield data to devise transfer pricing adjustments in the context of the CUP method. For the purposes of the example in this chapter, following standard practices, we have identified the spread between the yield of five-year EUR-denominated industrial bonds rated BBB and five-year EUR-denominated industrial bonds rated BBB–. It quantifies the additional premium embedded in the subordinated loan with respect to the senior loan.

The spread between the two yields is illustrated in Figure 2.3.

Figure 2.3 Daily Historical Yields Observed in Five-Year Tenor EUR-Denominated Industrial Bonds Rated BBB and BBB– Between 1 January 2021 and 1 January 2022

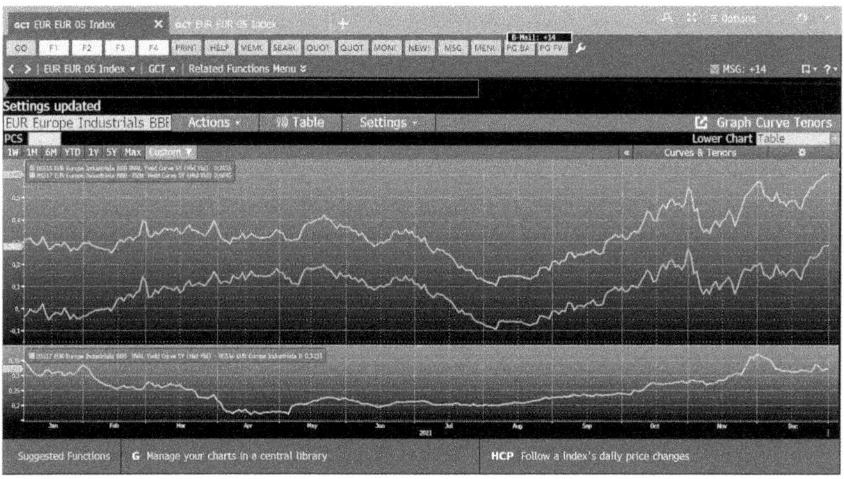

Source: Screenshot of Bloomberg Professional Services database.

The identified yield spread, i.e., the difference between the BBB and the BBB– rated bonds (the bottom line in Figure 2.3), is considered the additional spread required to assume the extra risk embedded in a subordinated loan compared to a senior loan. Therefore, it is considered that the identified comparable transaction (i.e., senior loan) should include an additional premium of 32.31 bps (i.e., 60.45 bps minus 28.15 bps, the difference between the BBB and the BBB– rated bonds as of 1 January 2022) that should be added to the previously determined rate to neutralize the effect on pricing due to differences in ranking.[49] After applying this comparability adjustment, the fully

49. For the purposes of this example and for illustrative purposes, the authors have used a single market data point applicable to the date of the transaction to determine the arm's length

adjusted arm's length rate of the comparable loan is 3M EONIA plus 163.71 bps (i.e., maturity-adjusted rate: 3M EONIA plus 131.4 bps, plus a ranking premium of 32.31 bps).

Step 3: Identify external comparable transactions and apply reliable economic adjustments to address the differences in comparability

It can occur that no internal comparable transactions are carried out by the MNE with unrelated parties or that a transaction between a member of the MNE and an independent party can be regarded as a reliable comparable. In those cases, the identification of comparable transactions would be based on external transactions, i.e., market transactions between two (or more) unrelated parties outside of the MNE group of companies.

Having already performed the comparability analysis, this step begins with the established macroeconomic factors to set up a search strategy, including the market circumstances around the time the loan is entered into, the country where the borrower is located as well as the currency and maturity of the loan. Furthermore, where possible, it could be considered to screen for the specific industry in which the borrower operates. To take into account the creditworthiness of the borrower in the analysis, screening should be performed for companies with a similar credit rating as the tested company.

The resulting comparables can be further narrowed down by restricting the comparables set based on features that are deemed non-comparable. Based on this general strategy, a set of transactions that have characteristics similar to the intercompany transaction that is being reviewed for transfer pricing purposes can be identified. If differences in comparability arise, similar approaches to those described in the previous section would be generally applied.

6 KEY TAKEAWAYS FOR PRACTITIONERS WHEN ASSESSING INTRAGROUP LOANS

From the guidance contained in Chapter X of the OECD TPG and UN TP Manual, the following key takeaways can be distilled for practitioners with respect to the accurate delineation of intragroup loans and subsequent selection and application of the appropriate transfer pricing method:

(1) *Accurate delineation*: The terms and conditions of intragroup loans should be aligned with the intent of the parties and the purpose of the transaction. The latter should be in accordance with the financing needs of the respective borrower and properly documented in the transfer pricing documentation.
(2) *Consideration of options realistically available*: When structuring new (or reviewing existing) intragroup loan transactions, the options realistically

maturity risk premium. In practice, it is common to apply time series and statistical analyses to arrive at a range of market premiums based on historical data available around the time of the analysed transaction.

available to both parties involved (e.g., lender and borrower) should be considered. If any of the parties involved has a realistic alternative option that would result in a better outcome (e.g., a lower interest rate for a borrower), this fact should be taken into account when performing the transfer pricing analysis.

(3) *Control over risk and financial capacity*: A functional analysis should be performed in order to determine whether the lender has sufficient substance to allocate the relevant risks and subsequent returns of the intragroup loan. In practice, a lack of substance could create a risk of the transaction's recharacterization (i.e., reallocating returns to the entity ultimately assuming and controlling the relevant risks). Furthermore, the delineation of intragroup transactions should also take into account the financial capacity of the borrower, e.g., through a debt capacity analysis.

(4) *Documenting the intent and actual conduct*: The intent and actual conduct of the parties should be reviewed and documented closely when assessing the delineation of intragroup financing transactions. Whereas the intent should be clearly documented in the contractual arrangement between the borrower and the lender, the actual conduct should be reviewed on a continuous basis. Differences between the intent and actual conduct of the parties involved in the intragroup loan transaction may create a risk of recharacterization of the transaction by local tax authorities.

(5) *TP method selection and application*: In practice, the CUP method is most commonly applied for determining arm's length pricing for intragroup loans. This follows from the widespread occurrence of borrowing and lending transactions in the global financial markets and data available on these transactions in publicly available data sources.

CHAPTER 3

Financial Guarantees

Andrew Hickman & Marcelo H. B. Moura

1 INTRODUCTION TO FINANCIAL GUARANTEES

1.1 Definition

This chapter discusses the transfer pricing aspects of intra-group financial guarantees. The term refers to an undertaking by one member of a controlled MNE group to stand behind the obligation of another member of the MNE group in relation to a financial transaction with another party that is commonly in the form of a loan.[1] Thus, in a typical scenario as illustrated below (Figure 3.1), a lender may provide a loan to a subsidiary, and the parent company may provide a guarantee to that lender with the effect that the parent will perform in place of the subsidiary in the event of the subsidiary's default.

Figure 3.1 Typical Intra-group Guarantee

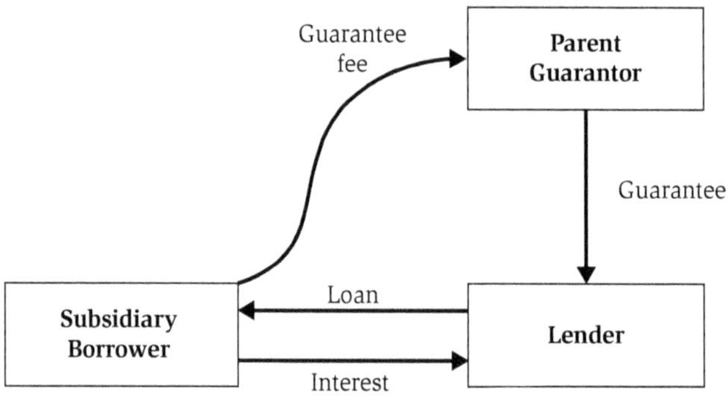

In a normal case, the lender's risk is reduced as a result of the wider recourse provided by the guarantor with the consequence that the price of credit is reduced to reflect the lender's perception of the guarantor's creditworthiness.[2]

The fee for the guarantee, if any, that the borrowing enterprise should pay to the affiliated guarantor causes a transfer pricing issue. In determining the issue, it is a prerequisite that the undertaking can be legally enforced against that entity. A second

1. Financial transactions are one of the most debated topics within the transfer pricing framework and strictly related to thin-capitalization rules; *see* Axel Eigelshoven, *Art. 9 Verbundene Unternehmen, in Doppelbesteuerungsabkommen* (Klaus Vogel & Moris Lehner eds., C.H.Beck 7 ed. 2021) m.no. 28a; Michael Schwenke & Stefan Greil, *Art. 9 MA Verbundene Unternehmen, in Doppelbesteuerung: Kommentar zu allen deutschen Doppelbesteuerungsabkommen* (Franz Wassermeyer et al. eds., C.H. Beck 156 Supplementary Delivery ed. January 2022) m.no. 97; Werner Rosar, *Verrechnung konzerninterner Finanztransaktionen, in Handbuch Verrechnungspreise* 376 (Werner Rosar & Florian Rosenberger eds., Linde Verlag 3. Auflage. ed. 2022).
2. Thus reducing the financing costs of the subsidiary; *see* David S. Miller, *Federal Income Tax Consequences of Guarantees: A Comprehensive Framework for Analysis*, 48 Tax Law 103–166, 109 (Autumn 1994).

key aspect is whether the borrower benefits from any reduced financing costs charged by the lender as a direct result of the guarantee alone.

1.2 Conceptual Challenges

The transfer pricing of financial guarantees is generally admitted to be difficult and contentious.[3] Commentators take different views on their treatment for transfer pricing purposes and choose different outcomes: some say there should be no fee, some indicate there should be a substantial fee, and others recommend an intermediate position.[4] The latter currently seems to be the majority view and endorsed by the leading guidance; however, its correctness from a theoretical or practical perspective is questionable.[5]

There is an oddity about financial guarantees in a transfer pricing context. In typical circumstances, a guarantee is not a transaction between associated enterprises[6] but between one member of an MNE group, normally the parent, and an independent lender. Indeed, the borrower in an MNE group with an active and centralized treasury function that takes responsibility for obtaining external financing for group affiliates may not be aware of the negotiations leading to the loan terms it is offered. In strictly legal terms, there is no automatic requirement for the borrower to be aware of the guarantee nor for the independent lender to transfer the benefit of any enhanced credit terms to the borrower.[7]

The guarantee comes within the transfer pricing rules only if the guarantor seeks to levy a charge to the affiliated borrower or if it is determined that there is a benefit for that entity that derives from the action of the parent or other associated enterprise.[8]

There are various reasons for the contentious nature of guarantees. They may be perceived to be a source of profit shifting since they are risk-transfer agreements that

---

3. 'The transfer pricing issues of guarantee fees will remain, in the long term, one of the most contentious areas of transfer pricing.' *See* Vera Averyanova & Jigna Sampat, *Transfer Pricing Aspects of Intra-Group Financial Guarantees in Light of the BEPS Action Plan*, 22 International Transfer Pricing Journal 361–368, 365 (IBFD October 2015).
4. For a selection of views, *see* Thomas Horst, *Debt Guarantee Fees and the Arm's-Length Standard*, 65 Tax Notes International 537–543 (Tax Analysts February 2012) et seq.; J. Gregory Ballentine, *A Transactional Approach to Parent Debt Guarantee Fees*, 27 Tax Notes International 133–136 (Tax Analysts July 2019) et seq.; Sophie Rukhadze, *Pricing of Intra-Group Guarantees and the Arm's Length Principle, in International Group Financing* (Christian Massoner et al. eds., Linde 2012).
5. For a detailed critique of the problems presented by guarantees under the current transfer pricing guidance and suggested solutions, *see* Andrew Hickman & Marcelo Moura, *Transfer Pricing of Financial Guarantees: The Limits of Arm's Length and a Practical Solution*, 3 Intertax (2023).
6. Which, in general, would not fall within the scope of transfer pricing rules; *see* Alexander Vögele & Wolfgang Wilhelm Fischer, *Kapitel A: Nationales Recht, in Verrechnungspreise: Betriebswirtschaft, Steuerrecht* (Alexander Vögele et al. eds., C.H. Beck 5 ed. 2020) m.no. 10.
7. The subsidiary has no role in the substance of the transaction thus the parent could tell the lender to remit the interest reduction to the parent directly. *See also* Ballentine, *supra* note 4, at 136.
8. John M. Breen, *Evaluating the Arm's-Length Price of Financial Guarantees: A Review of the OECD Framework*, Tax Notes International – Special Reports 869–882, 875 (Tax Analysts September 2010).

can be created relatively easily.[9] Since guarantees can support very significant borrowings in the billions, a guarantee fee priced at, for example, fifty basis points can represent a significant proportion of profits. The valuation of guarantee fees is not straightforward and sometimes has wide variations in the outcomes of available methods depending on whether the methods reflect the provider's or the recipient's perspective and depending on the assumptions made.[10] These outcomes are considered to indicate minimum or maximum amounts depending on which perspective is adopted, and guidance suggests that they may be expected to be modified in an unspecified manner as a result of arm's length bargaining. In addition, guarantees confront two of the most theoretically challenging aspects of the arm's length principle.

The first is the inability of the transfer pricing rules as currently understood to deal with capital allocation within an MNE group.[11] This is particularly problematic for financial guarantees since, in the illustrative case of a guarantee granted by a parent of the group in favour of the borrowing of its subsidiary, the reason for any such guarantee, its effect, and supposed value are consequences of how the parent has chosen to capitalize the subsidiary. A guarantee could be considered as replacing a deficiency in capital, and any guarantee fee apparently supported by the arm's length principle could be regarded as a reward to the parent for under-capitalizing the subsidiary and as a penalty to the subsidiary for not having appropriate capital.

The second challenging aspect is the articulation of the independence hypothesis under the arm's length principle[12] and the current focus on implicit support.[13] The two are related. The general understanding of implicit support involves the contention that lenders may consider affiliated enterprises to offer lower risk than unaffiliated borrowers and would consequently be willing to offer improved credit terms because of affiliation alone.[14] Transfer pricing guidance indicates that the impact of this does not give rise to compensation under the arm's length principle. In order to achieve this outcome, refinement is required of the independence hypothesis under the arm's length principle so that it does not consider standalone entities but affiliated entities that are affiliated to a different group. This proposition may seem inconsistent with the application of the arm's length principle in other situations in which group affiliation is disregarded and comparison is made with standalone entities.

9. In general, financial transactions follow this pattern. With illustrative examples, *see* Otto H. Jacobs et al., *5. Kapitel. Steuerplanung mit Verrechnungspreisen und Konzernumlagen, in Internationale Unternehmensbesteuerung: Deutsche Investitionen im Ausland – Ausländische Investitionen im Inland* 1052 et seq. (Dieter Endres & Christoph Spengel eds., C.H.Beck 8 ed. 2016).
10. Breen, *supra* note 8, at 878.
11. Transfer pricing rules also fail to consider unintended effects of MNE's investment decisions; *see* Ruud de Mooij & Li Liu, *At a Cost: The Real Effects of Transfer Pricing Regulations*, 68 IMF Economic Review 268–306, 269 et seq. (Palgrave Macmillan UK 2020).
12. Georg Kofler & Jens Wittendorff, *Article 9: Associated Enterprises, in Klaus Vogel on Double Taxation Conventions* (Ekkehart Reimer & Alexander Rust eds., Wolters Kluwer Law International 2022), m.no. 192.
13. Implicit support remains 'an ambiguous issue worldwide'. *See* Birhanu T. Daba, *Valuation of Implicit Support from a Transfer Pricing Perspective*, 28 International Transfer Pricing Journal 132–143, 132 (IBFD March–April 2021).
14. *Ibid.* at 132 et seq.

Two leading cases on transfer pricing and financial guarantees have endorsed this articulation of the independence hypothesis in relation to financial guarantees.

Court Case

The *General Electric* case[15] has proven to be influential in determining the approach in both the OECD and UN guidance on guarantee fees and implicit support. In that case, an explicit parental guarantee provided by GE Capital US (GECUS) extended the parent's investment grade credit rating of AAA to the subsidiary, GE Capital Canada (GECCAN), and the concept of implicit support was taken into account in valuing the guarantee fee payable. The tax court of Canada dismissed the government's claim that the explicit guarantee provided no additional benefit since the parent already implicitly supports the subsidiary. The case also attempted to determine the hypothesis required to apply transfer pricing rules to the provision of guarantees, taking into account implicit support. The taxpayer had advanced the view that implicit support is rooted in the non-arm's length relationship and cannot exist between independent parties; implicit support should, therefore, be dismissed in applying the arm's length hypothesis. The tax administration had opined that all of the economically relevant factors have to be considered, including the impact of affiliation. The judge seemed to take the view that there are external commercial pressures on GECUS to support GECCAN that are relevant characteristics of the transaction that should be included in the arm's length hypothesis.[16]

It seems that the hypothetical transaction envisaged in the *General Electric* case would be between parties having exactly the same credit ratings as the actual parties, operating in a similar manner as the actual parties with interdependent activities, and exactly the same ownership structures but with different parties. It would have to be hypothesized that the debtor is a subsidiary of an AAA-rated parent but different than the actual parent in order to retain the existence of a party that could provide implicit support that might be taken into account by the actual guarantor. Otherwise, the conundrum could not be solved that an unrelated guarantor would not acknowledge implicit support.[17]

15. *General Electric Capital Canada Inc v. Her Majesty The Queen* (2009) TCC 563. The ruling of the tax court was appealed, but the federal Court of Appeal confirmed the judgment notwithstanding criticism of the judge's reliance on the effect of removing the guarantee (2010 FCA 344).
16. General Electric, para. 199. One commentator suggests that Justice Hogan 'smartly avoided the fundamental transfer pricing question he said he was going to address' by suggesting that implicit support had nothing to do with the ownership of shares but was rooted in the reputational pressure exerted by external debt holders; *see* Erik Kamphuis, *How to Deal with Affiliation in Interpreting the Arm's Length Principle: The GE Case Reviewed*, 17 International Transfer Pricing Journal 292–297 (IBFD July–August 2010).
17. General Electric, para. 250.

Court Case

In *Chevron*,[18] similar challenges to the relevance of implicit support were also submitted by the taxpayer in this Australian case. At issue was a related party loan between the US subsidiary, Chevron Texaco Funding Corporation (CFC) and its Australian parent, Chevron Australia Holdings Pty Ltd (CAHPL). CFC borrowed money externally in the United States at 1.2% using commercial paper supported by a guarantee from the ultimate parent. CFC lends the borrowed funds of USD 2.5 billion to its Australian parent, CAHPL, at 9% with no security. The interest rate was determined by the taxpayer based on estimations of CAHPL's creditworthiness. Expert witnesses for both sides considered the effect of implicit support and reached different conclusions about the extent to which implicit support would have affected CAHPL's credit rating and the resulting interest rate. The case was decided by finding that explicit support should be included in the characterization of the transaction.

As in *General Electric*, the taxpayer advanced the view that implicit support is rooted in the non-arm's length relationship and should be dismissed when applying the arm's length hypothesis.[19] Similar to *General Electric*, in *Chevron*, the judge recognized that implicit support may be relevant when assessing a borrower's credit rating. Therefore, the proposition was dismissed that implicit support should be disregarded under the claim that the arm's length hypothesis relies on treating the controlled parties as independent.[20] The arm's length hypothesis was further examined in the federal Court of Appeal[21] which upheld the reasoning of the tax court and importantly confirmed that the independence hypothesis does not require the detachment of the taxpayer from the group it inhabits or the elimination of all of the commercial and financial attributes of the taxpayer.[22] Thus, the articulation of the independence hypothesis in *Chevron* potentially enabled the consideration of the existence of implicit support for the borrower as it did in *General Electric*. This is because the attributes of the actual borrower, including being a subsidiary of a strong parent, would remain the same under the independence hypothesis. Indeed, the trial judge accepted the relevance of implicit support since the independence proposition based on disregarding the relationship between the borrower and a strong parent failed.[23]

Thus, two courts in different jurisdictions analysed their respective transfer pricing rules and determined that the independence hypothesis does not require the controlled

18. *Chevron Australia Holdings Pty Ltd v. Commissioner of Taxation*, No. 4 [2015] FCA 1092 (23 October 2015).
19. Chevron Tax Court, para. 485.
20. *Ibid.*, para. 605.
21. *Chevron Australia Holdings Pty Ltd v. Commissioner of Taxation* ([2017] FCAFC 62) (Chevron Appeal).
22. Chevron Appeal, para. 43.
23. *Ibid.*, para. 605.

parties to be deemed to be standalone and detached from the group relationship. Hence, conceptually, the transfer pricing rules can recognize the evidence of implicit support since a group relationship is not ignored under the arm's length principle.

The following section 2 discusses the transfer analysis of financial guarantees involving the accurate delineation of financial guarantees and control of risk, recognition of the transaction, and selection and application of the most appropriate transfer pricing method.

2 INTRA-GROUP FINANCIAL GUARANTEES UNDER THE ARM'S LENGTH PRINCIPLE

2.1 Identification of the Commercial or Financial Relations

2.1.1 OECD and UN Guidance

Both the OECD (TPG or Guidelines)[24] and the UN (UN Manual)[25] provide guidance on the transfer pricing considerations for financial guarantees. The OECD guidance was published in February 2020,[26] and it became Chapter X of the TPG devoted to financial transactions and includes a section on financial guarantees.[27] The new guidance specifically endorses the application of the general principles to financial transactions for determining arm's length conditions of controlled transactions that are particularly found in Chapter I of the TPG. The UN Manual was revised in 2021 and takes account of the developments leading to the revisions in the OECD guidance and focuses special attention on the experience of developing countries and issues of most practical relevance to them.[28]

Both sets of guidance make key points that are summarized as follows:

(1) Commercial value of a financial guarantee derives from a transfer of obligations from the guaranteed party to the guarantor that are legally enforceable. Letters of comfort, letters of intent, keep-well agreements, or other documents that describe a promise of good management do not constitute legally enforceable transfers of obligations from one party to another and are not considered to require payment at arm's length.[29]

24. OECD, *OECD Transfer Pricing Guidelines for Multinational Enterprises and Tax Administrations 2022* (OECD Publishing 2022).
25. United Nations, *Practical Manual on Transfer Pricing for Developing Countries 2021* (2021).
26. *Transfer Pricing Guidance on Financial Transactions: Inclusive Framework on BEPS: Actions 4, 8–10 – OECD*, https://www.oecd.org/tax/beps/transfer-pricing-guidance-on-financial-transactions-inclusive-framework-on-beps-actions-4-8-10.htm (last visited 10 December 2021).
27. *See* OECD, *supra* note 24, Ch. X section D.
28. United Nations, *supra* note 25, at iii.
29. OECD, *supra* note 24, para. 10.155; United Nations, *supra* note 25, para. 9.13.1.2.

(2) The analytical process established for all transactions in the guidance applies to a guarantee and includes determining its purposes, its commercial significance, and benefit to the guaranteed party.[30]
(3) Since an explicit guarantee transfers risk, the framework to verify the assumption of risk through functional control applies, including the guarantor's financial capacity to bear the risk outcomes and offer additional recourse to a lender.[31]
(4) Implicit support is relevant in considering the value of the guarantee.[32]

In relation to the last point, the respective guidance of both the OECD and UN acknowledges the relevance of implicit support in evaluating guarantees. The OECD guidance notes that MNE group members are financially interdependent irrespective of any formal guarantee arrangement in the sense that the guarantor's economic risk may not change materially due to an explicit guarantee.[33] Stated differently, granting a formal guarantee acknowledges the MNE group's incentive to support the performance of the borrower.[34] If the guaranteed borrower, however, is not benefitting beyond the level of credit enhancement due to the implicit support of the MNE group, then no guarantee fee should be charged.[35] The UN Manual makes it clear that implicit support represents an assumption on the part of a lender and provides no legally enforceable rights. It is not itself a financial guarantee; nevertheless, the borrower may be able to obtain terms that are more favourable simply by being a member of an MNE group since the lender perceives the credit risk to be less.[36]

Both the OECD and UN guidance illustrate the impact of implicit support in valuing guarantee fees by reference to the interest rate differential between guaranteed and unguaranteed debt but taking into account the enhancement of the borrower's credit rating that results from implicit support. The relative importance of the subsidiary is considered to be an indicator of whether that entity would be likely to receive support in the absence of an explicit guarantee.[37] The UN Manual tables the potential impact of implicit support on credit ratings depending on the strategic importance of the subsidiary.[38] The guidance is influenced by the judgment in *General Electric* case[39] which is interpreted as endorsing implicit support since it was taken into account in measuring the additional benefit arising from the guarantee alone.

30. *See* OECD, *supra* note 24, Ch. X section D.1; United Nations, *supra* note 25, section 9.13.2.
31. The application of the control of risk framework to financial guarantees is an inference drawn from the stated application of the analytical principles in the respective guidance. However, the UN Manual does refer to 'control over risks' as a factor in Example 12 at 9.13.2.10, and the TPG refers to the capacity of the guarantor to bear risk (paras 10.166–168).
32. OECD, *supra* note 24, Ch. X section D.1.2; United Nations, *supra* note 25, para. 9.13.2.6.
33. OECD, *supra* note 24, para. 10.164.
34. *Ibid.*, para. 10.164.
35. *Ibid.*
36. United Nations, *supra* note 25, para. 9.13.1.5.
37. OECD, *supra* note 24, para. 10.78.
38. United Nations, *supra* note 25, para. 9.8.11.
39. *General Electric Capital Canada Inc v. Her Majesty The Queen* (2009) TCC 563.

Additionally, the OECD guidance emphasizes that guarantees may not give rise to compensation and that even an explicit guarantee does not necessarily lead to conferring a benefit to the borrower.[40] The UN Manual highlights three circumstances in which an intra-group financial guarantee is unlikely to require a fee at arm's length:

- when there is no improvement to creditworthiness;
- when the purported borrower has no debt capacity; and
- when the guarantee has been requested to ensure that the parent company does not divert the borrower's funds.[41]

The leading guidance therefore tends to express caution about assuming that a guarantee will attract payment under the arm's length principle.

2.1.2 The Analytical Framework to Accurately Delineate Financial Guarantees

Chapter I of the TPG provides guidance on the identification of the commercial and financial relations between the related party and on the accurate delineation of a controlled transaction.[42] It applies to any transaction, including financial guarantees. The guidance requires an understanding of how the MNE group operates in its sector[43] and then narrows to identify the economically relevant characteristics of the transaction consisting of its conditions and the circumstances in which it takes place.[44] The economically relevant characteristics are described under the following categories: contractual terms, functions performed taking into account assets used and risks assumed, characteristics of the property transferred or services provided, the economic circumstances of the parties and of the market in which they operate, and the business strategies pursued by the parties.[45] The UN Manual concisely describes the analytical process and identifies the following economically relevant characteristics that should be considered when considering financial guarantees:[46]

- contractual terms of the financial guarantee, including terms and conditions of the guaranteed instrument, as supported by the conduct of the parties;
- the borrower's risk profile after taking into account the impact of any implicit support by considering the functions performed and assets used;
- the guarantor's risk profile and financial capacity;
- the financial guarantee's characteristics and any benefits provided by it;

40. OECD, *supra* note 24, para. 10.168.
41. United Nations, *supra* note 25, para. 9.13.2.5.
42. OECD, *supra* note 24, para. 1.33.
43. *Ibid.*, para. 1.34.
44. *Ibid.*, para. 1.35.
45. *Ibid.*, para. 1.36.
46. United Nations, *supra* note 25, para. 9.13.2.1.

- both the guarantor's and borrower's economic circumstances, including an economic analysis of the market(s) in which they operate; and
- business strategies pursued by the guarantor and the guaranteed entity.

The potential benefits of a given guarantee cannot properly be determined without performing this analytical process. There is an instructive example in the UN Manual of how the business strategies and economic circumstances of a group issuing bonds through a special purpose vehicle determine whether a guarantee gives rise to any fee. In that example, the purpose of the guarantee and its commercial significance indicate that the explicit guarantee of the special purpose vehicle should attract no guarantee fee.[47] The purpose of guarantees and their commercial significance can vary widely. In some cases, they will provide access to capital or enhanced terms for accessible capital. However, in other cases, a guarantee may serve different purposes: it may be required by regulators as a precondition for a transaction;[48] it may relieve costs and administrative effort in providing evidence such as credit assessments at a subsidiary level;[49] it may avoid the imposition of financial covenants[50] allowing financial flexibility; it may be a requirement for cash-pooling[51] arrangements.[52]

Example[53]

The substantive contractual terms of a financial guarantee and the characteristics of the instrument could be identical in the case of Company A, an associated enterprise of MNE Group ABC, and Company Z, an associated enterprise of Group XYZ. Their respective parents each provide explicit enforceable commitments to assume all obligations arising from external borrowings taken on by Company A and Company Z.

However, assume that the remaining categories of economically relevant characteristics reveal the following evidence (Table 3.1).

47. *Ibid.*, para. 9.13.2.10, Example 12.
48. Particularly in the financial services sector.
49. In the case of a parental guarantee, *see also* Miller, *supra* note 2, at 109; Stephen L. Curtis, *Transfer Pricing for Corporate Treasury in the Multinational Enterprise*, 20 Journal of Applied Corporate Finance 97–112, 104 (Blackwell Publishing March 2008).
50. American Bar Association Section of Taxation, *Comments and Recommendations for Guidance Pertaining to the Transfer Pricing of Related Party Guarantees* 19 et seq. (September 2012).
51. Vögele & Wilhelm Fischer, *supra* note 6, m.no. 50.
52. All of those purposes allow the conclusion that guarantees 'typically arise when projects are politically desirable but financially infeasible'; *see* Howard B. Sosin, *On the Valuation of Federal Loan Guarantees to Corporations*, 35 The Journal of finance (New York) 1209–1221, 1212 (Blackwell Publishing Ltd December 1980).
53. The following example illustrates the importance of this analytical process.

Table 3.1 Description of MNE Groups ABC and XYZ

MNE Group ABC	*MNE Group XYZ*
The group operates in the real estate sector and specializes in the development and ownership of retail sites in several countries. Retail preferences differ across those countries, and the group's management relies on the local experience of its subsidiaries to make property acquisitions and disposals as well as arrange external financing with oversight from the group. Company A is based in Ruritania and has significant experience in the retail business and sources of external financing in that country. Company A is in the process of realigning its property portfolio in accordance with changes in the retail market and sees an opportunity to convert retail property into residential. Company A has a strong balance sheet, is not highly leveraged relative to the sector or to the consolidated group, and its income has been static for the past two years.	The group operates in the industrial sector, and Company Z is part of its financial services subgroup that offers leasing services to the group's industrial customers in several countries. The subgroup requires external funding for its subsidiaries from a variety of sources at the lowest possible cost in order to pursue its leasing activities competitively. It centrally manages capital requirements and the terms of external funding for all of its subsidiaries. Company Z provides leasing services in Ruritania and accesses funding from external sources there. Company Z implements strict policies determined by the central management of the subgroup relating to leasing terms and expected financial returns on capital. Company Z has experienced rapid growth because of its competitive terms. Its balance sheet is more highly leveraged than that of the consolidated group.

In these two scenarios, the nature of the guarantee instrument provided by the respective parents is substantively similar.[54] However, the evidence provided about the economically relevant characteristics of the circumstances of the respective parties is likely to lead to diverging conclusions about the purpose of the guarantee and its commercial significance. The result will be that the guarantee transactions may be delineated differently.

In the case of Group ABC, the economically significant characteristics may suggest that Company A has security represented by land and buildings that could be pledged to a lender in order to reduce the lender's risk and expected return. Pledging assets may be commercially restricting for Company A, particularly when it is conducting a business strategy to reconfigure its portfolio of assets. It would seem appropriate in this scenario to further investigate whether evidence exists to indicate that Company A

54. Although further enquiry would be required about the scope of the guarantees in each case.

could have obtained funding at the same cost in the absence of the parental guarantee. From the lender's perspective, it may perceive the parent's larger and more diverse portfolio as reducing its risk. It is possible to envisage reaching a conclusion on the further evidence that the guarantee granted more flexibility to Company A than providing security relating to its own assets but did not materially enhance its borrowing terms.[55]

In the case of Group XYZ, the economically significant characteristics may suggest that the parental guarantee is fundamental to the viability of Company Z's business. It would seem appropriate in this situation to further investigate the history of the guarantee, whether Company Z operated without a guarantee in any period and under what conditions, the commercial motivation for the guarantee, and any changes in funding procedures and costs that the guarantee made possible. It is possible to envisage reaching a conclusion on the further evidence that the guarantee underpinned the entire business of Company Z, given the importance of being able to access low-cost sources of funding.[56]

In these two scenarios, there is limited evidence about the control of risk. There is no suggestion in the example that the risks assumed by Company A in taking on funding were not controlled by Company A. However, there is some suggestion that Company Z may not control the risks assumed in acquiring the funding and that the funding risks may be controlled centrally in the XYZ Group. The relevance of control of risk to verify risk assumption is discussed in the following section 2.1.3.

2.1.3 Control of Risk

A guarantee is a contractual undertaking to assume risk on behalf of another party.[57] Chapter I of the TPG devotes considerable attention to determining and verifying the assumption for transfer pricing purposes of economically significant risks by the parties to the transaction based on a six-step process.[58] One aspect of the guidance focuses on whether the conduct of the parties is consistent with the written agreement leading to an outcome that the written terms may not reflect the substance of the transaction.[59]

55. The purpose of this scenario is not to illustrate valuation of the guarantee, but the likely outcome of such a conclusion is that any guarantee fee would be minimal because of the limited benefit to Company A and because of the limited risk assumed by the parent given the strength of Company A's assets.
56. The purpose of this scenario is not to illustrate valuation of the guarantee, but the likely outcome of such a conclusion is that any guarantee fee would be significant because of the substantial benefit to Company Z in conducting its business and because of the additional risk assumed by the parent.
57. Miller speaks rightfully of 'a contractual relation whereby one person engages to be answerable for the debt or default of another'; *see* Miller, *supra* note 2, at 106.
58. OECD, *supra* note 24, para. 1.60.
59. 'Where there are material differences between contractual terms and the conduct of the associated enterprises in their relations with one another, the functions they actually perform, the assets they actually use, and the risks they actually assume, considered in the context of the contractual terms, should ultimately determine the factual substance and accurately delineate the actual transaction.' *See Ibid.*, para. 1.46.

Differences between written contractual terms and factual substance are likely to be unusual in cases when a guarantee document exists and is with a third-party lender such as a commercial bank. This is because the third party will be motivated to negotiate the terms carefully and to hold the guarantor to its obligations.[60] There may be circumstances in which the conduct of the parties differs from the contractual undertaking when the guarantee is provided to a related party lender for the benefit of a related party borrower. An example is when the guarantor does not intervene to perform the obligations of the borrower, notwithstanding the existence of the written guarantee. Evidence as to why the guarantee was not enforced and whether the guarantor had the capacity to assume the risk may be relevant in determining the factual substance in such a case. It is also possible that an examination of the circumstances of the related parties in the context of intra-group debt leads to the conclusion that a guarantee should be included in the accurate delineation of the arrangement for transfer pricing purposes even though no written guarantee exists. Such a conclusion was reached in the Australian tax case of *Chevron*.[61] Evidence regarding the external borrowing policies of the MNE group and about the borrowing capacity of the borrower may be relevant in determining the factual substance in such a case as is proved in *Chevron*.

Guarantees are agreements to transfer risk, and factual conduct is also relevant in evaluating whether risk has been transferred from the borrower to the guarantor such that a lender would perceive a reduction in its lending risk.[62] This implies that there are two requirements for a guarantee to transfer risk: legal enforceability and additional security.

The commercial value of a financial guarantee derives from a transfer of obligations from the guaranteed party to the guarantor that are legally enforceable. Value being derived from letters of comfort, letters of intent, keep-well agreements,[63] or other documents that describe a promise of good management would generally be excluded.[64] Distinctions may be difficult because instruments that enhance an affiliate's standing in the eyes of creditors take many forms and represent points along a spectrum of enforceability. What creates an enforceable obligation may differ from one jurisdiction to another, and whether comfort letters, for example, create an enforceable obligation has been tested in the courts with differing outcomes.[65]

Second, the guarantor should evidence additional security that may derive from its cash flows, assets, and diversity such that its creditworthiness would provide reassurance to the lender. The concept of an expanded asset pool, wider recourse, and diversity is important. If the guarantor has correlated assets located in similar markets to the guaranteed entity, then the market shocks that could render the guaranteed entity susceptible to default may also affect the guarantor. The result is that the

60. Breen, *supra* note 8, at 876.
61. *Chevron Australia Holdings Pty Ltd v. Commissioner of Taxation*, No. 4 [2015] FCA 1092 (23 October 2015), hereinafter 'Chevron Tax Court'.
62. Curtis, *supra* note 49, at 104.
63. Miller, *supra* note 2, at 109.
64. United Nations, *supra* note 25, para. 9.13.1.3; OECD, *supra* note 24, para. 10.163.
65. American Bar Association Section of Taxation, *supra* note 50, at 12.

guarantor may also be unable to meet its obligations, and the risk transfer has not been effective. The OECD guidance recognizes the effect of such correlation between related parties.[66]

A further aspect of the guidance on determining and verifying assumption of risk concerns the concept of control of risk. The Guidelines provide the concept of control over risk as the means of verifying assumption of risks in a transaction once its economically significant risks have been identified and evidence is assessed as to how those risks have been transferred and assigned to the parties.[67] In addition to the control of risk, the party supposedly assuming risk is also required to have financial capacity to bear the anticipated risk.[68]

Essentially, therefore, the assumption of risk requires verification of whether the party contractually assuming risk not only has the capability to but also actually does perform the evaluation of risk and has the financial capacity to bear the risk outcomes. The guidance requires consideration of the involvement of the party contractually assuming the risk in the decision-making related to taking on the risk. When applied to guarantees, the guidance would require competence and experience to evaluate the risks being taken on.[69]

Example[70]

Group DEF is an industrial company parented by Company D located in Australia. It establishes a new company in Europe, Company E. Company E is funded through borrowing from the Group's Treasury Centre located in Company T which operates to optimize the group's borrowing costs and reports directly to Head Office management in Company D under whose direction it operates. Company T borrows from external sources under a guarantee from its parent, Company D. The lending to Company E is supported by a guarantee provided by Company F that acts as the group's Intellectual Property (IP) holding company and has significant assets and cash flows. Company E pays a guarantee fee to Company F, and the rate of interest Company E pays to Company T takes into account its enhanced creditworthiness derived from the guarantee. In this example, it is assumed that the guarantee is legally enforceable and that risk is transferred since the guarantor does offer additional security that reduces the lender's risk.

In the scenario depicted above, Company F has contractually assumed the risk since it assumes the default risk of its subsidiary, Company E. However, an examination of

66. 'In situations where the guarantor and the borrower operate under similar market conditions, an adverse market event that affects the performance of the borrower and increases its risk of default might also affect the guarantor and its capacity to fulfil its obligations.' *See* OECD, *supra* note 24, para. 10.168.
67. *Ibid.*, para. 1.67.
68. *Ibid.*, para. 1.64.
69. Steve Labrum et al., *United Kingdom, in Transfer Pricing & Intra-Group Financing: Country Tax Guides* (Anuschka Bakker & Sharvari Kale eds., IBFD 2021), section 4.
70. This example illustrates the relevance of control of risk in analysing financial guarantees.

the parties' functions ascertains that Company F's management was not involved in the financing of Company E, did not evaluate its default risk, and did not consider the impact of assuming Company E's default risk. Company F has no commercial interaction with Company E, it engages in no other intra-group financing transactions, it has no income-producing assets other than the group's IP assets, and its management is mainly comprised of IP lawyers. The guarantee document was drafted by the Group's Treasury Centre and signed by the appropriate officer of Company F following the board's approval.

In the light of this evidence, it is doubtful that Company F demonstrates that its management possessed the capability to make decisions to take on the risk relating to the guarantee or actually performed the decision-making function. Company F cannot show how it evaluated that taking on the default risk of Company E represented a prudent and appropriate investment for the company. The control of risk criteria in the Guidelines would not seem to be met. Company T, through its treasury centre, appears to have devised the financing arrangements and the accompanying guarantee, but it cannot guarantee its own lending. Further evidence about the direction provided to Company T by Company D is required, including that of decision-making relating to the implementation of a guarantee. However, it seems likely that Company D performed the decision-making function relating to assuming Company E's default risk through the guarantee instrument because Company D guarantees external debt and is ultimately responsible for managing the group's borrowing costs. Under the guidance, the risk return representing the entire guarantee fee would be reallocated to Company D, and Company F would not be expected to bear the cost of the guarantee being called upon in the event of Company E's default.

2.2 Recognition of the Accurately Delineated Transaction

The Guidelines envisage circumstances in which the accurately delineated transaction would not be recognized. The criteria for non-recognition focus on commercial irrationality inherent in the controlled transaction as accurately delineated that prevents determination of a price acceptable to both parties.[71] The guidance proceeds to provide that the structure that replaces the one disregarded for transfer pricing purposes should remain as close as possible with the initial scenario and achieve a commercial rationality that would be expected from third parties.[72]

71. Sayee Prasanna & Raffaele Petruzzi, *Accurate Delineation and Recognition of Actual Transactions, in Fundamentals of Transfer Pricing: General Topics and Specific Transactions*, 64 et seq. (Raffaele Petruzzi et al. eds., Wolters Kluwer 2021); Kofler & Wittendorff, *supra* note 12, m.no. 94. The OECD guidance provides that the 'transaction as accurately delineated may be disregarded, and if appropriate, replaced by an alternative transaction, where the arrangements made in relation to the transaction, viewed in their totality, differ from those which would have been adopted by independent enterprises behaving in a commercially rational manner in comparable circumstances, thereby preventing determination of a price that would be acceptable to both of the parties taking into account their respective perspectives and the options realistically available to each of them at the time of entering into the transaction'. *See* OECD, *supra* note 24, para. 1.122.
72. OECD, *supra* note 24, para. 1.144.

There is no explicit reference to the guidance on non-recognition in the discussion of guarantees in Chapter X TPG, but guidance on dealing with situations in which the effect of a guarantee is to permit a borrower to borrow a greater amount of debt than it could in the absence of a guarantee seems to demand such a reference. Two issues are identified in that guidance. This first is whether a portion of the loan from the third-party lender to the borrower might be accurately delineated as a loan from the third-party lender to the guarantor. It would then be channelled to the borrower by means of an equity contribution from the guarantor.[73] The second is whether the guarantee fee regarding the portion of the loan that is recognized as being from the lender to the borrower could be considered to be at arm's length.[74]

The essence of the circumstances envisaged in this guidance is excessive riskiness. The borrower may be so highly leveraged and may have no creditworthiness that default is highly likely at the outset. The result is that giving a guarantee looks commercially irrational, and its price would be extremely high such that reaching a price acceptable to the parties would be unlikely. The UN Manual is definitive on this point, stating that the debtor in such a case would have neither debt capacity nor credit status. Therefore, it would not be able to access the financial market without a guarantee, and a third party would consequently never provide a loan to this debtor without a guarantee.[75]

The outcome envisaged by the Guidelines and the UN Manual requires the substitution of a loan, which could be a third-party loan, to the actual group borrower with a loan to a different associated enterprise accompanied by an equity contribution from that enterprise to the actual borrower. However, such a transformation is not accurate delineation; instead, it involves conforming the observed transaction to one that meets perceived standards of arm's length behaviour and substituting a different transaction to the one observed. It is difficult to determine how the outcome can be reached through accurate delineation as stated in the Guidelines.[76] The process of accurate delineation depends on evidence that can be observed, and it can detect excessive riskiness, but it cannot change it.

The proper method to arrive at the solution presented in the guidance would involve reaching the conclusion that the transaction as accurately delineated reveals commercial irrationality that prevents the analysis from proceeding to considering pricing. Instead, it moves to a second stage of considering the application of the guidance on non-recognition. The guidance seems very relevant to the circumstances outlined. The replacement structure that is proposed is similar to the facts of the actual transaction in that a loan continues to be recognized, and the party assuming the risk under the loan (the guarantor) retains it as the substantive borrower. Thus, the desired outcome can be supported by the Guidelines, but it causes confusion to imply that the outcome results from the process of accurate delineation. Accurate delineation cannot be used to

73. *Ibid.*, para. 10.161.
74. *Ibid.*
75. United Nations, *supra* note 25, para. 9.13.2.5.
76. Critical to the unsolved interplay between delineation and recognition in Ch. X TPG, *see* Raffaele Petruzzi & Raphael Holzinger, *Accurate Delineation vs. Recognition of Intragroup Loans*, TNI 1111–1120, 1116 (Tax Analysts June 2020).

correct observations of excessive riskiness and replace the transaction with something that is deemed to conform to a commercial standard of risk. The sole sanction for substitution of transactions is found in the guidance on non-recognition.

2.3 Selection and Application of the Most Appropriate Transfer Pricing Method

Once the arrangements involving intra-group financial guarantees have been accurately delineated and the conclusion reached that the guarantee is compensable under the arm's length principle, the next step in a transfer pricing analysis is to determine an arm's length price.[77] This section discusses approaches to valuing intra-group financial guarantees for transfer pricing purposes. The methods are complex to apply and tend to reflect maximum or minimum prices from the perspectives of either the guarantor or the guaranteed borrower. In addition, the application of the methods is affected by the position taken on the relevance of implicit support and the framing of the independence hypothesis under the arm's length principle. All of the methods are based on the assumption that it is possible to differentiate the creditworthiness of the borrower and that of the guarantor notwithstanding that they are part of the same MNE group.

2.3.1 Economics of Guarantees

A financial guarantee requires an underlying financial transaction that is typically a loan to the associated enterprise from a third-party lender such as a bank. The guarantor assumes the responsibility of satisfying the outstanding debt obligations in the event that the borrower defaults. Thus, the lender has additional and enforceable recourse as a result of the guarantee. If it perceives its credit risk to be reduced, then the price of credit is modified to reflect its perception of the creditworthiness of the guarantor. The guarantor may allow the borrower to benefit from any reduced financing costs charged by the lender. However, the borrower may also be required to compensate the guarantor since the latter will be disadvantaged unless it is recompensed for the risk it incurs that it will be required to pay any shortfall on the loan as a result of the guarantee.[78] If the net effect of the reduction in loan costs plus the guarantee fee is not greater than the loan costs without the guarantee, then the borrower will not be at a disadvantage.

It is important to note that the borrower's default risk has not changed as a result of the guarantee. The default risk remains the same but has been assumed by the guarantor instead of the lender. Consequently, the guarantor has effectively swapped the borrower's default risk with the lender. Therefore, any outcome for which the borrower is financially advantaged because the reduction in loan costs is greater than

77. Raffaele Petruzzi et al., *Chapter 1: Introduction to Transfer Pricing, in Fundamentals of Transfer Pricing: General Topics and Specific Transactions* 3–38, 22 et seq. (Raffaele Petruzzi et al. eds., Wolters Kluwer 2021).
78. Notwithstanding the fact that the guarantor has a right of recovery from the principal debtor in the event that the guarantee is indeed enforced; *see* Miller, *supra* note 2, at 107.

the guarantee fee would result from differing evaluations of the borrower's default risk. The lender's assessment of the borrower's default risk is higher than the guarantor's assessment of the same risk.[79] Indeed, Schwarcz shows that lenders demand substantially higher pricing than financial guarantors for taking the same amount of risk. He attributes that outcome to abstraction bias resulting from the contingent nature of the guarantee.[80] Financial guarantors do not actually transfer their property at the time they make a guarantee which is unlike a bank that pays out capital at the outset of a project.[81] As a result, 'they may view their risk-taking more abstractly (the abstraction bias), causing them to underestimate the risk'[82] even after appropriate discounting for the contingency.

In addition, for intra-group financial guarantees, the guarantor may evaluate the risk differently than an independent guarantor because they are affiliated. Since they are members of the same MNE group, the guarantor may exert control over the borrower's financial management and be motivated to maintain its commercially interdependent operations in order to prevent the occurrence of circumstances that could otherwise lead to default irrespective of the explicit guarantee. While an independent lender could insist on covenants to manage its risk, neither an independent lender nor an independent guarantor would be likely to have the management control potentially exerted by an intra-group guarantor or the commercial interdependencies.

Differing evaluations of the same risk by independent parties compared to associated enterprises present challenges for a transfer pricing analysis since all transfer pricing methods depend on an evaluation of the borrower's default risk.[83] Those methods include:

- market observations of guarantee transactions between independent parties;
- methods that indirectly estimate the guarantee fee by constructing the interest benefit, or yield, as a result of the guarantee compared with what the lender would have charged; and
- cost-based models that estimate the expected loss.

All of them depend on determining the borrower's default risk so that appropriate comparisons can be made with guarantees involving similar risk, with the actual interest rate charged under the guarantee, or so that calculations can be made based on the likelihood of default. Determining the borrower default risk involves approximating the methods of credit-rating agencies.

79. Ashoka Mody & Dilip K. Patro, *Valuing and Accounting for Loan Guarantees*, 11 The World Bank Research Observer 119–142, 124 (Oxford University Press February 1996).
80. Steven L. Schwarcz, *Regulating Financial Guarantors*, 11 Harvard Business Law Review 159–192, 162 (Winter 2021).
81. *Ibid.*
82. *Ibid.*
83. Apart, theoretically, from an internal CUP when there is a third-party guarantee in place for the same borrower for which the price incorporates the guarantor's assessment of default risk. Nonetheless, this situation is unlikely to occur; *see* Breen, *supra* note 8, at 875 et seq.

2.3.2 *Overview of Credit-Ratings Approach*

Credit-rating agencies provide an assessment of the vulnerability of an assessed entity to default on financial obligations, such as the issue of bonds, known as an issuer rating. The assessment uses a predefined framework comprising several quantitative and qualitative factors, including:[84]

- sector risk profile;
- country risk;
- management strategy/governance;
- group structure;
- business profile;
- cash flow and profitability;
- financial structure; and
- financial flexibility.

Those factors are then taken into account within the methodology of estimating an issuer credit rating (ICR) for a borrowing entity. Importantly, the process involves consideration of both the group to which the issue belongs and the issuer itself. The credit-rating agency S&P, for instance, identifies a six-step approach that begins with the group assessment:[85]

(1) The identification of the parent entity and the group members is established.
(2) There is an assessment of the group's creditworthiness in order to determine a group standalone credit profile (SACP) and the group credit profile (GCP). Both the SACP and GCP are opinions of the group's creditworthiness. The former does not take into account government sources of potential extraordinary support or negative intervention considered to be available to the group, whereas the latter does.[86] The relevant sovereign constraints are subsequently considered to determine the GCP.
(3) The group status of each group member is assessed. The importance of each of them within the group falls under one of five categories: core, highly strategic, strategically important, moderately strategic, and non-strategic.[87] A core subsidiary would be given a potential ICR equal to the GCP.
(4) There is a determination of the group members' SACPs. This assessment takes into account sources of extraordinary support, including those from the group, guarantees, governments, and any other loss-absorbing capacity. The S&P considers that groups influence the group member's SACP when there are regular interactions with the issuer. Examples of positive influences from

84. Fitch Ratings, *Corporate Rating Criteria: Effective from 1 May 2020 to 21 December 2020* (May 2020).
85. S&P Global, *General Criteria: Group Rating Methodology* (July 2019), para. 9.
86. *Ibid.*, para. 19.
87. *Ibid.*

the group include: recurrent operating or capital subsidies, access to preferential funding, availability of centralized group liquidity resources, conferring monopoly powers, use of group brand, provision of services, and support of financial systems.[88]

(5) A potential ICR is assigned to group members based on the entity's SACP and adjusted to account for the highest source of extraordinary support.

(6) The final ICR is specified after a consideration of relevant sovereign constraints.

2.3.2.1 *Effect of Group Affiliation*

Two points are clear from this summary that are highly relevant to transfer pricing uses of credit-rating methodologies. The first is that an assessment of a group member's credit profile begins from and is referenced to the group's credit profile and, second, interactions with the group influence a group member's credit profile. Table 3.2 provides examples provided by the S&P for these group interactions and their potential for increasing or reducing the group member's SACP.[89]

Table 3.2 SACP and Ongoing Interaction or Influence

Positive Influence on SACP	*Negative Influence on SACP*
Frequent operating or capital subsidies	Price ceilings
Possibility of preferential funding	Risky projects
Centralized group liquidity resources	Commands for the provision of loss-making goods and services
Conferring monopoly powers	Double leverage, high shareholder-distribution policies
Favourable government contracts	Aggressive financial goals from owners
Friendly regulation	Unfriendly regulatory, tax or legal framework
Dividend policies, equity issuance flexibility or restriction	
Applicable tax regime	
Existing guarantees of credit facilities	

88. S&P Global, *General Criteria: Stand-Alone Credit Profiles: One Component of a Rating* (October 2010), para. 14.
89. *Ibid.*, Table 1.

Positive Influence on SACP	*Negative Influence on SACP*
Use of group brand	
Provision of intra-group services (investment, payroll, shared services centre)	
Committed capital or liquidity injection	
Support of financial system	

Source: S&P Global, General Criteria: Stand-Alone Credit Profiles: One Component of a Rating (October 2010), Table 1.

It may be observed that several of the positive influences are typical features of an MNE group, particularly perhaps centralized group liquidity, group brand, intra-group services, and common financial systems. It seems therefore likely that the group member's SACP may be positively influenced by group affiliation.

In addition to these group influences, the S&P approach determines categories of group status for a group member that are taken into consideration when determining the group member's SACP relative to the GCP (Table 3.3).[90]

Table 3.3 Extraordinary Group Support at Entity Level

Group Status	*Definition*	*Potential ICR*
Core[91]	Integral to group's identity and future strategy. Support from the rest of the group is likely to occur under any foreseeable circumstances.	GCP
Highly Strategic[92]	Almost integral to group's identity and future strategy. Support from the rest of the group is likely to occur under almost all foreseeable circumstances.	One notch lower than GCP if SACP < GCP. If entity SACP > GCP, then potential ICR = GCP.
Strategically Important[93]	Less integral to group than 'highly strategic'. Support from the rest of the group is likely to occur under most foreseeable circumstances. Some factors raise doubts about group support's extension.	Three notches above SACP with one notch below GCP cap. If SACP ≥ GCP, then potential ICR = GCP.

90. S&P Global, *supra* note 85, Table 1. This table is reproduced in the UN Manual in 9.8.11.
91. For a detailed description, *see Ibid.*, para. 45.
92. *Ibid.*, para. 46.
93. *Ibid.*, para. 47.

Group Status	*Definition*	*Potential ICR*
Moderately Strategic[94]	No support from the rest of the group in some foreseeable circumstances. However, potential for some group support.	One notch above SACP with one notch below GCP cap. If SACP ≥ GCP, then potential ICR = GCP.
Nonstrategic[95]	No strategic importance to the group.	SACP, but SACP ≤ GCP.

Source: S&P Global, General Criteria: Group Rating Methodology (July 2019), Table 1.

The way that the effect of group affiliation is considered by the rating agency Fitch is illuminating. In essence, it examines the link between the parent and the subsidiary and when it is very strong, the parent and subsidiary will be rated at the consolidated level irrespective of the individual SACPs.[96] The framework described by Fitch distinguishes between legal, strategic, and operational incentives as proxies to ascertain the level of connection between the stronger parent with the weaker subsidiary for which the more substantial the link, the higher the equalization of the SACP with the GCP.[97] What is significant for a transfer pricing analysis is that the subsidiary's SACP would be the same as the group's rating in eight of the fifteen outcomes described by Fitch.[98] Many groups would typically display high or medium operational and strategic incentives, and thus equalization of the subsidiary's credit rating with that of the group could result even in the absence of significant explicit guarantees.

2.3.2.2 Implications of Credit Ratings for Pricing Guarantees

All approaches for pricing guarantees depend on determining the borrower's default risk which involves approximating the methods of credit-rating agencies.[99] The discussion of their approach in the preceding paragraphs emphasizes that the borrower's affiliation to an MNE group can affect assessments of creditworthiness and, consequently, the risk of default. Affiliation is an actual characteristic of the intra-group borrower that is relevant from the perspective of rating agencies for determining risk. From the perspective of rating agencies, it can provide real and assessable benefits for ascertaining risk.

It can also be deduced from the discussion of the methods of credit-rating agencies that a credit rating of a group company as if it were an independent entity does not exist

94. *Ibid.*, para. 48.
95. *Ibid.*, para. 49.
96. Fitch Ratings, *Parent and Subsidiary Linkage Rating Criteria* 1 (December 2021).
97. *Ibid.*, at 5.
98. *Ibid.*, at 11.
99. Gary Lambert et al., *Implicit Support and Its Implications on Guarantee Fee Pricing: Fact or Fiction*, 47 Intertax 1077–1086, 1082 et seq. (Kluwer Law International 2019).

as their characteristics are different. Those that are relevant for determining default risk derive from the group affiliation.

In principle, the OECD guidance recognizes these points, although the affiliation benefits that rating agencies identify are more tangible and extensive than the OECD's concept of implicit support. The incidental benefit that an associated enterprise may receive solely by being affiliated to an MNE group, i.e., implicit support, is acknowledged and does not require adjustment or compensation. The OECD recognizes that a borrower's rating from a credit-rating agency will ordinarily reflect its MNE group membership. Thus, no adjustment would be required to reflect implicit support since it is already taken into account in the rating assessment.[100]

Thus, the credit-rating and the OECD approaches in relation to guarantees are aligned; there is no justification to evaluate the borrower's default risk as if it were unaffiliated.

2.3.3 Methods for Pricing Financial Guarantees

Both the OECD TPG and UN Manual suggest several methods for determining the arm's length price of the accurately delineated and recognized guarantee. All of the methods assume that the transaction has been accurately delineated as described in section 2.1.2 and that there is value in the guarantee that could not have been generated by the borrower itself, for example, by pledging its own assets. In addition, all of the methods assume that the purpose of the guarantee is to reduce interest costs and not to provide the borrower with debt capacity that it would not otherwise demonstrate.

2.3.3.1 CUP Method

The CUP method is usually mentioned as the most reliable way of determining pricing in the open market. At the same time, the practical difficulties in finding data that is sufficiently reliable to be used and in making reliable comparability adjustments challenge its applicability.[101] This is the case for finding data to apply the CUP method in the case of financial guarantees.[102] It would seem that there is little likelihood of locating information about the pricing of a guarantee provided by an independent guarantor for a loan to the same borrower (an internal CUP) or to a sufficiently comparable borrower with the same default risk (an external CUP) in order to apply the CUP method.[103] Nevertheless, both types of the CUP would, in principle, take into account affiliation benefits/implicit support. In the case of an internal CUP, this is

100. OECD, *supra* note 24, para. 10.176.
101. Melinda Brown, *Chapter 3: Transfer Pricing Methods – Traditional Transaction Methods, in Fundamentals of Transfer Pricing: General Topics and Specific Transactions* 71–105, 78 (Raffaele Petruzzi et al. eds., Wolters Kluwer 2021).
102. OECD, *supra* note 24, para. 10.172.
103. The UN Manual provides examples of internal and external CUPs in relation to guarantees; *see* United Nations, *supra* note 25, paras 9.13.2.11–12.

because the borrower remains the same; for an external CUP, the credit rating method should incorporate affiliation benefits.

The UN Manual casts the net wide for potentially useful information from market sources such as third-party financial guarantees (if available), bankers' acceptances, Credit Default Swap fees, letter of credit fees, commitment fees, some types of insurance, and put options.[104] Such market proxies for guarantees may be obtained from databases and can be selected to mimic the characteristics of the controlled guarantee arrangement. In all cases, a comparable default risk is required.

2.3.3.2 Are CUPs Really CUPs?

The CUP method highlights two conceptual difficulties in applying the arm's length principle to financial guarantees. First, an independent guarantor is unlikely to be in a position to influence the way that the borrower operates and is thus unlikely to be able to affect the risk of default. However, a group guarantor, particularly a parent guarantor, may be involved in the borrower's financial management with the result that it can directly intervene and take steps to prevent default from occurring. These circumstances may suggest that an independent guarantor incurs more risk than an intra-group guarantor and would charge a higher fee.[105] Adjustments for this comparability difference could be made in the borrower's credit rating. Financial management and centralized liquidity resources are some of the features that may be taken into account in a credit-rating approach and would tend to converge the group member's SACP with the GCP. In such a case, the borrower's financial management by the parent guarantor in the controlled arrangement may be reflected in a higher or equalized credit rating which would reduce or eliminate a guarantee fee.

Second, an independent guarantor may not be inclined to take implicit support into account. It may reasonably be opined that a party would not take out insurance if the party intended to bear the losses out of its own resources. Similarly, a group company benefitting from a guarantee from an independent party may not be inclined to claim the benefit of any implicit support from the group. These circumstances may suggest that an independent guarantor would not discount the risk for any implicit support and would charge a higher fee.

In summary, it is doubtful from both a theoretical and practical perspective that the assumption of risk by the parent guarantor is replicated in an uncontrolled transaction and that an intra-group financial guarantee can reliably be compared with an uncontrolled transaction. Without adjustment, the guarantee fee charged by an independent guarantor is likely to reflect a higher evaluation of the risk.

104. *Ibid.*, para. 9.13.2.8.
105. A similar observation was made by the judge in *General Electric*.

2.3.3.3 Yield Approach

The yield method represents one of the most commonly used approaches when valuing financial guarantees[106] despite being theoretically impure and imprecise. Using it begins with comparing the interest rate actually charged by the third-party lender on the loan as a result of the guarantee[107] with the interest rate that would have applied in the guarantee's absence. The difference between the two interest rates represents the benefit or yield arising from the guarantee. The comparison depends on being able to determine the borrower's default risk and the corresponding market interest rate for borrowing given that level of credit risk. The borrower's calculated credit rating would accord with the methodology of the rating agencies and should therefore include the effects of affiliation.[108] The following example is taken from the UN Manual at 9.13.2.13.

Example[109]

ACo, located in Country X, is an associated enterprise of BCo, located in Country Y. BCo has requested a five-year loan from a third-party lender. ACo provides an intra-group financial guarantee for this loan. The third-party lender provides the loan to BCo at an interest rate of 2%. ACo's credit rating is A, while BCo's credit rating (after considering the effect of implicit support) is BBB. Based on information available from public sources, a comparable uncontrolled loan (i.e., considering all the economically relevant characteristics, except for the intra-group financial guarantee) would have an interest rate of 3.25%. Under the yield approach, the interest benefit received by BCo as a result of the guarantee (i.e., its reduced cost for the funding) amounts to 1.25% (i.e., 3.25%–2%). Therefore, the arm's length maximum intra-group guarantee fee might be 1.25%. However, this amount might be reduced by considering how the advantage deriving from the guarantee should be shared between ACo and BCo.

The outcome of this assessment represents a ceiling remuneration that the borrower would be willing to pay for the guarantee fee. If it would cost more than the calculated reduction in interest costs, there would not be an economic reason for entering into the arrangement.[110] After reaching this outcome, the OECD suggests that modification may be required since the maximum amount does not necessarily reflect the outcome of a bargain made at arm's length but provides no guidance on how to determine it.[111] The

106. In the *GE* case, the Canadian Tax Court relied on this method for valuing the guarantee fee. New Zealand also endorses this approach, although it 'would have to be considered on a case-by-case basis'. *See* Inland Revenue Department, *BEPS: Interest Limitation Rules*, 31 Tax Information Bulletin 1–179, 111 (Inland Revenue Department of New Zealand April 2019). *See also* United Nations, *supra* note 25, para. 9.13.2.9.
107. Or a verified interest rate in the case of an intra-group lender.
108. OECD, *supra* note 24, para. 10.176.
109. United Nations, *supra* note 25, para. 9.13.2.13.
110. The conclusion that the yield represents a ceiling is questioned in the case of *General Electric*.
111. OECD, *supra* note 24, para. 10.177.

UN Manual emphasizes that it would not be appropriate to charge 100% of the yield as a guarantee fee.[112] It suggests using information from a cost approach to inform the split or a pragmatic approach of equal sharing between the guarantor and borrower.[113]

It seems questionable that the yield should be split with the borrower. The concept of the yield method is to identify the risk that the guarantor has assumed by determining the borrower's default risk in the absence of the guarantee and by determining the market price for that risk. Having determined the risk assumed by the guarantor and its market price in terms of interest rates, it seems doubtful that the borrower has any entitlement to share in that price. Otherwise stated, the borrower has not assumed any share of the guarantor's risk that would entitle it to share in the market price. It also seems questionable that the borrower needs an incentive to enter into the transaction. Strictly speaking, the guarantee is not something in which the borrower is involved, and the assumption of the borrower's default risk by the guarantor could take place between the lender and the guarantor without the knowledge of the borrower. The bargain is not made between the guarantor and the borrower. Splitting the yield is technically questionable but offers a pragmatic solution.

Court Case

A strong sense of pragmatism was also evident in *General Electric* in which the yield approach was used to determine a rating enhancement of three notches for the borrower as a result of the guarantee. This was found to equate to an interest rate reduction of 1.83%. Ultimately, the case did not determine how the yield should be split since the judge noted that the net economic benefit of the transaction exceeds the 1.83% rating differential calculated under the yield approach. The case was determined in favour of the taxpayer because the 1% guarantee fee charged by the taxpayer did not exceed an arm's length price and not because 1% was determined to be the appropriate split. The judge clearly indicated that the fee could have been higher than the differential of 1.83%.[114]

2.3.3.4 Cost Methods

Cost methods estimate the capital at risk under the guarantee in various ways. An expected loss or loss given default framework would estimate the probability of default on the loan adjusted for the expected recovery rate to provide the estimated capital at risk. An appropriate return on the expected capital at risk would then approximate the

112. United Nations, *supra* note 25, para. 9.13.2.9.
113. *Ibid.*, paras 9.13.2.13–14. Moerer makes a similar suggestion about using information from a cost approach and endorses a split of the yield so that both parties benefit from entering into the transaction. *See* Omar Moerer et al., *Chapter 5: Common Types of Intra-Group Financing Arrangements, in Transfer Pricing and Intra-Group Financing: The Entangled Worlds of Financial Markets and Transfer Pricing* (Anuschka Bakker & Sharvari Kale eds., IBFD 2021), section 5.4.4.
114. *General Electric*, para. 305.

required guarantee fee.[115] The method may take into account affiliation benefits to the extent that default rates are driven by credit ratings. Its supporters point to its use of third-party market data and its mirroring of the economics of the loan guarantee arrangement.[116]

A different cost method estimates the amount of capital that would be required to bring the borrower's credit rating up to that of the guarantor. The OECD guidance refers to this as a capital support method.[117] An appropriate return on capital would then be charged on this amount of notional capital in order to arrive at the guarantee fee. The approach should incorporate the effect of affiliation benefits when determining the borrower's credit rating. While this may seem to be a relatively simple approach, it does not reflect the contingent nature of a guarantee and may cause confusion between the notional hypothesis and the facts. This is because the borrower may not have required as much in loans if it had received a capital injection. In addition, the possibility of a capital injection may need to be extended to the borrower's credit rating since it would be a factor that could lead to a higher rating.

It is generally stated that cost methods are likely to indicate a minimum fee that the guarantor would expect to receive. The OECD guidance indicates that, like the yield approach, a cost method does not necessarily reflect the outcome of a bargain made at arm's length.[118] This is notwithstanding that there is no necessary bargain between the guarantor and borrower. As for the yield approach, the OECD provides no guidance on how to determine that bargain. Moerer opines that it is not uncommon to allocate one-half to two-thirds of the benefit to the guarantor.[119]

2.3.3.5 Statistical Tools and Financial Modelling

Pricing risk based on statistical tools and actuarial techniques are suggested by some commentators, and they are mentioned in both the OECD and UN guidance.[120] These may involve treating the guarantee as a contingent put option and establishing value by using option pricing models.[121]

115. The UN Manual provides an example of the cost approach; *see* United Nations, *supra* note 25, para. 9.13.2.14.
116. Stanley J. Hales et al., *Determining Arm's-Length Guarantee Fees*, 39 Tax Management International Journal 445-454 (Bureau of National Affairs August 2010).
117. OECD, *supra* note 24, para. 10.182.
118. *Ibid.*, para. 10.179.
119. Moerer et al., *supra* note 113, section 5.4.3.
120. OECD, *supra* note 24, para. 10.179; United Nations, *supra* note 25, para. 9.13.2.9.
121. Raffaele Petruzzi, *Chapter 3 Assessing the Arm's Length Nature of Intra-Group Financing: A New Approach, in Transfer Pricing Aspects of Intra-Group Financing* 138 (Kluwer Law International 2016); Omar Moerer & Antonio Russo, *Chapter 1 Introduction, in Transfer Pricing and Intra-Group Financing* (Anuschka Bakker & Marc M. Levey eds., IBFD 2012); Lambert et al., *supra* note 99.

3 CONCLUSION: WORKABLE GUIDANCE BUT THEORETICALLY CHALLENGING

The transfer pricing aspects of intra-group financial guarantees epitomize the challenges faced in dealing with how associated enterprises are capitalized under the arm's length principle. A guarantee could be regarded as compensating for a deficiency in a subsidiary's capital, and any guarantee fee apparently supported by the arm's length principle could be seen as a reward to the parent for under-capitalizing the subsidiary. They also question whether it is appropriate and possible for a transfer pricing analysis to separate out members of an MNE group and treat them as individual entities or whether the existence of the group affiliation is retained.

The current guidance provides workable solutions. It is based on accurately delineating the guarantee with particular regard to its legal enforceability and the credit enhancement directly attributable to it. That guidance requires an independence hypothesis that recognizes group affiliation and the potential for implicit support. Valuation methods, particularly the yield approach, provide pragmatic ways to estimate any guarantee fee.

However, current approaches require considerable effort to claim an arm's length price for a guarantee. The effort may seem misdirected since the value of the guarantee is referenced to the borrower's capital structure which is not determined by the open market but by the MNE group and often by the guarantor itself. Treating creditworthiness within an MNE group as indivisible and collective may reflect reality and would offer a practical solution either on justifiable grounds or as a safe harbour by eliminating the need to consider intra-group guarantee fees for transfer pricing purposes.[122]

122. For exploration of this suggestion, *see* Andrew Hickman & Marcelo Moura, *Transfer Pricing of Financial Guarantees: The Limits of Arm's Length and a Practical Solution*, 1 Intertax (2023).

CHAPTER 4

Cash Pooling

Sherif Assef, Marc Oliver Birmans & Elias Sobotka

1 INTRODUCTION

Cash pooling can be an effective way to optimize both excess and deficit cash positions within a group of affiliated companies for short-term cash management. A multinational group can minimize its overall interest costs by allocating internal funds to reduce dependence on external sources. Moreover, cash pooling can result in significant savings when the group marshals its combined market power when dealing with external banks. Savings can also result from centralization of cash management which may lead to additional efficiencies.

However, when a cash pooling system effectuates cross-border transfers among related parties in one or more currencies, it can lead to a range of tax issues, including transfer pricing. Cash pools involve frequent withdrawals from and deposits into a central pool of funds, and these transfers can cross tax jurisdictions. In addition, there is the question of allocating the benefits that cash pooling can generate for a multinational enterprise (MNE). With specific OECD guidance on financial transactions, including cash pooling, now being a part of the organization's transfer pricing guidelines,[1] tax authorities around the world are increasingly focusing on these issues as part of their efforts to protect their tax bases. Further, the OECD's BEPS Project has provided new tools for challenging financing structures through an emphasis on economic substance and arm's length divisions of functions and risks.

The objective of transfer pricing guidance is achieving consensus on the proper treatment of these arrangements. However, different countries can take their own approaches to intercompany issues raised by cash pools, increasing the challenges for multinational corporations' treasury functions.

2 TRANSFER PRICING ANALYSIS

2.1 Identification of the Commercial or Financial Relations

It is common for a MNE to centralize its internal treasury operations in one or more group companies around the world. Sometimes, this role is performed by an existing group company, perhaps the group's parent, even as that company performs other functions (e.g., headquarter services). Alternatively, one or more entities can be organized specifically to perform the treasury operations either globally or regionally.[2] In any case, the core activities of a treasury operation include advancing loans to meet the capital requirements of other group members. The loans can be short-term trading

1. OECD, *OECD Transfer Pricing Guidelines for Multinational Enterprises and Tax Administrations 2022* (OECD Publishing 2022), Ch. X.
2. This could be a 'special purpose vehicle'. Luxembourg, for example, has a strong presence of treasury centres of MNE groups. Among other functions, they are primarily acting as cash pool leaders for the benefit of the groups. Consequently, the arm's length compensation for the cash pool leader is a clear focus of the Luxembourg tax authorities. In particular, in the event of an imbalance in the cash pool that may lead to losses for the cash pool leader, they will audit the treasurer's conduct in terms of cash management and will analyse the economic rationale of the cash pool set-up.

balances or can satisfy longer-term requirements. In addition, the group treasury company may accept deposits from other group members that have surplus cash. It can also meet group capital needs by borrowing externally itself, or this may be done by the parent or other members of the multinational group. The treasury company may also have sufficient equity of its own that is available to fund lending operations.

One way that a group treasury company or other group entity can manage short-term liquidity needs is through cash pooling arrangements. These can generally be characterized as either 'physical' or 'notional':

- In a physical cash pool (set up in the form of either a 'zero-balancing' or 'target-balancing' approach), participating entities transfer funds, perhaps on a daily basis, to or from a master account. This is managed by the central treasury entity or cash pool leader (CPL), who is the group entity that manages the pool; it can play a variety of service-focused or more entrepreneurial roles. Separate subaccounts that are typically at the same bank with surplus or deficit balances are mechanically automatically swept to and from the master account so that the participants' subaccounts are zeroed/levelled out.[3]
- In contrast, with a notional cash pooling system, the debit and credit balances of all cash pooling participants are offset virtually and directly. This is typically done by a third-party bank; however, the pooling involves no actual transfer of funds. In effect, a group of accounts are treated as if they are one account.

Movements between actual or virtual accounts should be characterized as loans between the CPL and the participating entities.[4] As such, physical and notional cash pooling structures have similar transfer pricing implications although they can be quite different in practice. Further, they may have some elements of both physical and notional pools in practice. In either case, any excess cash deposited by participants is available to offset deficiencies of cash for either physical or virtual participants, and the pool as a whole calculates interest payable or receivable based on its combined net negative or positive position.[5]

Cash pools may be single currency or multicurrency. As the names imply, the former deals in one currency, while the latter involves deposits and withdrawals in multiple currencies. The latter can more readily create transfer pricing issues as they are more likely to involve transfers across tax jurisdictions. However, single-currency pools may also produce transfer pricing exposures when entities in different countries deal in the same currency.

Physical cash pools usually deal in a single currency, whereas those that are notional can handle multiple currencies. A mix of structures, such as a multi-currency notional pool header administering several single-currency physical pools, is possible.

---

3. Zero-balancing cash pools are also known as physical or sweeping cash pools. They are the most commonly used form in the United States.
4. There can be situations in which tax authorities may characterize account balances as loans directly between the pool participants if the pool arrangement is not properly structured. This situation can raise difficult tax issues but will not be explored in this chapter.
5. Positive and negative positions in a cash pool are also referred to as credit and debit positions, respectively.

2.1.1 *Role of the CPL*

A CPL can undertake a variety of functions including accepting deposits from cash pool participants, making loans to those participants, and dealing with external banks. The CPL manages the master account and administers participants' positions in a zero-balancing pool or calculates interest on combined credit and debit balances of the participating positions in a notional pool. The CPL can be a mere administrator of the cash pool or function more as an in-house bank, thereby bearing the risks inherent in these activities.

For a zero-balancing cash pool, if a specific participant's cash pool account has a positive balance at the end of a given business day,[6] the excess funds are swept into the CPL's master account so that the balance in the cash pool participant's subaccount is zero. The participant is subsequently credited with interest on that balance. In a notional pool, each participant may have its own account with the external bank, while the CPL records a mirror account and opens an account in the name of each participant. Balances are virtually pooled into the mirror accounts, and the CPL administers the required record-keeping.

Much the opposite occurs if a participant's cash pool account has a negative balance. Funds are withdrawn from the master account and transferred into the participant's cash pool account and interest is charged. In a notional pool, a loan is recorded on the participant's own bank account, and the CPL records the transaction in the mirror account in order to calculate net positive or negative positions for the pool.

The CPL may also be responsible for investing excess funds from the cash pool, generally in short-term, low-risk, fixed-income securities for the purpose of maintaining liquidity while also achieving capital appreciation for the cash pool participants. Excess funds may also simply be deposited with external banks. The company's treasury department may provide guidelines and establish investment limits within which the CPL must operate.

A CPL also often performs certain administrative services to support the pool, including routine treasury and banking services such as currency conversion, vendor invoice payments, cash management, and credit evaluation. The CPL is functioning mostly as a service provider if these services are its primary focus. This may be the case with a notional cash pool. Alternatively, the CPL may take on the role of an in-house bank by holding a master account that accepts deposits from pool participants and makes loans to them. This can be the case with a zero-balancing cash pool.

2.1.2 *Role of the External Bank*

In many ways, the role played by an external bank in a cash pooling arrangement is dependent on that played by the CPL. In situations when the CPL acts as a true bank,

6. Cash pool deposits and loans should be short term in nature that are typically overnight or otherwise a similarly limited tenor with regular sweeping of positive and negative positions.

the role of the external banks may be limited to depositing excess pool cash or providing a source of funds when the pool is in a net negative position. Alternatively, external banks play a more central role in dealing with individual pool participants if the CPL is focused on administrative services such as those described above. In that case, the banks are more directly compensated through the interest rate spreads earned on pool credit and debit positions.

Note that the precise functions performed by external banks and CPLs and, in the latter case, the arm's length remuneration should be determined on a case-by-case basis whether dealing with a zero-balancing or notional cash pool. For example, it is possible for a CPL to follow the limited service-provider model in a zero-balancing pool.

2.1.3 Accurate Delineation of Cash Pooling Transactions

2.1.3.1 Economically Relevant Characteristics

The OECD TPG emphasize the importance of accurate delineation for financial transactions.[7] Under this approach, the characterization of a financial transaction can be challenged by a tax authority based on the economically relevant characteristics[8] of that transaction which may include the following:

(1) *The contractual terms* – Legal agreements among the parties involved should clearly lay out terms, rights, and obligations. This is often not the case when the parties are related, including with regard to cash pooling arrangements. The absence of or inconsistency between the agreements that do exist and the behaviour of the parties involved could lead to challenges by tax authorities regarding the characterization of the intercompany transactions.

(2) *Functional analysis* – The functions performed and risks borne by the parties to a cash pooling arrangement, in particular with respect to the CPL, should be in harmony with the transfer pricing policies that are applied. A functional analysis of the parties involved, particularly with respect to the lender's ability to bear and manage the risks inherent in the financing transaction, may be essential in accurately delineating the transaction (*see* the previous discussion of the CPL as service provider versus entrepreneur, for example).

(3) *Characteristics of financial instruments* – The terms of any intercompany loan will inform its accurate delineation and arm's length pricing. Cash pool deposits and withdrawals should be very short term in nature, and their pricing will be impacted by the presence or lack of any group guarantees.

---

7. OECD, *supra* note 1, paras 10.14–50, 10.115–127; United Nations, *Practical Manual on Transfer Pricing for Developing Countries 2021* (2021), para. 3.3.2.
8. OECD, *supra* note 1, paras 10.21–38; United Nations, *supra* note 7, para. 9.12.2.

(4) *Economic circumstances* – The pricing of cash pool balances will also depend on such factors as the currency in which they are denominated with multi-currency pools presenting particular challenges. In addition, due to the short-term nature of the balances (properly structured and delineated), government interest rates can be important benchmarks. The same is valid for the group's external borrowing costs.

(5) *Business strategies* – Cash pools are typically used to meet short-term working capital needs. An MNE should differentiate their purpose, use, and pricing policies from those of other financing channels, e.g., longer-term capital needs, funding acquisitions, etc. In addition, aggregating the participants' surplus and deficit cash positions should result in synergies for the group as a whole. This can hopefully be quantified and lead to superior outcomes for each participant rather than if they were to manage short-term cash needs in isolation.

Various aspects of these economically relevant characteristics find form in such elements as an enforceable obligation to pay interest (for both the CPL and cash pool participants); a borrower's ability to meet those obligations (i.e., analysis of debt capacity); the ability of a borrower to obtain funds externally; various industry factors; and alternatives realistically available to the lender and borrower.

Example

A common pitfall concerns long-term balances. It is often observed that – over periods of multiple years – individual participants are either structural depositors or borrowers in the cash pooling arrangement. These long-term balances are often not monitored, and no consideration is given to reclassifying parts of the long-term balances as either a long-term deposit or loan. However, tax authorities have issued such challenges at times.

For cash pools, the application of an accurate delineation analysis might lead to recharacterization of debit and credit balances in the pool that are meant to be short-term arrangements into long-term loans or deposits if they are left outstanding for a long period of time.[9] How long is too long may vary in different situations with consideration possibly given to patterns over multiple years and the context of the group's overall funding policies. The exposure for taxpayers may be that short-term rates charged or credit for cash pool balances may be adjusted up. It is also possible for long-term withdrawals or deposits to be recharacterized as capital injections with the denial of any associated interest deductions or income.

9. In Australia, for example, one particular challenge regarding the characterization of a cash pool is to clearly distinguish between (short-term) cash deposits and long-term loans.

Court Case

In the *Switzerland v. A GmbH* case,[10] Swiss A GmbH and Foreign F Co (the CPL responsible for global treasury and cash pooling), both subsidiaries of the same group entered into a cash pooling agreement for a short-term deposit of excess capital and short-term borrowing. In the agreement, if the balance was in A GmbH's favour, A GmbH would be credited interest based on the one-month London Interbank Bid Rate minus 6.25 basis points with an all-in minimum floor of 5 basis points for the deposit rate.

Tax authorities opined that part of the cash pooling agreement comprised a long-term loan to F Co and that the interest rate on such a loan had to be higher than the 2.25% set according to Swiss Safe Harbour Interest Rates. The tax appeal court then largely confirmed the decision of the tax authorities that transactions between A GmbH and F Co were not at arm's length and reduced the applicable interest rate from 2.25% to 2%.

Finally, the administrative court concluded that it was correct to qualify a portion of the cash pool receivable as a mid- or long-term loan. However, it held that the tax authorities did not need to refer to safe harbour interest rates for every case and that the interest rates paid by F Co on the 'long-term loans' were in accordance with the arm's length principle.

2.1.3.2 Benefits of Cash Pooling

By definition, cash pooling arrangements are not observed among unrelated parties. Related parties enter into these arrangements because they generate certain benefits that would not be achievable by the participants under any available realistic alternatives for managing their short-term cash needs. Some of these benefits are discussed below.

Efficient Use of Group Liquidity

Typically, a third-party bank earns the spread between credit and debit interest rates. This is an overall cost to the MNE, but a cash pool can eliminate or at least reduce it by first making use of available group liquidity before borrowing externally. This is what is known as the 'netting' or 'coordination' benefit of cash pools.

Negotiation with External Banks

A multinational group can typically negotiate better rates (i.e., higher deposit rates and lower lending rates) with banks than cash pooling participants could receive on their own by aggregating its positive and negative cash positions. Similarly, if cash pool balances are invested in short-term securities, aggregation across pool participants will

10. *Switzerland v. A GmbH*, No. SB.2017.00100 (Verwaltungsgericht des Kantons Zürich 12 September 2018).

likely lead to more advantageous terms and returns for the MNE. This is sometimes known as the 'volume' benefit or synergy benefit.

Reduced Transaction Costs

Cash pooling can minimize both external and internal costs associated with funding operations. Banking fees and other transaction costs will typically be reduced compared to a situation in which each pool participant would deal with external banks separately. This impact can be heightened by an enhanced bargaining position of the group when acting in concert. In addition, centralized liquidity management will likely require fewer internal resources than if each entity's working capital needs had to be dealt with separately perhaps by its own treasury staff.

Risk Management

It can be easier for a treasurer to anticipate and manage funding risks in a centralized process such as cash pooling which provides for a top-down perspective on the group's cash needs. There may also be opportunities to benefit from natural hedges throughout the system (e.g., currency).

As the authors will discuss later in this chapter, some of these benefits are measurable and may need to be allocated among the CPL and cash pool participants. More generally, the presence of such benefits is a key component of the economically relevant characteristics of a typical cash pooling arrangement which can make it a key part of an organization's overall funding strategy.

2.2 Recognition of the Accurately Delineated Transaction

Since cash pool arrangements are not observed among unrelated parties, the resulting intercompany transactions are often not easily evaluated and benchmarked using market data that might apply to traditional loans and treasury operations. As such, a pure comparison with third-party rates for credit and debit balances might be too simple and thus not fully appropriate. Below is a discussion of typical transfer pricing issues pertaining to cash pools and the applicable guidance for determining the commercial rationality of the transaction that would allow its recognition.[11]

2.2.1 CPL

For both a physical (zero-balance) and notional cash pool, an evaluation of the relevant transfer pricing issues that are raised often begins with examining the role of the CPL. For example, can the CPL be treated as a service provider to the pool and more generally to the multinational group, one that merely administers the cash pool, or does it take on significant credit risk? The former scenario might lead to transfer pricing policies that allow the CPL to earn no more than an administrative fee or a modest markup on its operating costs. If the CPL bears credit risk when lending to group

11. OECD, *supra* note 1, para. 10.7.

companies, however, the focus of the transfer pricing policies can shift to determining the market interest rates to be charged.

A CPL functioning as a service provider is mostly a conduit between external banks and the CPL's group affiliates. The banks are the actual lenders and borrowers (the latter through acceptance of group deposits) with the CPL only facilitating the process. Interest rates charged and credited within the cash pool might be based on the external bank rates with a spread added by the CPL to cover its expenses and an appropriate profit margin commensurate with its functional and risk profile.

Alternatively, the CPL can pass on the bank rates and charge cash pool participants separate fees. Presuming that the facts support it, this transfer pricing approach can be relatively easy to execute as the benchmarking of cash pool credit and debit charges is directly based on external prices.[12] However, in all scenarios, any excess profits (or losses) need to be reallocated to the cash pool participants. This can be done, e.g., by year-end compensation payments.[13]

Example

Assume a CPL is acting like a true in-house bank in that it takes on credit risk when lending to its affiliates (conversely, those affiliates bear credit risk when depositing with (i.e., lending to) the CPL).[14] In this case, a simple reimbursement of the CPL's costs with a modest markup may not be an acceptable transfer pricing methodology and could be subject to a challenge by the tax authority of the CPL's home jurisdiction. The financial risks borne by the treasury company and cash pool participants may need to be reflected in the debit and credit rates charged and ultimately in the profits earned by the CPL.

In addition, the credit risk borne by the CPL may have minimal connection to that borne by external banks that lend to it (or to another group company, e.g., the parent) so that the pricing of the former cannot be reliably based on that of the latter. A full-service treasury operation may be raising funds through a variety of sources – for example, bank borrowings, debt issuances (e.g., commercial paper), or its own equity – then using those funds to meet the capital requirements of its affiliated group companies. As such, there is no direct connection between the CPL's dealings with external banks and its transactions with related parties.

2.2.2 *Cash Pool Lending and Deposit Rates*

The rate charged on cash pool debit balances may depend on the creditworthiness of the cash pool participants if the group central treasury operation bears credit risk. That

12. Some ancillary intercompany issues may apply such as the impact of any guarantees and contributions to cash pool benefits. They will be discussed below.
13. *See* section 2.3.2 below.
14. The ability to bear risk, e.g., through sufficient capital, should be evaluated for all of the relevant parties.

creditworthiness can be established by reference to the participants' credit rating as assigned by an accredited rating agency such as Moody's or Standard & Poor's. No such stand-alone credit rating will exist for most individual entities within a corporate group in which case one can be estimated through the application of certain rating models. They generally compare an entity's relevant financial metrics, such as leverage and interest coverage ratios, to that of publicly rated companies either directly or through the application of mathematical algorithms. The rates charged on overnight loans would be commensurate with the credit risk borne by the CPL.

In practice, evaluating the creditworthiness of each participant can be a burdensome exercise if a cash pool has a large number of participants. It may be possible to group them into a manageable number of credit rating categories in order to limit the required credit analyses to a manageable level.[15]

Example

A common pitfall relates to the absence of an in-house bank risk premium. For deposits, cash pool participants often receive a market deposit rate offered by third-party banks. The counterparty risk of a regulated business bank is thus reflected in the interest rate. In Europe, for example, the average credit rating of leading banks is around A. In-house CPLs within corporate groups with a BBB rating or lower thus imply a greater counterparty risk for the cash pool depositor. As such, what is referred to as the 'inhouse bank risk premium' should be added to the third-party rate to compensate the depositor for the additional credit risk compared to the realistically available outside option.

Application of an appropriate base rate

Although the focus should be on applying appropriate debit and credit margins when benchmarking pool interest rates, the selection and application of an appropriate base rate should also be considered. In particular, in times of negative base rates, the question needs to be answered whether to implement a floor of 0% or apply negative rates in the cash pool. This decision should be primarily based on the external funding conditions of the group, if available, and mirror the banking rates in the cash pool. Consequently, a floor mechanism should be also reflected in the internal transactions if it is implemented in the external debt.[16]

Benefits must be shared among the participants (*see* section 2.3.2 below); therefore, it may also be appropriate to base the (short-term) credit rating on the group's credit

15. The next section of this chapter discusses available analytical approaches in more detail.
16. In the German court case I R 74/15, the associated entities did not have written agreements on their intra-group cash pooling. The tax court argued that rates within an interest floor were paid for the cash pool balances based on refinancing conditions of the parent company. The federal tax court ultimately ruled that there is a breach of the arm's length principle if, in the context of an intra-group cash pooling, only a minimum and a maximum interest rate is agreed and this leaves a significant margin for the calculation of the interest subsidy. *See* Bundesfinanzhof, 17 January 2018, BFHI R 74/15.

rating. Most cash pool participants can already realize a benefit from joining the cash pool arrangement due to this rating enhancement. The authors' observations ascertain that most MNEs do not apply different credit ratings and thus various interest rates for the individual cash pool participants. Therefore, the group credit rating approach to price cash pool balances is prevailing.

Crediting rates for cash pool deposits must also be established, and there are several approaches to benchmarking them. For example, these rates can be based on the creditworthiness of the CPL; that is, a deposit made by a cash pool participant is analogous to a loan from that participant to the CPL.[17] Alternatively, MNEs can reference comparable deposit rates observed in the market. The availability of comparable data may help determine if there is a need to assess and incorporate the CPL's credit rating into the analysis.

Court Case

In the *Denmark v. Bombardier*[18] case, a Danish subsidiary of the Canadian Bombardier group entered into a zero-balancing cash pooling arrangement with a Swiss subsidiary that was appointed as the cash pool administrator. It required the Danish subsidiary to deposit its surplus funds in the cash pool and allowed borrowing from it when required.

The cash pooling arrangement was based on a daily overnight bank rate plus a rate spread (minus 0.5% on the subsidiary's deposits and plus 1.15% on loans). There was no transfer pricing documentation explaining how the transfer pricing rates were determined or calculated. Consequently, the revenue authorities disregarded the difference in spreads on the short-term deposits and the simultaneous corresponding loans that, in effect, equalized the rates (i.e., the loan rate needed to be applied).

The administrative tax court upheld that the rate on the short-term deposits and the corresponding loans should be the same. It reasoned that there was very little or no creditor risk on these gross corresponding loans/deposits because of the possibility of offsetting the balance. In the absence of facts indicating that the deposit rate should be different, the rates on deposits and loans under a cash pooling arrangement should be the same. Further, the administrative tax court confirmed the decision of the revenue authorities that a remuneration of 0.25% for the CPL's services on all deposits and borrowings is appropriate.

2.3 Selection of the Most Appropriate Method

Overall, regulations on cash pooling arrangements are similarly structured with minor differences in some countries. Most international tax authorities adhere to the

17. *See* section 2.4.
18. *See* Landsskatteretten dom af 21 October 2013 i sag nr. SKM2014.53.LSR.

case-specific treatment and application of appropriate transfer pricing methods in the OECD TPG, thus can be regarded as a rather common theme. A transfer pricing model incorporating the main characteristics of all major jurisdictions commonly dealing with cash pooling arrangements should therefore safeguard the business advantages by minimizing significant transfer pricing risk.

Attention must be focused on the finalized 2020 recommendations ('OECD guidance' or 'final guidance') regarding the arm's length treatment of various financial transactions among related parties, including in the context of cash pooling arrangements. Relevant aspects of that guidance that have been incorporated in the 2022 OECD TPG as Chapter X are summarized below.

2.3.1 Transactions with Cash Pool Members

Cash pool members are rewarded or charged with respect to their participation in the pool through arm's length interest rates for debit and credit positions in the pool. The determination of these arm's length rates is not straightforward due to the lack of comparable cash pooling arrangements among unrelated parties. In situations when the CPL is acting as a service provider, e.g., administrative/coordination functions with external banks, the rates to be charged within the pool may be relatively directly linked to those charged and credited by the banks. There must be appropriate adjustments to remunerate the CPL for its role. If the CPL is instead bearing significant credit risk, a participant-by-participant analysis may be needed (at least for major cash pool participants) similar to that described above. In either case, MNEs should take into account the appropriate allocation of cash pooling benefits as described below.

The determination of cash pool debit and credit rates should also consider realistic alternatives available to the pool participants (including the CPL). They should not be financially disadvantaged due to participation in the pool relative to funding arrangements that could be accessed outside the pool. Note that the benefits of a cash pool may be largely measured in terms of the external interest rates made available to the group and the pool participants, though not necessarily entirely so. For example, they may desire a reliable source of short-term financing that may be difficult to access outside the cash pool. It is important for taxpayers to comprehensively document the business rationale behind a cash pooling arrangement in order to minimize the risk of recharacterization by a tax authority.

Example

The recent *SingTel*[19] case (which relates to a shareholder loan) has reaffirmed the Australian Taxation Office's ability to reconstruct transfer pricing arrangements (or terms of arrangements) that are not considered commercially realistic

19. *Singapore Telecom Australia Investments Pty Ltd v. Commissioner of Taxation*, No. [2021] FCA 1597 (Federal Court 17 December 2021).

(i.e., would not have been entered into by unrelated parties). As such, the need for taxpayers to discharge their onus of proof to support the commerciality of cash pooling arrangements (or key terms within such arrangements) has heightened.

2.3.2 *Allocation of Benefits*

Cash pooling arrangements can generate a number of benefits for an MNE. The first is by making it possible for the enterprise to efficiently allocate internal surplus cash to meet funding needs, thus reducing external borrowing costs. The second is that the group can realize volume benefits on both loan and deposit rates with external banks by aggregating cash deficits and surpluses. Ideally, both of those group benefits should be measured relative to the results that would be available to each individual cash pool member dealing with external banks one-on-one.[20]

The OECD TPG direct that any synergies accruing to the multinational group from the operation of a cash pool, such as aggregate savings on external borrowing, should be allocated to the pool participants.[21] For example, those who account for a larger share of total withdrawals might pay a lower rate of interest. Similarly, large depositors might be credited with higher rates on their surplus balances.[22]

It may also be reasonable to allocate at least a portion of the benefits to the CPL if it plays a significant role in securing cash pool benefits. This may be the case, for example, if attractive bank interest rates are a result of negotiations by the CPL as opposed to the amount of participant balances (though the latter can also be a contributing factor). Any guarantees provided by the CPL may also need to be taken into account, as described below. It is less likely to deserve credit for netting and volume benefits realized by the cash pool in situations when it is operating only as an administrative service provider.

Example

Another common pitfall relates to the insufficient allocation of benefits. The OECD states that all participants should be in a more financially advantageous position than in the absence of a cash pooling arrangement.[23] As such – regardless of the classification of the CPL – the intra-group borrowing conditions must be at least as favourable as the realistically available options. This does not solely refer to enhanced interest rates but can also imply access to a permanent

20. With or without the benefits of a guarantee, which may need to be separately compensated.
21. OECD, *supra* note 1, paras 10.143–146.
22. The next section will discuss methodologies for allocating benefits.
23. OECD, *supra* note 1, para. 10.146.

source of financing, reduced exposure to external banks, and access to liquidity, among others. Note that benefits other than enhanced interest rates may be more difficult to demonstrate in practical situations.

The guidance recognizes that identifying and collecting the data required to measure and implement such allocations is a challenge for MNEs and the tax administrations evaluating the arrangements.[24] However, disregarding the implications of cash pool benefits, for example, by benchmarking loan and deposit rates as if they are market transactions outside of a cash pool structure, could lead to challenges with respect to the accurate delineation of the intercompany arrangement. Consequently, taxpayers are requested to prepare comprehensive documentation of the returns to the CPL and pool participants in the context of the cash pool structure.

2.3.3 Remuneration of CPLs

As with an in-house treasury operation, arm's length remuneration for a CPL should be determined based on its functions and incurrence of economically significant risks. As discussed above, the remuneration should consider, among other factors, the proper delineation of the CPL as either a routine service provider, a full-service in-house bank, or something in between. The OECD guidance indicates that CPLs generally perform coordination or agency functions as opposed to engaging in activities and bearing risks that are similar to those undertaken and risks borne by a bank; consequently, arm's length remuneration for a CPL will generally be limited (e.g., return on costs).[25] Whether this characterization and corresponding transfer pricing approach are supportable in any particular case depends on the facts and circumstances of that case.

The accurate characterization of the CPL's role along with its arm's length compensation should be coordinated with the benchmarking of interest rates for loans and deposits.

2.3.4 Guarantees[26]

Cash pool structures often include guarantees from group affiliates. They can take a number of forms, including a guarantee from the CPL, the parent company, or another group entity to external banks. There may also be a system of cross-guarantees among the participants in the pool. The latter would basically result in all pool members guaranteeing the ability of their affiliates to meet their obligations in the pool (external banks often require cross-guarantees among cash pool members).[27] A question arises as to whether the presence of guarantees should lead to the payment of guarantee fees.

24. *Ibid.*, paras 3.20–23.
25. *Ibid.*, para. 10.130.
26. Chapter 3 of this book deals with financial guarantees.
27. Similar to cross-guarantees are 'set-off rights' under which any unsettled balances in a participant's account can be satisfied using balances from other participants. This is typically an integral feature of a notional cash pooling structure.

A guarantee provided by a group entity, such as the parent, may result in the availability of interest rates that are more advantageous to cash pool participants from external banks. This could mean that the participants should compensate the guarantor for helping to lower their costs of short-term financing (or for enabling such financing available in the first place). However, if the guarantor is also benefiting from the arrangement, for example, by allowing its operating entities to manage their capital needs and generate business opportunities, the guarantee may not need to be compensated (at least not fully) since the guarantor is deriving benefits from its provision. An analogous perspective is that the external banks may already be assuming that the guarantor will support the pool participants even in the absence of a formal guarantee (especially if the guarantor is the parent), so the guarantee does not bestow any incremental economic benefit.[28] Determination of the need for and quantum of a guarantee fee depends on the facts and circumstances of each case.[29]

Concerning cross-guarantees, the analysis may be more straightforward. The cash pool participants enter into the cross-guarantee arrangement as a requirement for being in the pool. Stated differently, there is no formal decision by any participant to provide a guarantee on behalf of another participant, much less evaluate the risk exposure inherent in such guarantees.[30] Consequently, a system of cross-guarantees is mostly an acknowledgement that it is in each participant's best interest to not allow another participant or the CPL to default on a cash pool loan. This can be seen as a form of implicit support with each participant deriving benefits from the provision of the cross-guarantees (e.g., access to short-term funding) and is therefore not compensable. The author's observations ascertain that guarantees are generally not charged in cash pooling arrangements.

Court Case

In the *Portugal v. S.A. Cash Corp* case,[31] a Portuguese company (S.A. Cash Corp, subsidiary) and a German company (P Co, parent) entered into a notional cash pooling arrangement with a Dutch bank. Both companies held accounts and provided cross-guarantees for each other's liabilities in respect of their account balances under the agreement.

The Portuguese revenue authorities assessed the substantial corporate income tax for the 2008 fiscal year which reflected a guarantee fee for the cash pooling arrangement. They stated that the more advantageous financial situation of S.A. Cash Corp contributed to a better overall credit rating in comparison to P Co.

28. For example, the guarantee may be an administrative or legal requirement.
29. OECD, *supra* note 1, para. 10.148; United Nations, *supra* note 7, para. 9.13.1.
30. Each participant's exposure would be difficult to measure given that other participants are guaranteeing the same balances.
31. *Portugal v. Cash Corp.*, No. 55/2012-T (Centro de Arbitragem Administrativa 24 Dez 2012).

The arbitral tribunal upheld the revenue authorities' reasoning that the cash pooling arrangement was more than a virtual merger of balances for optimizing debit and credit interest. It was determined that its true nature was that of an exceptional contract and, for all practical purposes, a guarantee was rendered by S.A. Cash Corp to its parent, P Co.

2.4 Application of the Most Appropriate Method

As discussed above, cash pooling arrangements raise a number of transfer pricing issues, including remuneration of the CPLs, deposit rates earned by the pool participants, and withdrawal rates charged to them. There is also the question of how to determine and allocate the group benefits generated by the pool. In establishing the proper policies on these and other important questions, as with any intercompany pricing issues, a comprehensive functional analysis of the cash pool structure and the entities involved is paramount.

2.4.1 Functional Analysis

The functional analysis has been made even more crucial by Chapter X of the 2022 OECD TPG that emphasizes the need to accurately delineate all intercompany financial transactions. Regarding cash pools, accurate delineation takes on unique characteristics and can encompass many factors. As described in the OECD TPG:

> The accurate delineation of the cash pooling transactions will depend on the particular facts and circumstances of each case. As cash pooling is not undertaken regularly, if at all, by independent enterprises, the application of transfer pricing principles requires careful consideration.[32]
>
> The accurate delineation of cash pooling arrangements would need to take into account not only the facts and circumstances of the balances transferred but the wider context of the conditions of the pooling arrangement as a whole. For example, a cash pool is likely to differ from a straightforward overnight deposit with a bank or similar financial institution in that a cash pool member with a credit position is not depositing money as a transaction in isolation with a view to a simple depositor return.[33]

This guidance points to the need to adapt the functional analysis to cover issues that are particularly important for cash pools. These include:

- the role played by the CPL or central treasury company;
- the risks borne by the CPL and the pool participants (and perhaps external banks);

32. OECD, *supra* note 1, para. 10.115.
33. *Ibid.*, para. 10.116.

- realistic alternatives available to participants for short-term funding; and
- the quantum and allocation of any group benefits generated by the pool.

The latter is unique to cash pools versus other financing arrangements, and thus the functional analysis should address the source of any savings or efficiencies from the pool and the role of the strategic group policies in generating them.

Example

One common pitfall concerns the insufficient substance for the CPL. In order to be classified as a CPL entitled to earn parts or all of the spreads between the balances that it adopts, a robust factual and functional analysis needs to prove that it controls the financial risks and has the financial capacity to bear these risks. In practice, some structures lack the people functions and/or a sufficient equity base to qualify for more than a coordination function and might thus be overrewarded. For such set-ups, either more substance needs to be created or the transfer pricing model should be aligned to the actual (leaner) functional and risk profile.

2.4.2 Benchmarking Debit & Credit Rates

Intercompany transactions are likely to be present due to the transfer of funds from/to individual participants' accounts to the master account of the CPL under a physical cash pooling arrangement. These positions should earn or pay arm's length interest rates. In general, the rates should be indicative of what would be earned or charged in similar transactions between unrelated parties. Consequently, rates credited on deposits with unrelated banks or charged on short-term loans can be identified. The former can be based on available market benchmarks for rates at which banks are willing to borrow funds in various currencies and/or by jurisdiction. Rates for pool withdrawals can be compared to yields on short-maturity financial instruments. For both deposit and withdrawal rates, the credit ratings of the relevant parties – the CPL for deposit rates (i.e., the CPL as the 'borrower') and the particular pool participants for withdrawals – may need to be matched. Interest rates charged between the CPL and external banks may provide a beneficial commencement for benchmarking internal pool deposits and lending rates, not including any needed adjustments for volume, creditworthiness, and other relevant factors.[34]

There can be a question as to whether intercompany transactions are actually created in a notional pool. Some have argued that there may not be an intercompany transaction between a pool participant and the CPL, for instance, if the participant has access to its own (mirror) bank account with a third-party bank. The participant's mirror account with the CPL is considered to be part of a group of accounts that are virtually pooled as one. Consequently, with a deposit into or withdrawal from the pool, is the actual transaction between the participant and the third-party bank with the CPL

34. Also *see* the discussion on allocation of pool benefits below.

separately administering mirror accounts? While this argument finds some favour with certain taxpayers, most tax authorities tend to see past the virtual dealings in a notional pool. They conclude that deposits and withdrawals should be characterized as related-party transactions between participants and the CPL in the same manner as that with zero-balancing cash pools.

2.4.3 Accounting for Pool Synergies

Cash pooling differs from situations in which the participants may individually deposit funds overnight with a bank or borrow from it when they have short-term funding needs. The cash pool represents a broad group strategy to efficiently use available cash and minimize external financing costs. The accurate delineation of a cash pooling arrangement therefore requires taking into account the impact of this strategy on the group and each participant's contribution to it (as well as that of the CPL). Under the arm's length standard, the benefits realized by the group through a cash pool may need to be allocated to the related parties.

Broadly, cash pool benefits are divided between: (i) netting benefits and (ii) volume or aggregation of benefits. Netting benefits refer to the savings realized by the group for external financing by efficiently using internal surplus cash to meet participants' short-term working capital needs. If a pool participant can borrow USD 1 million from the pool rather than from a third-party bank, for example, the interest payable on that loan does not leave the group. Volume benefits result from the ability of the group to obtain a more favourable deposit and lending rates from outside banks by pooling its resources and thereby enhancing its bargaining power.

One of the more challenging aspects of a transfer pricing analysis is the measurement of netting and volume benefits. Netting benefits are the savings resulting from pool participants borrowing internally what they would have otherwise borrowed externally. If it is assumed that any pool negative balances represent financing that would otherwise have been obtained from a third-party bank, then the resulting benefits to the group would be based on the interest rates that each participant would have been charged by a bank. However, this may not be easy to determine as it may require an individual credit assessment of each participant, not to mention taking into consideration the possible impact of any implicit group support or explicit guarantees. Further, it is possible that easy access to internal funds changes the behaviour of some pool participants. It may prompt them to more readily rely on loans for their working capital needs as opposed to such needs being met through external borrowing.

The measurement of volume benefits will also present challenges as it would require comparing the interest rates that a bank is offering and charging the CPL on pool surpluses and shortages versus what the bank would offer and charge each individual participant. However, the latter would be difficult to establish without actual transactions occurring between each participant and the bank. The bank could be asked to provide quotes for each participant or some sort of indicative pricing, however, this may not be a reliable method for benchmarking actual market pricing.[35]

Assuming that netting and volume benefits can be reliably measured or can at least be estimated, this still leaves the challenge of allocating those benefits among the CPL and cash pool participants. The allocation should be commensurate with each entity's relative contribution to generating the benefits and the risks incurred:

(1) The CPL earns returns based on its role in raising funds, bearing credit risk, or simply administering the pool, as the case may be (*see* an earlier discussion of the role of the CPL and section 2.4.4 below).
(2) The parent company or other entities as relevant are paid for any services that they may provide on behalf of the cash pool.
(3) The borrowing and lending pool participants are rewarded based on their contributions to the netting and volume benefits realized by the group.

The benefits are often allocated based on a residual profit split analysis wherein 'routine' functions are remunerated first from the pool benefits perhaps based on cost-plus payments. The residual is allocated among the pool participants and the CPL based on some relative measure of contribution such as magnitude of borrowings, headcount, sales, or some combination of allocation keys.

The actual execution of the resulting allocation of benefits can be accomplished by differentiating deposit and lending rates among participants, e.g., large borrowers would pay a lower rate on loans than smaller borrowers.

2.4.4 Compensating the CPL

The spectrum of roles that a CPL can play in a cash pooling structure from the service provider/administrator model to more of a full-service in-house bank is discussed earlier in this chapter. If the CPL is only administering the pool, providing a service to the participants by maintaining accounts, and liaising with outside banks, among others, then a fixed return on its associated costs will likely be sufficient remuneration. Alternatively, the CPL can sometimes function more like an in-house bank, for example, taking the lead in raising and managing funds for the pool and bearing credit risk on withdrawals by pool participants (as well as being a source of counterparty risk to those participants on deposits). It should then earn returns commensurate with those that would be earned by a true lending institution perhaps through the spreads between deposit and lending rates.

The profit and loss situation of a CPL should be monitored and reviewed to ensure that it is commensurate with its characterization. For example, a mere service provider with a high degree of imbalance between credit and debit positions leading to overall losses might likely not be accepted by the tax administration in the CPL's county.

35. The OECD TPG warn against depending on bank quotes for financial transactions; *see* OECD, *supra* note 1, paras 10.107–108.

Example

Another common pitfall deals with monitoring the profitability of the CPL. For routine CPLs, only a minimal reward is attributed (often based on the cost-plus method). The German tax authorities, for example, consider a markup between 5% and 10% as adequate.[36] However, it is advisable for entrepreneurial CPLs to also prepare (segmented) profit and loss statements to ensure that the pricing does not lead to a loss situation. Typical expense positions – such as arrangement fees and commitment fees paid to banks for facilities attributed to the cash management function – can drive cash pools into losses. It should thus be considered if certain treasury costs need to be recharged to the cash pool participants separately if the CPL lacks sufficient income to absorb these losses.

In the context of the above discussion on allocating the benefits of a cash pool, the CPL's contribution to those benefits can include skilful negotiations with external banks, efficiencies in the raising of funds, structuring of pooling arrangements tailored to the group's expected cash needs, and optimal management of participant accounts. In a similar manner as that for the cash pool participants, the transfer pricing policy can allocate to the CPL a share of pool profits through the interest rate spreads it earns on pool deposits and loans relative to the rates credited and charged by external banks (that spread may be structured to provide a fixed return on its costs if the CPL does not significantly contribute to the benefits).

Depending on the specific case at hand, the netting benefits might not be sufficient to cover the CPL's costs such as commitment fees or hedging costs in the case of multi-currency cash pools.[37] This might require the implementation of a separate fee or cost allocation mechanism.

Example

Tax authorities in Germany have demonstrated an increasing focus on cash pooling systems in recent years. In most cases, they consider that the CPL functions as a pure routine service provider as opposed to a more independently operating entrepreneur and therefore assumes only limited functions and risks for the cash pool. Accordingly, the compensation of the CPL is often determined on a cost-based method. Since July 2021, this view has also been formulated in

36. *See* Bundesministerium der Finanzen, *Verwaltungsgrundsätze Verrechnungspreise Grundsätze für die Korrektur von Einkünften gemäß § 1 AStG.*
37. In one of the first of its kind, the court case *Norway v. Conoco Philips* dealt with the benefits of a multi-currency cash pool arrangement in which the court held that the decisive question was whether the allocation of the cash pooling benefits was done at arm's length. It dismissed the argument that the benefits should only accrue to the parent company. In order to achieve an arm's length price, the comparison had to take into account all characteristics of the controlled transaction except the parties' association with each other. *See Norway v. ConocoPhillips Skandinavia AS*, No. HR-2016-988-A, Doc. No. 2015/1044 (2010).

new transfer pricing administrative principles that are binding for all tax inspectors performing tax audits.[38] This entails that a non-entrepreneurial CPL is to be compensated for its administrative costs plus a markup on those costs between 5% and 10%. The remaining benefits generated from the cash pool are then to be distributed among the cash pool participants.

An entrepreneurial CPL, the alternative classification for German tax authorities, would earn an interest margin for its additional functions performed and higher risks assumed.[39] This requires proof that control over risk functions are performed by the CPL and that sufficient capital is available.

In general, most tax authorities in Europe and the United States Internal Revenue Service follow the OECD guidance that the compensation of the CPL needs to be commensurate with its functional and risk profile, i.e., if the CPL is characterized as an entrepreneur or service provider.

2.4.5 Guarantees

Cash pooling arrangements often include either cross-guarantees among the participants and/or general guarantees on behalf of the pool by the parent or other entities.

In the case of a guarantee from the latter, a guarantee fee may be required if it results in measurable interest savings for the CPL and/or the cash pool participants that exceed any savings resulting from implicit parental support of the pool. The fee may be paid by the CPL rather than by each participant individually, though the participants may bear the cost through the deposit and withdrawal rates extended by the CPL.

A system of cross-guarantees wherein each pool participant is severally and jointly responsible for any cash shortfalls arising from pool activity is fairly common in cash pool arrangements. Deficiencies can result when a participant who has withdrawn from the pool is unable (temporarily or otherwise) to repay its borrowing, for example. It is difficult if not impossible to quantify the risk of an individual participant due to cross-guarantees as no participant can generally control membership in the pool or the magnitude of borrowing. Consequently, the OECD TPG suggest that a system of cross-guarantees effectively reflects the group's implied and full support for the pool and all of its participants.[40] The result would be to enhance each participant's credit standing to that of the group as a whole.[41] No guarantee fee would be necessary since the support is implicitly rather than explicitly guaranteed. Among other things, this conclusion can significantly reduce or eliminate the need to perform a credit assessment of each pool participant in order to benchmark lending rates. Consequently, the rates paid to external banks may become closer comparables.

38. Bundesministerium der Finanzen, *supra* note 36, m.no. 3.98–100.
39. *Ibid.*, m.no. 3.99; OECD, *supra* note 1, paras 10.131–142.
40. OECD, *supra* note 1, paras 10.147–148.
41. A similar result is obtained through what is known as *rights of set-off* wherein pool participants allow the CPL (or, through the CPL, external banks) to automatically offset defaults on outstanding withdrawals with available excess cash (deposits).

2.4.6 *Thin Capitalization Rules*

As discussed above, physical or notional cash pooling transactions will create intercompany loans in most jurisdictions (if separate entities are involved).[42] Many countries, particularly in Europe, have formal thin capitalization rules, e.g., earning stripping rules/interest-to-pretax-earning-limits, or debt/equity ratio limitations.[43] Although it is not clear in most affected countries whether thin capitalization rules will also extend to cash pool arrangements in all cases, this is certainly an element to be considered in advance when setting up a cash pool. Pool loans granted by the CPL to a participating company may be added to the total of group loans relevant for determining whether the participant has excessive debt taken up from group companies.

In addition, a growing number of countries have special provisions for the non-deductibility of interest above certain thresholds or with respect to interest paid to tax haven jurisdictions. This is largely a result of the OECD's BEPS initiative.

3 CONCLUSION

In recent years, the use of cash pooling arrangements by MNEs has become more prevalent. They are part of a broader effort by global firms to apply advanced treasury techniques to minimize their external funding costs. Not surprisingly, this development has been met by heightened scrutiny from tax authorities, particularly in those jurisdictions where cash pooling entities tend to be most active. The revised OECD TPG have afforded tax inspectors additional tools with which to challenge the structures of cash pools and the associated intercompany pricing issues.

Overall, regulations on cash pooling arrangements are similarly structured, with minor differences in most countries. Most international tax authorities adhere to the case-specific treatment and application of appropriate transfer pricing methods in the OECD TPG, and this can thus be regarded as a rather common theme. A transfer pricing model incorporating the primary characteristics of all major jurisdictions commonly dealing with cash pooling arrangements should therefore safeguard the business advantages by minimizing significant transfer pricing risk. Multinationals should ensure that their cash pooling arrangements are operationalized in a manner consistent with the arm's length standard. The following are of particular importance:

(1) A complete functional analysis should be performed in order to develop a narrative as to each affiliated entity's role within the pool and to validate the desired characterization of the pool transactions and relationships.

42. In the court case *Poland v. M. sp. Z.o.o.z*, the Polish Supreme Administrative Court found that a cash pooling arrangement can be considered as a loan for the purpose of thin capitalization rules even in the absence of a loan contract and related obligations or consents, *see Poland v. Cash Pool B sp z.o.o.*, No. II FSK 3798/17 (13 November 2013).
43. Examples include France, Germany, Portugal, Spain, and the United Kingdom.

(2) It should be ensured that group entities tasked with monitoring and controlling cash pool risks have adequate economic substance to do so.
(3) Intercompany deposit rates, borrowing rates, and other payments should be established in a manner that does not financially disadvantage each pool participant relative to realistic alternatives to dealing within the pool (and hopefully in a more prosperous condition).
(4) The CPL should be adequately remunerated for the role that it plays and the risks that it bears.
(5) Practical yet supportable methods should be considered for measuring and allocating cash pool benefits.

As is always the case in any transfer pricing matter, the facts, characterizations, economic analysis, and relevant conclusions with respect to a cross-border cash pooling arrangement should be carefully documented with information that is revisited annually as the business evolves.

CHAPTER 5

Hybrid Financing

David Ledure, Wouter Moelands, Rocío López & Tomás Hermida

1 WHAT IS HYBRID FINANCING?

1.1 Characteristics of Hybrid Financing Instruments

A distinction is typically made in corporate finance between debt and equity capital (or financing) as they have fundamentally different characteristics.

Equity capital represents the amount of money that would be returned to the company's shareholders if all of its assets were liquidated and all of its debt was settled in the case of liquidation. It is a popular method for raising capital and is often used to meet the funding needs of an organization by selling a company's stock in exchange for cash.[1] The most typical characteristics of equity are that it has a claim on the residual value of the company in the event of liquidation, its holder has voting rights, and there is no finite maturity date.[2]

Debt capital occurs when a company raises funds via the issuance of debt instruments (e.g., loans, bonds, notes, etc.). The individuals or institutions become creditors and receive a promise that the principal and interest on the debt will be repaid in return for the provision of (debt) capital. Some of its characteristics are that the creditor has unconditional rights to the repayment of the principal amount, and there is a finite maturity date.

Equity and debt financing have clear characteristics that make it relatively easy to distinguish them from each other; however, hybrid instruments are more difficult to categorize. As the name already implies, being a 'hybrid' form of financing, these instruments show some characteristics that are typical for equity financing and a number of features generally associated with debt financing.[3] To add even more complexity, hybrid instruments can take various forms. However, there are common features when assessing their different types. The main characteristics of hybrid financing are typically as follows:[4,5]

(1) There is either no or a very long maturity date.
(2) Hybrid instruments are typically subordinated in relation to other debt obligations. Depending on the instrument, this may vary from ordinary subordination through a junior instrument to an instrument with priority only over common shares.
(3) The rate and/or payment of interest or dividends can be contingent upon the income achieved by the borrower.

1. Richard A. Brealey et al., *Principles of Corporate Finance* 4 (McGraw Hill Education 13th ed. 2020).
2. Ferdinando Bruno & Andrea Rozzi, *The Hybrid Financial Instruments in Italy: A First Attempt to Define This Category*, 7 International In-house Counsel Journal 1–6, 2 (International In-house Counsel Journal Subs 2014).
3. *Ibid.*, at 1–2.
4. Peter J. Green et al., *Hybrid Securities: An Overview*, Multi-Jurisdictional Guide Capital Markets 2 (Practical Law Company Spring 2012).
5. Grzegorz Namiotkiewicz et al., *Issuance of Hybrid Debt Instruments and So-Called Contingent Convertible Bonds (CoCo)*, Clifford Chance, at 2 (August 2016).

(4) There is the possibility of suspending the repayment of the principal amount in specific circumstances such as the occurrence of a loss or the deterioration of certain financial indicators of the borrower.

Besides these more generic characteristics, there are also types of hybrid financing that include additional features such as:

- the right to exchange the instrument into the issuer's share capital or even carry out a compulsory conversion of the hybrid instrument; and/or
- the right to remain after the satisfaction of all obligations, for instance, in the case of a liquidation, on a par with the other shareholders.

As hybrid instruments are sui generis, there is often no legal framework or definition for them.[6] The characteristics as described above are not an exhaustive list, and there are many other variations. The potential set of terms and conditions for hybrid financing are almost unlimited, provided that the instruments are in compliance with the local laws and regulations.

Hybrid instruments combine the benefits of debt (lower risk) and those of equity financing (e.g., potential claiming of residual benefits, higher inference in the operation of the business) when considering their characteristics and when juxtaposed with more traditional financing instruments. As such, hybrid instruments are a relatively safe source of capital from an issuer perspective albeit they are typically more expensive than traditional debt financing due to their subordination to other debt obligations. Further benefits may include the fact that they do not deteriorate the borrower's lending indicators in some cases, and it is possible to suspend payments or even to write off part of the liabilities with certain instruments in the case of future financial difficulties.

This chapter covers transfer pricing aspects of hybrid financial instruments used between related parties; some are more commonly applied than others. As such, the next sections of this chapter address how to select and apply transfer pricing methods to these transactions, considering the added complexities of having both debt and equity-like characteristics. This chapter does not cover 'hybrid mismatch arrangements' that can occur for certain hybrid instruments whereby the tax treatment of the instrument is different in the country of the issuer and that of the subscriber.[7]

6. Bruno & Rozzi, *supra* note 2; Bart Peeters & Lars Vanneste, *The Hybrid Financial Instruments: The Effects of the OECD BEPS Action 2 Report and the ATAD*, 48 Intertax 14–45 (Kluwer Law International 2020).
7. Mismatch arrangements have been addressed in the OECD's report concerning BEPS Action 2; *see* OECD, *Neutralising the Effects of Branch Mismatch Arrangements, Action 2: Inclusive Framework on BEPS* (OECD Publishing 2017).

1.2 Examples of Hybrid Instruments

As previously described, there is no strict definition of hybrid instruments. From a practical perspective, the following types of hybrid financial instruments are commonly observed:

(1) *Mezzanine financing*: As the name implies, this is a form of a traditional loan; however, the lender can assume ownership if it is not paid back on time and in full; this makes it a relatively safe loan.
(2) *Convertible preferred shares*: Convertible preferred shares retain a lower risk profile but with the potential for higher yield when they are converted to common stock for capital appreciation. An advantage of this type of hybrid financial instrument is that preferred shares do not dilute existing common shareholder's value. For financial institutions, convertible preferred stocks are considered part of Tier 1 capital.[8]
(3) *Convertible bonds*: Similar to convertible preferred shares, convertible bonds include an option to convert each bond into shares of the bond issuer's common stock. Convertible bonds issuance is generally a more rapid process than a common shares issuance, and the new capital does not affect the firm's earnings. Moreover, the issuers of these bonds typically pay less interest compared to traditional debt financing. A subcategory of convertible bonds is the contingent convertible bond (known as CoCo bonds). The concept is the same as with the regular convertible bond; however, the initiative of converting lies with the issuer of the bonds and not with the holders. It is also possible for a CoCo bond to be converted automatically in the event of a trigger, for example, when the issuer's capital ratio or other financial ratios fall under a certain threshold.
(4) *Profit participating loans/bonds*: This type of hybrid instrument is typically subordinated to another debt financing. It can be defined as a transfer of money to a company by which the lender is rewarded with variable interest

8. Tier 1 capital is composed of the sum of common shares (equivalent for non-joint stock companies) and stock surplus, retained earnings, other comprehensive income, qualifying minority interest, and regulatory adjustments plus the sum of capital instruments meeting the criteria for Additional Tier 1 capital (AT1) and related surplus, additional qualifying minority interest, and regulatory adjustments. Common Equity Tier 1 capital (CET1) is the highest quality of regulatory capital as it absorbs losses immediately when they occur. AT1 also provides loss absorption on a going-concern basis, although AT1 instruments do not meet all of the criteria for CET1. For example, some debt instruments, such as perpetual contingent convertible capital instruments, may be included in AT1 but not in CET1. *See* Bank for International Settlements, *Definition of Capital in Basel III: Executive Summary*, https://www.bis.org/fsi/fsisummaries/defcap_b3.htm (last visited 1 August 2022).

rates usually depending on profits.[9] The loan provider's yield thus depends on the economic result of the company.[10]

(5) *Perpetuals*: This is a fixed security with no maturity date (or a very distant one) that provides a steady stream of income.

1.3 Some Definitions of Hybrid Financing

There is no transfer pricing definition of hybrid financing, and the Organisation for Economic Co-operation and Development transfer pricing guidelines (OECD TPG)[11] do not provide any specific comments on these types of financing. While the OECD issued its Chapter X on financing transactions in February 2020,[12] this chapter does not cover specific guidelines on hybrid financing. Nevertheless, it is useful to refer to other regulations for guidance in interpreting its specific features that are used in an independent context to apply to an intercompany context as well. As such, this section briefly discusses hybrid financing covered in international accounting standards (i.e., IAS 32)[13] and regulatory requirements such as Basel I[14] for banks and Solvency II[15] for insurers.

1.3.1 International Accounting Standards

Some accounting standards, like the IAS, cover hybrid financing. The IAS 32 requires that the component parts be accounted for and presented separately according to their substance based on the definitions of liability and equity. The split is made at issuance

9. Jakob Bundgaard & Katja Joo Dyppel, *Profit-Participating Loans in International Tax Law*, 38 Intertax 643-662, 643, 644 (Kluwer Law International 2010).
10. Libena Tetrevova & Jan Svedik, *Mezzanine Financing Instruments in Comparison to the Classic Financing Sources*, 16 Business, Management and Education 133-146, 136 (Gediminas Technical University, Department of Construction Economics & Property 2018).
11. OECD, *OECD Transfer Pricing Guidelines for Multinational Enterprises and Tax Administrations 2022* (OECD Publishing 2022).
12. Incorporated in the OECD TPG in January 2022.
13. The IAS 32 specify the presentation for financial instruments classified into financial assets, financial liabilities, and equity instruments. Differentiation between a financial liability and equity depends on whether an entity has an obligation to deliver cash (or some other financial asset). *See* International Financial Reporting Standards, *IAS 32 Financial Instruments: Presentation*.
14. Beginning with the Basel Concordat, first issued in 1975 and revised several times since, the BCBS has established a series of international standards for bank regulation, most notably its landmark publications of the accords on capital adequacy that are commonly known as Basel I, Basel II and, most recently, Basel III ('Basel Accords'). Under Basel I, banks that operate internationally must maintain capital (Tier 1 and Tier 2) equal to at least 8% of their risk-weighted assets. This ensures banks hold a certain amount of capital in order to meet obligations. *See* Bank for International Settlements, *History of the Basel Committee*, https://www.bis.org/bcbs/history.htm (last visited 1 August 2022).
15. The Solvency II regime introduces a framework for insurance firms in the European Union (EU). It is based on the risk profile of each individual insurance company in order to promote comparability, transparency, and competitiveness. *See Directive 2009/138/EC on the Taking-Up and Pursuit of the Business of Insurance and Reinsurance (Solvency II)*, No. 2009/138/EC.

and not revised for subsequent changes in market interest rates, share prices, or other events that change the likelihood that the conversion option will be exercised.[16]

The most important element that differentiates a financial liability from an equity instrument within the meaning of the IAS 32 is the presence of a contractual obligation on the issuer to deliver cash or other financial assets to the other party (the holder).[17] The existence of this obligation means that there is a financial liability or with an equity instrument in the case of a lack thereof. Classification always depends on the content of the specific financial instrument which should be regarded as prevailing over its name or form for the purpose of describing it in the accounts. In practice, it is assumed that if payments to the holders of the given instrument are at the sole discretion of the issuer who has the right to unconditionally avoid a cash payment, then such an instrument may be deemed an equity instrument in principle.

1.3.2 Basel Accords

As presented before, the Basel Accords were a series of three sequential banking regulation agreements (Basel I, II, and III) set by the Basel Committee on Bank Supervision (BCBS). They were established with the sole purpose of creating an international regulatory framework for managing credit risk and market risk.

The Basel Accords set criteria for measuring capital adequacy and divide capital into two different categories, Tier 1 (or core capital) and Tier 2 (or supplementary capital) capital. The former includes the common stock, disclosed reserves, and minority interest in the equity accounts of consolidated subsidiaries. The latter includes the undisclosed reserves, asset revaluation reserves, and hybrid capital instruments.[18]

Hybrid securities are often issued by financial institutions, including banks. The issuer of hybrid securities seeks out these instruments that qualify for a favourable equity treatment from rating agencies and without diluting existing shareholders. Issuers therefore attempt to structure these instruments as Tier 2 capital.

Whether a hybrid instrument should be considered as being 'equity-like' or 'debt-like' depends on the institution assessing this qualification. From a rating agency and bank regulatory perspective, more equity-like instruments receive a more favourable treatment.

Banks are required under the Basel capital requirements[19] to maintain certain ratios between Tier 1 and total capital to assets. The Basel Framework at the time before the Global Financial Crisis[20] did not address the features of hybrid instruments, and there

16. *Supra* note 13, at A1358.
17. *Ibid.*, at A1341.
18. Green et al., *supra* note 4, at 3.
19. Defined as the percentage of risk-weighted assets as cash reserves that banks with international presence are required to hold. This percentage and these minimum capital requirements were changing with several modifications over the years. *See supra* note 14.
20. The Global Financial Crisis refers to the massive financial crisis the world faced from 2008 to 2009 that affected individuals and institutions around the globe. Certain financial institutions began to experience financial distress, many were absorbed by larger entities, and the government was forced to offer bailouts to keep many institutions afloat. The crisis, often referred to as

were minimal legal frameworks or guidelines for banks and regulators. The only available instrument was the Sydney Agreement of 1998.[21]

The 2008 financial crisis exposed the weakness of the international financial system and led to the creation of Basel III. This new regulation was created in November 2010 to reform and rectify some anomalies that caused the financial crisis linked to weaknesses in corporate governance and liquidity management, over-leveraged capital structures due to lack of regulatory restrictions, and misaligned incentives in Basel I and II. It emphasized the rationale behind the distinction between Tier 1 and Tier 2 capital. The former must contribute in order for the bank to remain as a going concern and must be subordinated to a depositor and general creditor; cannot be secured nor guaranteed; cannot hinder recapitalization; and must be capable of principal loss absorption[22] (including a mandatory conversion to common shares or principal write-down at a prespecified trigger point). When financial instruments do not meet these criteria, the capital can be qualified as Tier 2 capital provided that the financial instrument has a minimum original maturity of at least five years with no incentive to redeem and is callable only by the issuer after a minimum of five years with prior supervisory approval.

1.3.3 Solvency II

Solvency II consists of a risk-based capital regime applicable to regulated insurance companies with head offices based in the EU. The spirit of this regime is similar to that established in Basel II and is based on and supported by three pillars. The first is grounded on an arm's length calculation of insurance liabilities in the market and risk-based calculation of capital. The second involves a process of review and supervision and, lastly, the third imposes reporting and transparency requirements and obligations.

The process known as 'technical provisions' consists of the calculation of insurance liabilities under Solvency II and includes a 'best estimate' of liabilities and a risk margin (when the liability is not appropriately hedged).

Solvency II defines a series of directives that stipulate that EU insurers are required to maintain a specific amount or percentage of capital. These can be categorized into three different levels or 'tiers', i.e., high-quality capital ('Tier 1'); good-quality capital ('Tier 2'); and low-quality capital ('Tier 3').[23] Financial instruments are classified under the concept of a tier based on the valuation of their pre-bankruptcy and

'The Great Recession', began with the housing market bubble created by an incredible load of mortgage-backed securities that bundled high-risk loans.

21. The 'Sydney Agreement' is the term commonly applied to the 27 October 1998 press release of the Basel Committee on Banking Supervision. *See* Bank for International Settlements, *Instruments Eligible for Inclusion in Tier 1 Capital: Press Release*, https://www.bis.org/press/p981027.htm (last visited 1 August 2022).
22. Common stock provides 'loss absorption' for an issuer, meaning that common stockholders are the last class of security holders to receive distributions in a liquidation.
23. Kamil Liberadzki & Marcin Liberadzki, *Hybrid Securities: Structuring, Pricing and Risk Assessment* 81 (Palgrave Macmillan UK 2016).

post-bankruptcy loss-absorption features. Insurers with access to hybrid capital are able to improve their financial strength which allows them to increase their solvency or liquidity position by providing additional loss-absorbing capacity.

In order to cover the solvency capital requirement (SCR), at least 50% of all eligible funds should be comprised of Tier 1 capital. In addition, surplus funding from high-quality hybrid issues above the level of 20% may be classified as Ancillary T2. The remainder of funds may consist of T2 capital, including subordinated debt which is defined as dated or undated bonds. Moreover, a maximum of 15% of funds may be from Tier 3 capital (Figure 5.1). Finally, a minimum of 80% of minimum capital requirements must be common shares and reserves.[24]

Figure 5.1 Solvency II Hybrid Limits from Standard & Poor's

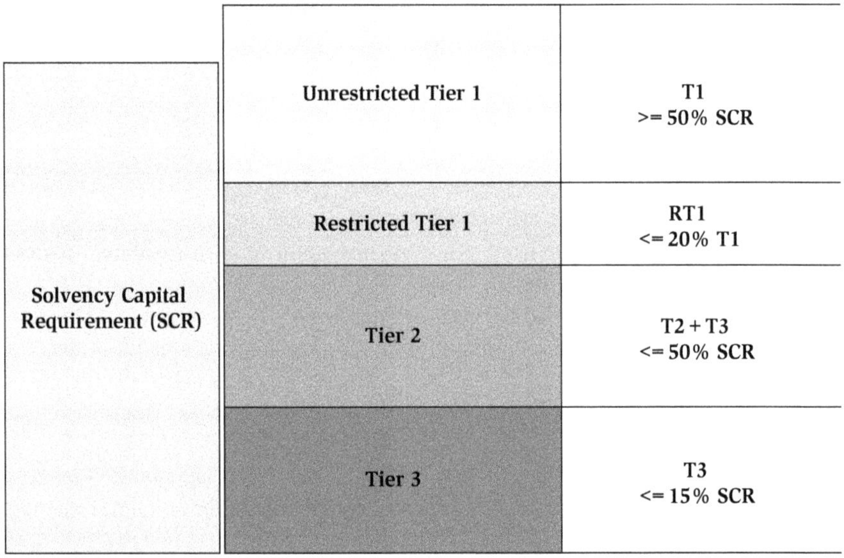

Source: S&P Global.[25]

2 IDENTIFICATION OF THE COMMERCIAL OR FINANCIAL RELATIONS

In order to identify the commercial and financial relations between the related parties, the OECD TPG and transfer pricing regulations such as the US Transfer Pricing Regulations as included in Internal Revenue Code (I.R.C.) §1.482 require that the

24. *Ibid.*
25. S&P, *Solvency II Gives European Insurers Room to Issue More Hybrid Debt, but Not Without Risk to the Ratings*, https://www.spglobal.com/ratings/en/research/articles/190529-solvency-ii-gives-european-insurers-room-to-issue-more-hybrid-debt-but-not-without-risk-to-the-ratings-10969145 (last visited 1 August 2022).

comparability factors be assessed.[26] This evaluation has two objectives. First, it enables assessing whether the transaction has been 'accurately delineated'. Once this occurs, then the comparability analysis allows comparing the conditions and economically relevant circumstances of the tested intercompany transaction with comparable transactions between unrelated parties.[27] While the current section comments on each of the comparability factors, they are further applied in the next sections covering the accurate delineation and the selection of the transfer pricing method.

2.1 The Contractual Terms of the Transaction

As indicated above, hybrid instruments cover a wide range of instruments with different characteristics for which a careful analysis is required due to the hybrid nature. Typical contractual features of hybrid instruments cover one or more contractual characteristics such as the absence of or a very long maturity, subordination, and no guaranteed fixed return, option, or obligation to convert.

2.2 Functional Analysis

A functional analysis is the cornerstone of any transfer pricing analysis. While all of the former's aspects are relevant, the 'control over risk' is likely at the centre of the functional analysis for hybrid instruments. Compared to traditional debt instruments, hybrid instrument risks may be allocated differently between the issuer and the subscriber. Therefore, all of the economically significant risks should be identified.[28] Subsequently, the functional analysis of the entity bearing such risks should demonstrate that it performs 'control functions and risk mitigating functions'.[29] For hybrid instruments, the control over risk functions are seldom only at the subscriber level.

Example

If the issuer's profits are lower than expected under a profit participating loan, this is first linked to the issuer's operations. This entity has obvious control over these risks. However, it should be demonstrated that the subscriber also has the relevant substance and expertise to understand the risks and have access to sufficient information to assess them just as an independent investor would have. However, this does not necessarily require that risk can be influenced or

26. *See* OECD, *supra* note 11, para. 1.36.; US I.R.C., para. 1.482-1(d). As local country transfer pricing regulation generally contains similar requirements as the OECD TPG, the following sections focus on the latter.
27. *Ibid.*, para. 1.33.
28. *Ibid.*, para. 1.38.
29. *Ibid.*, para. 1.60.

that uncertainty can be completely removed from the transaction by the subscriber.[30]

2.3 Characteristics of Property or Services

Differences in specific characteristics should be considered as they may determine the (un)comparability of controlled and uncontrolled transactions.[31] This comparability factor is arguably less relevant for financial transactions compared to goods or services transactions as hybrid instruments are primarily driven by their contractual terms. However, as the arm's length pricing of these instruments is often determined by CUPs, adjusted CUPs, or other economic methods relying on open-market information, attention is required in relation to items that can influence these price points. For example, liquidity premiums may be required to take into account differences between over-the-counter instruments and those that are traded.

2.4 Economic Circumstances

Particular economic circumstances that exist in specific markets may influence arm's length pricing.[32] For financial instruments in general, financial markets are considered as global and interconnected. Consequently, it is typically considered that financial markets are 'perfect'; i.e., any differences between markets would create some arbitrage opportunities that should minimize such differences by the pure force of the market. This would eliminate the differences and return it to its original status of 'perfection'. While this level of perfection may not always occur, it is typically an assumption related to financial markets.

An economic circumstance that is generally a key consideration concerns the situation of the borrower or issuer. More in particular, the borrower's or issuer's credit risk is a key parameter for financial transactions in general. While a credit rating estimation is also key for many hybrid instruments, other measures might be required for some of these instruments. In the case of convertible bonds, for example, the conversion risk/opportunity requires modelling and scenario analyses that are not captured by traditional credit risk measures.

Finally, government regulations are also a relevant element reflecting specific economic circumstances. This is particularly true for regulated industries, i.e., banking and capital markets, insurances, and asset management, among others. Such regulations are often a driver for crafting the specific characteristics of a hybrid instrument. While such consideration is key for the accurate delineation of the transaction, as explained below, the comparability analysis should verify whether country or region-specific regulations also influence the arm's length pricing.

30. *Ibid.*, para. 1.67.
31. *Ibid.*, para. 1.67.
32. *Ibid.*, para. 1.133.

2.5 Business Strategies

Business strategy is the final comparability factor prescribed by the OECD.[33] For hybrid instruments, it might become a relevant element for accurate delineation; e.g., tapping from additional subordinated funding may be a key element for a borrower in the deployment of its business strategy. For the actual comparability assessment of controlled and uncontrolled transactions, the business strategies should be less of an influencing factor.

3 RECOGNITION OF THE ACCURATELY DELINEATED TRANSACTION

The accurate delineation of the actual transaction begins with a thorough identification of the economically relevant characteristics of the transaction - consisting of the commercial or financial relations between the parties as well as the conditions and economically relevant circumstances. Hereto, the comparability factors of the previous section should be carefully considered.

While a written contract is the commencement of any transfer pricing analysis, it must be supplemented with other relevant information in order to accurately delineate the transaction. Therefore, it should be ensured that the written contract is in accordance with the actual conduct of the parties by also considering the other comparability factors.[34] Stated differently, implementing an intercompany hybrid instrument is not just a matter of legal documentation as it should also be supported by each of the five comparability factors. If not, tax authorities might re-delineate (some aspects of) the contract when assessing the arm's length nature of such a transaction or even disregard the transactions in specific circumstances.

Only in exceptional circumstances can tax authorities disregard a transaction for transfer pricing purposes. The determinant here is the 'commercial rationality of the arrangement'. Hereto, a transaction cannot be disregarded if unrelated parties under comparable circumstances would have agreed to it. Whether it can or cannot be observed between unrelated parties is not of relevance.[35] An appropriate example of the accurate delineation can be found in the new Chapter X of the OECD TPG[36] on whether an 'advance of funds' can be accurately delineated as (hybrid) debt funding instead of equity funding for transfer pricing purposes. It provides a non-exhaustive list of economically relevant characteristics to be considered:

- the presence or absence of a fixed repayment date;
- the obligation to pay interest;

33. *Ibid.*, para. 1.137.
34. *Ibid.*, para. 1.140.
35. *Ibid.*, paras 1.122–123.
36. *Ibid.*, Ch. X.

- the right to enforce payment of principal and interest;
- the status of the funder in comparison to regular corporate creditors;
- the existence of financial covenants and security;
- the source of interest payments;
- the ability of the recipient of the funds to obtain loans from unrelated lending institutions; the extent to which the advance is used to acquire capital assets; and
- the failure of the purported debtor to repay on the due date or to seek a postponement.[37]

As hybrid instruments represent, by definition, different characteristics compared to plain vanilla debt or equity instruments, it is important to clearly describe the business drivers of such specific features and the control over risk functions in order to ensure that the contract is in accordance with the conduct of the parties.[38] To do so, the options realistically available to the parties should be analysed to justify the characteristics that are unique to hybrid financing. In some industries, these options are also driven by regulations such as the Basel Accords and Insolvency.

Example

In order to qualify as Tier 2 capital, the issuer has no other choice than to include certain hybrid features. If not, it can be in breach of the regulatory capital requirements and ultimately lose its banking or insurance licence. Under Basel Accords and Insolvency regulations, a hybrid debt capital instrument may be included in the supplementary (Tier 2) capital if it has close similarities to equity, particularly when it is able to support losses on an ongoing basis without effectuating liquidation. Hybrid debt capital instruments that may qualify as Tier 2 capital under Basel Accords and Insolvency regulations include perpetual preferred shares carrying a fixed charge (or coupon), long-term preferred shares in Canada, perpetual debt instruments in the United Kingdom, and mandatory convertible debt instruments in the US, among others. Subordinated term debt instruments with a minimum original term to maturity of over five years may also be included within the supplementary (Tier 2) elements of capital but only to a maximum of 50% of the core (Tier 1) capital element and subject to adequate amortization arrangements.[39]

4 SELECTION OF THE MOST APPROPRIATE METHOD

There are no specified methods (as the 'specified methods' term is defined in Chapter II of the OECD TPG) to establish arm's length remuneration for hybrid financing (nor

37. *Ibid.*, para. 10.12.
38. *Ibid.*, paras 1.122–123.
39. Basel Committee on Banking Supervision, *The Basel Framework* 1273 et seq.

for traditional debt financing, for that matter). However, the OECD TPG state that the selection of a transfer pricing method should always aim at finding the most appropriate method for a particular case. To do so, the selection process should take into consideration the respective strengths and weaknesses of the OECD-recognized methods.[40]

Considering this, the pricing of hybrid financing is often based on the (adjusted) CUP method or an 'unspecified method'. Section 5. describes the application of these methods on practical examples of hybrid financing.

Direction can be obtained from the OECD Guidance for applying the CUP method for hybrid financing. It states that the arm's length interest rate for a tested loan can be benchmarked using publicly available data for other borrowers with the same credit rating for loans with sufficiently similar terms and conditions as well as other comparability factors.[41] In addition to the credit rating, the OECD Guidance mentions maturity and currency as other relevant comparability factors.[42] It notes that the issuance rating should also be factored in addition to considering the borrower's rating (e.g., whether the seniority of the instrument would cause it to have a different rating from that of the issuer). Furthermore, it notes that an issuer's credit rating may be impacted by the implicit support from its parent or other related parties.[43] Finally, it briefly mentions the other methods that may be considered when evaluating the pricing of a loan that can be applied to hybrid financing and economic modelling.

In the US, I.R.C. §1.482-2(a) addresses transfer pricing regulations for debt financing which can also be used to evaluate hybrid financing. The general rule is that an arm's length remuneration shall be a rate that was charged or would have been charged at the time the transaction was entered into in independent transactions with or between unrelated parties under similar circumstances.

There are no specific methods for establishing arm's length remuneration for hybrid financing nor concerning debt financing. With respect to the latter, the US Transfer Pricing Regulations state that all relevant factors should be considered. These include:

- the principal amount and duration of the loan;
- the security involved;
- the credit standing of the borrower; and
- the interest rate prevailing at the situs of the lender or creditor for comparable loans between unrelated parties.[44]

The OECD accepts that methods that are not listed in the OECD TPG could also be used. In such cases, their selection should be supported by an explanation of why

40. OECD, *supra* note 11, para. 2.2.
41. *Ibid.*, para. 10.91.
42. *Ibid.*
43. OECD, *supra* note 11, paras 10.76–77.
44. US I.R.C., para. 1.482-2(a).

OECD-recognized methods were considered as less appropriate or unworkable.[45] This is often the case for some classes of hybrid financing instruments. Therefore, they rely on generally accepted economic methods involving variables that are often sourced with open-market information. While this is not the application of the CUP method stricto sensu, it is close to this method as the open-market information is used for the relevant parameters.

5 APPLICATION OF THE MOST APPROPRIATE METHOD

5.1 Mezzanine Debt and Preferred Stock

As mentioned in section 5.1.2, mezzanine financing is a financing agreement in which funds are provided in the form of a traditional loan, but the lender can assume ownership if the loan is not paid back on time and in full, making it a relatively safe loan. Preferred stock, on the other hand, is a component of share capital that has priority over common stocks in relation to dividend payments and in the event of a liquidation and includes properties of both an equity and a debt instrument.

Under the framework of the CUP method, there are typically two key economic components to consider when determining what interest rate may be applied by an independent entity in a comparable uncontrolled transaction. These are:

(1) creditworthiness of a financing instrument; and
(2) terms and conditions of the instrument.

5.1.1 Creditworthiness of Mezzanine Debt and Preferred Stock

A credit rating of a certain financing instrument evaluates its risk based on an estimation (on a forward-looking or forecasted basis) of: (i) the likelihood of the borrower/issuer defaulting on its financial obligations which is measured by the issuer's credit rating and (ii) the expected loss in the case of the issuer's default considering the instrument's security and priority of claim.

(i) Credit Rating of the Issuer

The creditworthiness of the borrowing entity is one of the primary drivers of the interest rate of a financing arrangement. Hence, identifying or estimating this creditworthiness is a crucial step for the benchmarking analysis.

If there is a published credit rating for the borrower issued by a rating agency,[46] the preferred approach would generally be to rely on it. However, it is important to

45. OECD, *supra* note 11, para. 2.9.
46. The main credit rating agencies are Standard & Poor's (S&P), Moody's Investor Service (Moody's), and Fitch Ratings (Fitch). There are also smaller agencies such as DBRS Morningstar and Egan-Jones.

consider if this credit rating is contemporaneous with the mezzanine instrument under analysis or if it was issued before that instrument. In the case of the latter, the published credit rating might need to be revised in light of the borrower's current capital structure by taking into account its recent mezzanine issuance.

In the absence of a recent published credit rating for the borrower, its creditworthiness can be estimated for the purposes of transfer pricing analyses following the guidance provided by credit rating agencies. In this regard, the credit rating of the borrowing entity can be determined either as a distinct and separate enterprise (i.e., on a 'standalone' basis)[47] or in the context of its membership in a larger group.[48]

Using the 'standalone approach', a borrower within a multinational group is treated as a distinct and separate enterprise. Its creditworthiness is evaluated on the basis of its own financial standing and disregards the influence of the parent company and other members of the multinational group. For this purpose, most credit rating agencies (including S&P and Moody's) developed industry-specific models that take into account the main qualitative and quantitative factors that are relevant for each industry. This offers the best possible relative ranking of a borrower's creditworthiness vis-à-vis similar companies in the same industry.

On the other hand, the 'member of the group' approach evaluates the creditworthiness of the subsidiary and recognizes that the subsidiary is a part of a multinational group. This approach considers the willingness of the parent company/group to intervene if the subsidiary encounters financial difficulties, given the level of affiliation and strategic importance of this entity for the rest of the group.[49]

While the standalone approach used to be recommended and generally applied, based on the authors' experience, tax authorities in the broader transfer pricing context, case law, and recent transfer pricing guidelines discuss the appropriateness of taking into account a company's group affiliation when assessing its creditworthiness.

Example

In the *GE* Case,[50] the issue was the validity of the payment of a guarantee fee by a Canadian subsidiary to a US parent. In this case, the Tax Court of Canada (TCC) applied both the standalone approach and the concept of implicit support by the parent company to arrive at an appropriate credit rating for the Canadian subsidiary of GE Capital. The TCC recognized that implicit support is not equivalent to explicit support by a parent company but still has some value in the determination of a subsidiary's credit rating.

In particular, the OECD Guidance on financial transactions states that implicit support from the group may affect the borrower's credit rating that of any debt that it

47. Moody's Investor Service, *Assessing Affiliate Support in the Absence of a Guarantee* (July 2021).
48. S&P Global, *General Criteria: Group Rating Methodology* (December 2021).
49. *Ibid.*
50. *General Electric Capital Canada Inc v. Her Majesty the Queen* (2009) TCC 563.

issues.[51] The relative status of an entity within the group may help to determine what impact that potential group support has on a debt issuer's credit rating.

This OECD Guidance is in accordance with the methodology published by S&P that provides notching guidance in the case of core/highly strategic entities of a multinational group. In particular, S&P's Group Rating Methodology establishes qualitative criteria to rate entities that are part of a group based on their level of affiliation with other group entities, their strategic importance for the group, and the likelihood of receiving support from the rest of the group in the case of distress.

(ii) Credit Rating of the Issuance

The estimated creditworthiness of the issuer may differ from the specific ratings of its debt instruments. The issuer's rating evaluates the company's overall risk of default, whereas a specific issue rating evaluates the ultimate repayment of only the issue (i.e., including the expected recovery in the event of default). The ultimate repayment of a specific issue depends on the features of that particular debt instrument. In particular, the issue rating considers specific features of the financial instrument, for instance, guarantees, securities, and level of seniority.[52]

To recognize the lower priority and recovery prospects of financial obligations that do not have a specific claim on the debtor's assets, both S&P and Moody's consider the principles of notching down. This is used to establish an implied credit rating for lower recovery prospects and is a method used to identify financial obligations that are disadvantaged in relation to more secured obligations. The notching principle does not seek to predict exact recovery levels because this requires knowing the exact mix of assets and values at a particular time in the future. Instead, it is used to identify debt issues with a material disadvantage relative to better-positioned obligations.

Moody's uses a loss given default methodology to determine a credit rating for lower-ranked obligations of a company (e.g., unsecured and/or subordinate) and provides general guidance indicating that debt subordinated to more senior obligations would be rated one credit rating notch lower than a senior unsecured obligation for investment-grade obligors and up to two credit rating notches lower in the case of non-investment grade obligors.[53]

Table 5.1 provides subordination-based rating guidance from Moody's.

51. OECD, *supra* note 11, para. 10.78.
52. *Ibid.*, para. 10.69.
53. Moody's Investor Service, *Notching Corporate Instrument Ratings Based on Differences in Security and Priority of Claim* (October 2017).

Table 5.1 Guidance on Subordination-Based Notching from Moody's

Debt Type	*Notches*
Senior Secured Debt	**+1 or +2**
Senior Unsecured Debt	**0**
Subordinated Debt	**–1 or –2**
Junior Subordinated Debt	**–1 or –2**
Preferred Stock[54]	**–2**

Source: Moody's Investor Service.[55]

In addition to general guidance, as mentioned above, Moody's also provides specific notching guidance in some of its rating methodologies.

Example

The real estate investment trusts and Other Commercial Real Estate Firms Methodology[56] provide specific guidance for notching hybrid instruments considering their lower priority in the capital structure. In particular, for hybrids other than preferred stock, specific terms of the hybrids would be considered in order to assess whether the instrument is more like ordinary subordinated debt or more like preferred securities. Among other terms, Moody's would assess whether any coupon-skipping mechanisms may imply delayed repayment of the hybrid coupons prior to a default of the firm's senior unsecured debt, and they may also consider any convertibility terms. If the hybrid instrument is considered to be more like ordinary subordinated debt, the notching guidance for subordinated debt would typically be followed. On the other hand, if the hybrid is more like preferred securities, the hybrid is generally rated at the same level as preferred securities, i.e., one or two notches below senior unsecured debt.[57]

In addition, S&P also provides some general principles for assigning an issue credit rating to a hybrid instrument. In particular, S&P assigns an issue credit rating for instruments that are rateable by notching down from the starting point for that issuer. Notching for hybrid instruments generally combines: (1) one or two notches for subordination and (2) one or more notches to reflect the risk of loss absorption or cash

54. Minus two notches also applies to junior-most hybrid securities that may include both debt and equity characteristics. However, if a junior-most hybrid includes mandatory coupon skip triggers, then it is minus three notches.
55. *Supra* note 53.
56. Moody's Investor Service, *REITs and Other Commercial Real Estate Firms Methodology* (July 2021).
57. *Ibid.*

conservation. Such notching down is cumulative, thus doing so for subordination risk is in addition to any potential notching down for deferral risk.[58]

A debt instrument that transforms into a hybrid instrument upon a trigger event will be rated based on its hybrid features if the rating agency anticipates that the trigger will be activated at or before loss absorption or cash conservation on an equivalent hybrid instrument.

Regarding point (1) above, S&P provides criteria for how much to notch down the ratings on subordinated debt and preferred stock/shares (collectively, 'junior instruments') for the subordination risk of speculative-grade and investment-grade corporate issuers in all ranked and unranked jurisdictions.[59] Specifically, S&P notches down junior instruments for subordination risk as follows:[60]

- twice for speculative-grade issuers of junior instruments in Group A and Group B jurisdictions;
- once for speculative-grade issuers of junior instruments in Group C or unranked jurisdictions; and
- once for investment-grade issuers of junior instruments regardless of the jurisdiction ranking.

In relation to point (2), S&P reflects the risk of loss absorption or cash conservation; either may create payment risk by deducting one or more notches.[61]

If it is considered that the payment risk (i.e., likelihood of loss absorption or cash conservation) for a specific instrument is not reflected in either the starting point or the minimum notching, wider notching would be applied at issuance. They may also revise the notching as part of their surveillance if the payment risk increases or decreases over the life of the instrument. They do not impose a limit on the number of notches that may be deducted for payment risk.[62]

If the instrument includes features that enable the issuer to modify it in such a way that the risk of loss absorption or cash conservation would increase, S&P incorporates those features into the rating from the issue date. However, when an external event must occur before an issuer may modify the instrument, they do not typically incorporate the potential change in the terms of the instrument into the rating.[63]

Payment-in-kind (PIK) instruments (including toggle notes) are typically not subject to notching for the risk of loss absorption or cash conservation as the imputed promise will not generally be breached before the instrument's maturity date. However, if a PIK instrument's terms and conditions create an imputed promise that the investor will

58. S&P, *General Criteria: Hybrid Capital: Methodology and Assumptions* (March 2022). S&P Global Ratings considers an instrument to be a hybrid capital instrument if, and only if, it can absorb losses or conserve cash without causing a legal default or liquidation of the issuer; *see Ibid.*, para. 3.
59. S&P, *Ratings: Reflecting Subordination Risk in Corporate Issue Ratings* (March 2018), paras 48–49.
60. S&P, *Standard & Poor's Publishes Jurisdiction Ranking Assessments for the Insolvency Regimes of 30 Countries* (January 2016).
61. *Supra* note 58, para. 50.
62. *Ibid.*, para. 52.
63. *Ibid.*, para. 53.

receive payments in cash during the instrument's life (and these payments can be deferred), S&P typically treats the feature as being equivalent to cumulative coupon deferability and notch as if the instrument contained such a deferability feature.[64]

S&P caps their rating at 'CCC' on a hybrid instrument that has a contingent capital trigger leading to common equity conversion or principal write-down, or both, that is based on a specified rating change. They do not consider a contingent capital trigger to be based on a rating change if it is based on an entity entering into bankruptcy or similar proceedings.[65]

5.1.2 Identification of Arm's Length Interest Rates

The arm's length principle requires that intercompany financial transactions be undertaken on terms and conditions similar to those that would have been entered into by independent parties.

(i) Terms and Conditions of Indebtedness

Some of the components that directly affect the interest rate level on the transaction are:

- type of financing transaction (e.g., term loans, revolver loans, preferred stock);
- industry of the borrower;
- the tenor/maturity of the issuance;
- credit rating of the issuance;
- fixed versus floating rates (floating rates established as a base rate plus a spread typically represent less risk to lenders because they automatically reflect changes in the market conditions);
- currency in which the financial instrument is negotiated;
- embedded options (e.g., granting the borrower the ability to repay before maturity, allowing the lender to collect before maturity, or making the loan convertible to equity); and
- timing of the issuance.

For additional details, the authors direct the reader to Chapter 2 on loans.

(ii) Search for Arm's Length Interest Rates

Once the terms and conditions of the financial instrument have been identified, it is possible to search for third-party comparable financial instruments using the estimated credit rating of the issuance. Public information on loans, bonds, and preferred stock with similar credit ratings and characteristics could then be considered for the purposes of the analysis.

---

64. *Ibid.*, para. 54.
65. *Ibid.*, para. 55.

In general, two transactions do not need to be identical to be considered comparable but must be sufficiently similar to provide a reliable basis for determining arm's length results. When differences that materially affect the price or profit under analysis are identified and can be reliably quantified and adjusted, adjustments must be made to improve the comparability between the controlled and uncontrolled transaction. The main adjustments that can be performed to improve comparability are:

(1) *Tenor adjustment*: Longer-term financial instruments tend to be riskier than those with a shorter term. Given the tenor of the financial instrument under analysis, term adjustments could be made to account for the differences between this term to maturity and those of the selected external transactions.
(2) *Mark-to-market adjustment*: Historical market data may not be a reliable indicator of current market conditions. In order to increase comparability between the financial instrument under analysis and the third-party comparables, mark-to-market adjustments could be applied to the interest rates of the latter to reflect the market conditions at the time of origination of the tested financial instrument.
(3) *Currency adjustment*: In practice, third parties (issuers of debt, investors, and others) commonly use cross-currency basis swaps to convert cash flows from one currency to another on a floating rate debt. Under a cross-currency basis swap contract, one party borrows a certain currency from another party and simultaneously lends the same value of a different currency to that party at current spot rates. This adjustment could be applied to third-party comparables to increase comparability by eliminating the inherent risk of each currency.
(4) *Credit rating adjustment*: In order to match the estimated credit rating for the debt instrument under analysis, credit rating adjustments could be performed to the comparable observations.
(5) *Floating to fixed adjustment*: In practice, if the debt instrument analysis has a fixed rate and the interest rates for the comparable debt transactions identified in the searches are priced with a fixed credit margin over a base rate, the floating base rate must be converted into a fixed base rate for the interest rates to be comparable. Comparable fixed interest rates can be derived by adding the relevant fixed base rate (swap rate) to the credit margins to obtain the fixed interest rates for the comparable debt transactions.

For the identification of comparable transactions, one of the following two approaches can generally be considered:

(1) Focus on the credit rating comparability by searching for any type of financial instrument (including bonds and loans) with the same creditworthiness as the transaction under analysis. The reason behind this is that the issuance's credit rating, for instance, is already factored into its payment rank. Thus, all financial instruments with the same creditworthiness, regardless of the type, are expected to have similar interest rates.

(2) Alternatively, focus on the type of instrument by being more flexible with the rest of the search criteria such as the credit rating or industry. In order to illustrate this, consider the mezzanine market that is formed only by non-investment grade instruments and therefore focusing on the creditworthiness may not be relevant for this type of benchmark.

There is generally no preference between the two approaches mentioned above when performing a benchmarking analysis for testing intercompany mezzanine debt, and both can be equally considered. In particular, if the comparability is not focused on the type of instrument, it needs to be more specific on the credit rating, the type of industry, and the region, among other aspects.

However, when performing a benchmarking analysis for testing intercompany preferred stock, there is usually a preference for a combination of both approaches (i.e., search for comparable preferred stock with a similar credit rating). In this case, having additional publicly available information allows us to be more specific on the search criteria and therefore combine the two previously mentioned approaches.

5.2 Convertible Bonds

A convertible bond can be considered as a traditional fixed income instrument for which part of the interest payments has been replaced by a financial call option, often to lower the coupon rate. The investor in the convertible bond has agreed to receiving lower interest payments in exchange for an option to convert its bond into equity.

As a result, at issuance of the convertible bond, the market value of the fixed income instrument (without the conversion option) plus the market value of the call option should be equal to the subscription value of the convertible bond.

Under the framework of the CUP method, there are four key economic components to consider when determining what interest rate may be applied by an independent entity in a comparable uncontrolled transaction involving a convertible bond. These are:

- creditworthiness of the fixed income (only) instrument;
- terms and conditions of the fixed income (only) instrument;
- value of the underlying shares of the option; and
- terms and conditions of the financial option to convert the bond into an equity instrument.

As finding exact comparable transactions along all economic components is unlikely, adjustments related to the last two items of the economic components (linked to the call option) will usually be required. This approach is consistent with paragraph 2.16 of the OECD TPG.

5.2.1 *Market Value of the Underlying Shares of the Options*

The underlying shares of the option can be either: (i) quoted or (ii) unquoted. If the underlying shares of the conversion option are quoted, their price will be used in the estimation of the market value of the conversion option. If they are not quoted, their market value needs to be estimated. Some typical methods used to do so include: (i) the income approach (Discount Cash Flow), (ii) the market approach (multiples of quoted peers or comparable transactions), and (iii) the adjusted net asset approach.

5.2.2 *Market Value of the Conversion Option (Call)*

The market value of the conversion option is dependent upon the terms and conditions of the options, the characteristics of the underlying shares, and the level of interest rates. To be more specific, the key parameters are typically:

- maturity of the option;
- possibility to exercise early or not;
- exercise price of the option;
- existence of additional market or non-market conditions;
- expected dividend payments over the life of the option;
- market value of the underlying shares;
- volatility of the expected return of the underlying shares; and
- risk-free rate over the life of the option.

The models to be used to estimate the market value of the conversion option are dependent upon its characteristics and particularly upon the existence of market or non-market conditions, the possibility of early exercise, and the payment of dividends.

Once the value of the option has been estimated, it needs to be converted into an equivalent interest rate so that its impact on the market interest rate can be measured. Then, the arm's length interest rate of the convertible bond is equal to that for a similar non-convertible fixed income instrument[66] less this estimated option-equivalent interest rate.

Convertible bond arm's length interest rate
= Similar non convertible bond arm's lenght interest rate
–/– Estimated option equivalent interest rate

The authors refer to sections 5.1.1 and 5.1.2 for a detailed explanation of how to assess the creditworthiness of a fixed income instrument and the arm's length interest rate, respectively.

66. Refer to sections 5.1.1 and 5.1.2 for a detailed explanation of how to assess the creditworthiness and an arm's length interest rate of a non-convertible fixed income instrument, respectively.

5.3 Contingent Convertible Bonds

A CoCo bond can be considered as a traditional fixed income instrument for which the borrower is paying a higher interest rate to have the right to force the conversion into equity instead of reimbursing the bond in cash. The investor in the CoCo bond has agreed to receive higher interest payments in exchange for having to potentially accept a reimbursement in shares rather than in cash. He has also sold a put option (right to sell shares) to the borrower.

As a result, at issuance of the CoCo bond, the market value of the fixed income (only) instrument (without the conversion option) less the market value of the put option should be equal to the subscription value of the convertible bond.

Under the framework of the CUP method, there are four key economic components to consider when determining what interest rate may be applied by an independent entity in a comparable uncontrolled transaction. Similar as those for convertible bonds, these are:

- creditworthiness of the fixed income (only) instrument;
- terms and conditions of the fixed income (only) instrument;
- value of the underlying shares of the option; and
- terms and conditions of the financial option to convert the bond into an equity instrument.

Adjustments related to the last two items of the economic components (linked to the put option) will usually be required as finding exact comparable transactions along all economic components is unlikely.

Reference can be made to section 5.2 for the approaches to quantify these four economic components for testing the arm's length return of CoCo bonds.

5.4 Profit Participating Loans

In a profit participating loan, the creditor is entitled to participate in the profits of the operations of the debtor and/or in the appreciation of the fair value of a particular asset if the profit participating loan is used to fund that asset. The creditor of the profit participating loan generally receives a below-market interest rate (often 0%) but, as the name suggests, is entitled to participate in the profits of the debtor and/or market value appreciation of the asset. Another characteristic of profit participating loans is that they generally have the condition of subordinated debt in the order of credit priority in the event of a borrower's insolvency. The lender will consequently be negatively affected by an unfavourable evolution of the borrower's operations/fair value of the faded asset.

Industries or transactions for which profit participating loans tend to be more common are real estate or direct lending, where real estate and debt receivables portfolios are funded with profit participating loans. The returns on the underlying assets can often be established with relative accuracy, and the profit participating loan would shift a material part of its risk associated with the underlying assets from the borrower to the lender. This would require to clearly identify the commercial or financial relations between both from a transfer pricing discussion as previously described in section 5.2.

As the CUP method often cannot be reliably applied to intercompany profit participating loans, the transactional net margin method (TNMM) is more commonly selected to assess the arm's length nature of the remuneration paid to and earned from them. In applying the TNMM, the borrower of the profit participating loan is typically the tested party that is the more routine entity. The net profit indicator used in applying the TNMM is generally the borrower's return on equity capital employed compared to similar independent comparable companies (e.g., real estate investment companies or direct lenders in the previously provided examples). It will be remunerated for that part of the assets it has funded with its own equity capital that is often supplemented with a CUP analysis on the syndicate loan administration fees. It will be recompensed for its limited risk finance function on the portion of its assets funded with the proceeds of the profit participating loan.

Alternatively, the TNMM is applied with the lender of the profit participating loan as the tested party. The return lender's on capital or return on assets versus independent comparable companies will be assessed (again, for example, real estate investment companies or direct lenders in the previously provided examples).

Example

In a recent case in Luxembourg[67] that dealt with the arm's length interest rates on profit participating loans, the returns on these were deemed to be assessed by a comparison with the arm's length interest accrued during the same period for a similar fixed interest loan.

Otherwise stated, the arm's length nature of the return on the profit participating loan would then need to be assessed under the framework of the CUP method considering key characteristics as previously addressed such as:

- creditworthiness of a comparable fixed income instrument; and
- terms and conditions of a comparable fixed income instrument.

In this case, consistent with other hybrid transactions addressed in this chapter, evaluating whether a profit participating loan is consistent with the arm's length principle should not just be limited to the interest rate or expected returns on instruments with a similar level of risk (e.g., preferred shares or mezzanine loans). It should include a critical assessment and justification of the economic reasons justifying the choice of the profit participating loan form as opposed to other options realistically available to the borrower.

67. No. 43264 (Tribunal Administratif du Grand-Duché de Luxembourg 13 July 2021).

6 CONCLUSION

Hybrid financing is a container concept and encompasses a broad range of instruments that can have very different characteristics. What these instruments have in common are the combination of some typical debt features combined with a number of equity characteristics.

Although the OECD completed its OECD Transfer Pricing Guidelines with a chapter covering financial transactions, it did not address hybrid financing. Therefore, transfer pricing practitioners should only rely on the general transfer pricing principles.

Tax authorities are arguably less experienced in these transactions due to their unique features. Moreover, considering the hybrid features may have a significant impact on the return of these instruments, tax authorities might also scrutinize whether such characteristics are required. Hereto, a solid comparability analysis is key to evidence that the accurate delineated transaction is in accordance with the contract. While all comparability factors are important, some items merit a particular focus for hybrid financing. The functional analysis should detail the control over risk functions to back up more atypical risk allocation compared to traditional financing. Under the economic circumstances, the applicable regulations can justify or even impose certain hybrid features in order to adhere to capital regulations in, e.g., the banking and insurance industry. Finally, the business strategy should be appropriately considered, whereby hybrid features should be tested through the options realistically available.

Once the hybrid instrument has been accurately delineated, the transfer pricing method should be selected. Additionally, in this context, the five OECD transfer pricing methods can seldom be applied as such. While a CUP might be available in certain specific cases, more often, adjusted CUPs could be an appropriate approach for some instruments. For example, the higher risk could be captured by a notching-down approach compared to more traditional debt funding. In many cases, however, an (adjusted) CUP would not result in an arm's length outcome. Therefore, practitioners and tax authorities should often refer to economic methods that are commonly accepted by financial specialists. While the selection of the model itself should be documented by reference to economic literature, some parameters of these models typically rely on benchmarkable open-market information.

The features of hybrid financing effectuate specific transfer pricing challenges for both tax authorities and transfer pricing practitioners. This sometimes requires some untraditional thinking and cooperation with financial experts.

CHAPTER 6
Factoring

Bipin Dodhia, Pooja R. Shah, Rahul Mitra & Waman Y. Kale

1 INTRODUCTION

Companies generate accounts receivables in the normal course of business by selling goods or services to their customers on credit. Companies who extend credit to their customers may sell their accounts receivable in certain cases to a factor that is a financial intermediary who purchases accounts receivable at a discount.[1] Thus, factoring refers to the financing arrangement that involves outright selling of trade debts/accounts receivable invoices by one party to another, i.e., the factor at a discounted price. There are essentially three parties in a factoring arrangement:

(1) factor: one who purchases the invoice/account receivable of the client;
(2) client: one who has issued an invoice to a customer and sells the resulting receivable to the factor. The client may also be referred to as the 'seller'; and
(3) customers: those who owe the money represented by the invoices to the clients. They are also known as 'account debtors'.

1. Internal Revenue Service, *Factoring of Receivables: Audit Technique Guide* 1 (Department of the Treasury of the United States June 2006).

Factoring differs from routine loan financing arrangements because it involves a transfer of assets rather than a loan of money. Therefore, factors primarily evaluate the quality of the asset being purchased when assessing risk (i.e., the ability to collect client receivables) rather than the financial position of the seller/client. Further, factoring goes beyond financing/advancing funds as factors typically provide additional account receivable support services in most cases that may include:

- customer credit analysis;
- assumption of customer credit risk/bad debt risk;
- invoice handling, debtor follow-ups, and invoice collection;
- accounting and reporting related to accounts receivables including maintaining history of payments by customers and management reports on collections; and
- provision of expertise related to disputes, returns, and adjustments.

Thus, the functions that may be performed by the factor are likely to vary from a purely administrative to a completely risk management role depending on the type and terms of the factoring agreement. As a natural consequence, the cost/price of factoring services also varies depending on the type of factoring and risk coverage provided by the factor. Normally, the price of factoring, i.e., the discount rate, consists of the following two components:[2]

(1) an interest on funds advanced by the factor (which is typically a bit higher than the short-term bank lending rate); and
(2) a factoring commission that includes management and administration fees, handling costs, and risk premiums to cover the credit risk assumed by the factor.

The percentage of a discount depends on a number of variables, for example:

- the type of industry in which the client is operating;
- total number of customers;
- annual turnover;
- total number of invoices per year;
- average collection period;
- average receivables balance and quality of debtors/customers;
- type of factoring;[3]
- services covered by the factoring arrangement;
- the volume factored;
- term length;[4]

2. Irina Diakonova & Gesa Körner, *Where Do Financial Services Meet Transfer Pricing?*, 2 Derivatives & Financial Instruments. IBFD 55-73 (IBFD 2000).
3. For example, recourse or non-recourse factoring, disclosed or undisclosed factoring, advance or maturity factoring.
4. Term length means the duration of the factoring relationship.

- extent of advance;[5]
- float;[6] and
- other terms and conditions of the factoring arrangement.

It is imperative to understand why businesses enter into factoring arrangements in third-party dealings before commencing the analysis of a related party factoring transaction. Some of the most common reasons why businesses decide to do so include:[7]

- *cash flow management*: factoring helps in unlocking the funds tied up in accounts receivables and thereby helps finance sales growth;
- *availability*: difficulty in obtaining credit from traditional sources like banks or financial markets;
- *collateral preservation*: factors usually limit their collateral to client accounts receivable leaving other assets unencumbered; and
- *value-added services*: additional account receivable support services provided by the factor can help reduce direct expenses, improve collections, and reduce credit losses.

It is also noted that there are many regulatory issues associated with the factoring arrangement. It only exists in countries with laws that support buying and selling receivables. It is generally not effective for foreign account receivables that have more than 180-day terms.[8]

In a related party factoring, accounts receivable of one related party (the client) are transferred to another (the factor) at a discount from the face value. With related party factoring, the client obtains the required liquidity while the factor gains control of the client's accounts receivable and assumes the risk of holding it. Hence, the factor must be compensated for providing liquidity and bearing the risk with an arm's length fee, i.e., the discounting rate. All relevant terms and conditions of the factoring arrangement should be specified in the agreement between the parties (*Figure 6.1*).

5. The percentage of the account receivable/trade debt face value that the factor advances to the client upon acceptance of the invoice.
6. The time period between when the factor receives payment from the customer and when it transfers the reserve less the factor's fees to the client.
7. The Edwards Research Group, *The Basics of Accounts Receivable Factoring* 8 (1997).
8. *See also Factoring*, https://tfig.unece.org/contents/factoring.htm (last visited 1 August 2022).

Figure 6.1 Graphic Example of an Intra-group Factoring Arrangement

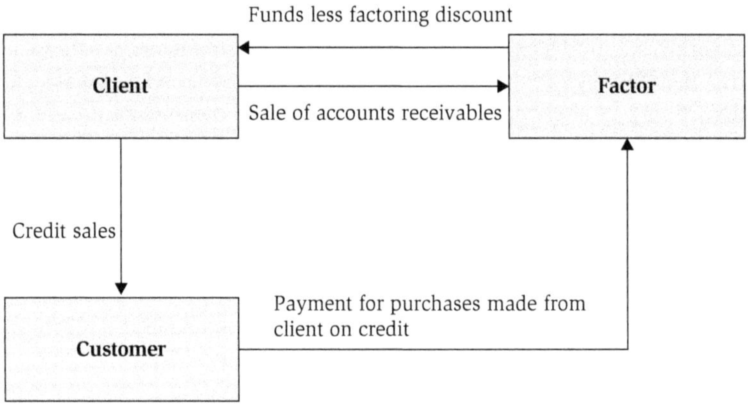

Example

Company A located in Country X and Company B located in Country Y are part of ABC Group. In order to have more liquidity to increase its sales, Company A requires additional financial resources that are neither available in its bank account nor can be obtained through traditional bank finance as Company A is in its start-up phase. Company B is engaged in providing support services to the ABC Group companies and has available financial resources that it does not need for its own business and also has the necessary human resources to provide accounts receivable support services. Therefore, Company A and Company B enter into a factoring agreement whereby the latter assumes the accounts receivable of the former at a discount of its face value and provides necessary cash to Company A. Company A (the client) and Company B (the factor) will need to assess whether the intra-group factoring agreement is at arm's length.

The broad construct of the example above has been used in subsequent sections of this chapter to explain different possible factoring arrangements and various transfer pricing concepts.

Different types of intra-group factoring arrangements exist, e.g.:

(1) Recourse and non-recourse factoring:[9] In a factoring arrangement with a recourse option, the factor can resort to the client in the event the customer does not pay for the invoice. Thus, the factor does not take the credit risk/bad debt risk. In the case of non-recourse factoring, the factor bears the risk of loss resulting from non-payment of an invoice by the customer and thus either has to absorb the loss or take direct enforcement action against the customer.

9. *Supra* note 7, at 4.

(2) Disclosed and undisclosed/confidential factoring: In a disclosed factoring, the customers are aware that the payment must be made to the factor contrary to an undisclosed/confidential factoring.

(3) Advance and maturity factoring:[10] In an advance factoring, the factor grants an advance to the client against the accounts receivable that is assumed (this is generally 70%–80% of the receivable's face value) and pays the balance after deducting fees following collection from the customer. In a maturity factoring, the factor does not pay any advance to the client but instead collects the sum due from the customers and pays the client on the date on which it is collected or on the guaranteed payment date.

2 ASSESSMENT OF ARM'S LENGTH NATURE OF INTRA-GROUP FACTORING ARRANGEMENTS

This chapter will now discuss how to assess the arm's length nature of intra-group factoring arrangements using a four-step analysis.

2.1 Identification of the Commercial or Financial Relations

The identification of the commercial or financial relations between related parties involves analysing the economically relevant characteristics (or comparability factors) of a transaction in order to accurately delineate the actual transaction.[11] This is the first step in a comparability analysis. In the specific case of intra-group factoring arrangements, it would be necessary to analyse the following economically relevant characteristics (or comparability factors) in order to identify the commercial or financial relations:

(1) *Contractual Terms and Characteristics of the Factoring Arrangement*

The following characteristics are of importance:

- type of factoring;[12]
- services covered by the factoring arrangement and whether they are to be performed by the factor or contracted back to the client;
- the volume factored;
- term length;[13]
- extent of advance;[14]

10. *Ibid.*, at 5 et seq.
11. OECD, *OECD Transfer Pricing Guidelines for Multinational Enterprises and Tax Administrations 2022* (OECD Publishing 2022), para. 10.22.
12. For example, recourse or non-recourse factoring, disclosed or undisclosed factoring, advance or maturity factoring.
13. Term length means the duration of the factoring relationship.
14. The percentage of the account receivable/trade debt face value that the factor advances to the client upon acceptance of the invoice.

- float;[15]
- days outstanding in receivable; and
- discount rate.

When a transaction has been formalized by the related parties through written contractual agreements, those agreements provide the starting point for delineating the transaction between them. However, the contractual arrangements between associated enterprises may not always provide information in sufficient detail or may be inconsistent with the actual conduct of the parties or other facts and circumstances. It is therefore necessary to examine other documents (e.g., communication between the parties other than the written contract), the actual conduct of the parties, and the economic principles that generally govern relationships between independent enterprises in comparable circumstances in order to accurately delineate the actual transaction.[16] Stated differently, for the purpose of a transfer pricing analysis, the contractual agreements form the starting point for the accurate delineation of the transaction. However, in the event of any observed inconsistencies between the contractual agreements and the conduct of the parties, the actual transaction should generally be delineated in accordance with the transaction characteristics that are reflected in the conduct of the parties.[17]

(2) *Functions Performed, Assets Used and Risks Assumed by Both the Related Party Factor and the Related Party Client*

The functional analysis seeks to identify the economically significant activities and responsibilities undertaken, assets used or contributed, and risks assumed by the parties to the transactions.[18] The risk allocation is an important step for identifying the economically relevant characteristics of the controlled transaction due to the relationship between risk and return.[19] In relation to factoring arrangements, the identification of the functions performed and risks assumed by the factor assumes added significance as they can vary significantly depending on the type of factoring arrangement. It involves an analysis of the services covered by the factoring arrangement that can vary from pure financing to the inclusion of additional administrative services to complete risk management services; an analysis of financial, human, and other resources contributed by the factor; and an analysis of financing and credit risk assumption by the parties.

(3) *Economic Circumstances of Both the Related Party Factor and the Related Party Client and of the Market in Which They Operate*[20]

In this step, issues that might be considered include:

15. The time period between when the factor receives payment from the customer and when it transfers the reserve less the factor's fees to the client.
16. *Supra* note 11, para. 10.22.
17. *Ibid.*, para. 10.22.
18. *Ibid.*
19. *Ibid.*
20. *Ibid.*

- geographic location of the related party factor and the related party client;
- the nature and extent of government regulations in relation to such factoring arrangements in the country of the related party factor and the client;
- the industry in which the related party client operates;
- the date and time of the transaction; and
- the availability of alternate sources of finance/the strength of financing systems in the client's location.

(4) *Business Strategies Pursued by the Related Party Factor and Related Party Client*[21]

In relation to factoring arrangements, business strategies could include the factor's market penetration strategy as well as the client's cost savings strategy/outsourcing strategy, financing, balance sheet considerations, and equity preservation strategy. The selected business strategy may have an impact on the transaction's price; for instance, the factor's market penetration strategy may result in a lower discount rate. Alternatively, the client's balance sheet consideration and equity preservation strategy may result in accepting a discount rate that is higher than the cost of an alternate source of funding. Hence, business strategies must be examined when delineating the transaction and determining comparability for transfer pricing purposes.

This step will lead to the accurate delineation of the actual transaction.

Example

Company A located in Country X and Company B located in Country Y are part of ABC Group. In order to have more liquidity to increase its sales, Company A requires additional financial resources that are neither available in its bank account nor can be obtained through traditional bank finance as Company A is in its start-up phase. Therefore, Company A and Company B (that has available financial resources that it does not need for its own business) enter into a factoring agreement. Company B takes over the accounts receivable of Company A (without assuming the customer credit risk) at a discount to its face value and provides necessary cash to Company A. Company B does not have the resources to provide Company A with the collection services; therefore, such function continues to be performed by Company A. The accurate delineation of the actual transaction makes it clear that the factoring arrangement between Company A and Company B is limited to providing short-term financing. This might imply that, at arm's length, Company A should pay a lower discount rate/short-term

21. *Ibid.*

interest rate to Company B in accordance with the fewer functions performed and lower risks assumed by Company B in the intra-group factoring arrangement.

Example

Company A located in Country X and Company B located in Country Y are part of ABC Group. To decrease the reliance on external debt and optimize their internal use of cash, ABC Group has centralized the collection of trade receivables in Company B that is also engaged in providing other support services to the ABC Group. Accordingly, Company A (that has significant accounts receivable balances and requires additional financial resources) and Company B enter into a factoring agreement. Company B takes over the accounts receivable of Company A (also assuming the customer credit risk) at a discount to its face value and provides necessary cash to Company A. Since Company B provides support services to the ABC Group and, accordingly, also assumes the collection function from Company A, the accurate delineation of the actual transaction makes it clear that the factoring arrangement between Company A and Company B is not limited to financing. It also includes support services, and the risk assumed by Company B is also higher as it bears the loss in the event of customers' insolvencies. The above facts help to identify two elements of the transaction, i.e., assumption of risk and pure support services. This might imply that, at arm's length, Company A should pay a higher discount rate to Company B in accordance with the increased number of functions performed and greater risks assumed by Company B in the intra-group factoring arrangement. The accurate delineation of the actual transaction may also result in identification of two intercompany transactions between Company A and Company B – one of factoring/financing and another of provision of support services. In such a case, Company B may be compensated for the support service at cost plus an arm's length mark-up based on the set of comparables and a discounting fee to cover the cost and risks associated with financing.

Example

Company A located in Country X and Company B located in Country Y are part of ABC Group. Company A has been in operation for only three years but has a significant and long-term contract to supply a few AA-rated customers. In order to fulfil the obligations under this contract, Company A requires additional financial resources that are neither available in its bank account nor can be obtained through traditional bank finance as Company A has been in operation for only a short while. Therefore, Company A and Company B (that has available financial resources that it does not need for its own business) enter into a factoring agreement. According to it, Company B takes over the accounts receivable of Company A at a discount to its face value and provides the necessary cash to Company A. Based on the terms and conditions of the intra-group factoring agreement, Company B has agreed to bear the risk of default by these customers of Company A. However, upon the accurate delineation of the actual transaction, it becomes clear that these customers of Company A are highly creditworthy and unlikely to default based on their credit history. Considering the above findings, it merits analysis why Company A and Company B have agreed on the specified terms and conditions of the intra-group factoring arrangement when Company A has such a high-quality accounts receivable. Thus, the accurate delineation of the actual transaction indicates that, at arm's length, Company A would not be required to pay any higher discount fee to provide for the assumption of credit risk by Company B.

The identification of the commercial or financial relations between the related parties and the conditions and economically relevant circumstances attached to those relations as explained above helps to accurately delineate the controlled transaction that is the essential element of transfer pricing.

2.2 Recognition of the Accurately Delineated Transaction

The recognition of the accurately delineated transaction consists of the assessment of the 'benefit test' and the 'willing to pay/perform for itself test'. It involves a determination of whether any compensation for the intra-group transaction could be charged having regard to the commercial rationality of the transaction. The key question in the analysis is whether the actual transaction possesses the commercial rationality of arrangements that would be agreed between unrelated parties under comparable economic circumstances and not whether the same transaction can be observed between independent parties.[22] In the specific case of intra-group factoring, it would be necessary to analyse whether the intra-group factoring arrangement has commercial rationality by addressing the following two fundamental questions:

(1) Could the related party client enter into a similar factoring arrangement with an unrelated factor?
(2) If answered affirmatively, would the related party client request a similar factoring arrangement?

22. *Ibid.*

Example

Company A located in Country X and Company B located in Country Y are part of ABC Group. Company A requires additional financial resources for its business and, accordingly, Company A and Company B have entered into a factoring agreement. Company B takes over the accounts receivable of Company A at a discount to its face value and provides the necessary cash to Company A. In order to assess whether the intra-group factoring arrangement has commercial rationality, it should be assessed if:

- an unrelated party (i.e., an unrelated factor) would provide similar financing to Company A under similar circumstances; or
- if Company A, if it was an unrelated party, would enter into a factoring arrangement similar to the tested factoring arrangement.

The answers to the questions above would require an assessment of the underlying reason for the factoring arrangement and the benefit created by it. Typically, it implies a detailed analysis of the facts and circumstances surrounding the arrangement, the purpose of the arrangement, the type of arrangement, the willingness and the capability of the related party factor to provide for the services agreed under the factoring arrangement and the alternatives available to both the parties.

An intra-group factoring arrangement will have commercial rationality if:

(1) the intra-group factoring arrangement provides direct and identifiable economic or commercial benefits to the related party client, such as:
  (a) when the client has opportunities to expand his business but does not have the required liquidity;
  (b) when traditional bank lending is not available due to the client's newly established business;
  (c) when the rate of return on the cash invested in the business exceeds the costs associated with factoring the receivables; and
  (d) when the objective of the factoring arrangement is to manage foreign exchange transactions.

(2) the related factor has the capability to provide the finance and the services agreed under the factoring arrangement;

(3) the intra-group factoring arrangement provides direct and identifiable economic or commercial benefits to the related party factor, such as:
  (a) the related factor has evaluated the available alternatives for investing;
  (b) the related factor is expanding his business presence in the jurisdiction of the related party client;
  (c) the centralization of the foreign exchange management function within the related party factor results in increased foreign exchange volumes and the ability to achieve exchange rates that are more beneficial, better cash flow planning, and foreign exchange hedging.

Example

Company A located in Country X and Company B located in Country Y are part of ABC Group. To decrease the reliance on external debt and optimize their internal use of cash, ABC Group has centralized the collection of trade receivables in Company B that is also engaged in providing other support services to the ABC Group. Accordingly, Company A and Company B enter into a factoring agreement whereby the latter takes over the accounts receivable of the former (also assuming the customer credit risk) at a discount to its face value and provides the necessary cash to Company A. Further, Company B also provides essential accounts receivable support to Company A.

Assume Company A requires additional financial resources to increase its sales and has significant accounts receivable balances that have a history of delayed payments/defaults. Further, Company A does not have sufficient resources for managing its accounts receivable. Based on the recognition of the accurately delineated transaction, the factoring arrangement appears commercially rational as it has provided a benefit to Company A in terms of liquidity and outsourcing of accounts receivable management. Accordingly, Country X's tax authorities should accept the payment of the discount fee by Company A to Company B for the intra-group factoring arrangement.

Example

Company A located in Country X and Company B located in Country Y are part of ABC Group. In order to have more liquidity to increase its sales, Company A requires additional financial resources that are neither available in its bank account nor obtainable through traditional bank finance as Company A is in its start-up phase. Therefore, Company A and Company B (that has available financial resources that it does not need for its own business) enter into a factoring agreement whereby the latter takes over the accounts receivable of the former (without assuming the customer credit risk) at a discount of its face value and provides the necessary cash to Company A.

Assume that Company A has offered cash discounts to its customers in the past and secured an early payment at a discount rate much lower than that charged under the factoring arrangement and that there is no reason to discontinue the practice of offering cash discounts. Considering these facts and based on the accurate delineation of the actual transaction, Country X's tax authorities can question the commercial rationality of the related party factoring arrangement and the arm's length nature of the agreed discount rate.

Example

Company A located in Country X and Company B located in Country Y are part of ABC Group. In order to have more liquidity to increase its sales, Company A requires additional financial resources. Therefore, Company A and Company B (that has available financial resources that it does not need for its own business) enter into a factoring agreement whereby Company B takes over the accounts receivable of Company A (without assuming the customer credit risk) at a discount of its face value and provides the necessary cash to Company A.

Assume that Company A has a better credit rating than most of its accounts receivable and can simply obtain a loan from a bank at a lower cost than factoring. Considering these facts and based on the accurate delineation of the actual transaction, Country X's tax authorities can question the commercial rationality of the related party factoring arrangement and the agreed arm's length nature of the discount rate.

Court Case

In the *Pacific* case,[23] the C Corporations paid management fees and factoring fees to the related partnership. The tax authorities asserted that such payments had no economic substance and were made only to eliminate substantial portions of the C Corporations' taxable income. The following evidence[24] was placed on record:

(1) The C Corporations did not perform due diligence when investigating the costs and benefits of factoring. They did not compare its cost to that of securing working capital via bank loans. They did no comparison shopping to ascertain whether more advantageous factoring terms could be obtained from an independent company.[25]

(2) The factoring fees that the C Corporations paid coupled with the expected turnaround time for collection yielded an effective annual percentage rate (APR) of 52% which was at the high end of (or above) the range of APRs that independent factors would have charged.[26]

23. *Pacific Management Group, Bsc Leasing, Inc., Tax Matters Partner, Et al., Petitioners v. Commissioner of Internal Revenue,* No. Memo 2018-131 (United States Tax Court 20 August 2018).
24. The list comprises only the most relevant evidence in relation to the disallowance of the factoring payments.
25. *Pacific Management Group, Bsc Leasing, Inc., Tax Matters Partner, Et al., Petitioners v. Commissioner of Internal Revenue,* No. Memo 2018-131, at 42.
26. *Ibid.*

(3) The payment practices under the arrangement were erratic and contrary to standard factoring practice that intends to provide the client with immediate liquidity.[27]
(4) Under the factoring arrangement, the client (C Corporations) was to function as a collection agent for the factor, and the factor was to reimburse the client for such services. However, there is no evidence of any such reimbursement being made. Additionally, there is no evidence of how such a reimbursement was to be calculated.[28]
(5) The arrangement was a circular flow of funds whereby the C Corporations provided funds to the partnership by paying management fees that were subsequently used to finance the transfer of accounts receivable. Thus, the factoring arrangement provided no meaningful working capital financing to the C Corporations.[29]

The US Tax Court disallowed the factoring fees and management fees. It stated that they lacked economic substance, failed to constitute 'ordinary and necessary expenses', and failed to reflect the arm's length pricing. It based its decision on the evidence gathered and having conducted in-depth legal and economic analyses on the factoring and management contracts entered between related parties.[30]

Court Case

In *McKesson*,[31] the taxpayer entered into a receivables sales agreement (essentially a factoring agreement) and a related servicing agreement with its parent company. Under the factoring agreement, the taxpayer sold its trade receivables to its parent at a discount of 2.206%. Under the servicing agreement, the parent company paid the taxpayer a fixed annual fee to continue servicing the receivables. The discount rate of 2.206% was calculated using a formula. At the time that the factoring agreement was entered into, the taxpayer had sales of USD 3 billion and profits of USD 40 million, credit arrangements with major financial institutions in the hundreds of millions of dollars, a sizeable credit department that collected the receivables within thirty days (on average), and a bad debt experience of only 0.043%. There was no evidence of pending imminent or future changes in the make-up, nature, or quality of taxpayer's receivables or

27. *Pacific Management Group, Bsc Leasing, Inc., Tax Matters Partner, Et al., Petitioners v. Commissioner of Internal Revenue*, No. Memo 2018-131, at 43.
28. *Ibid.*, at 45.
29. *Ibid.*, at 46.
30. *Ibid.*, at 41, 49.
31. *McKesson Canada Corporation v. The Queen* 2013 TCC 404.

customers. The taxpayer had also not identified a business need for a cash infusion or borrowing. Further, the taxpayer was profitable prior to the factoring agreement, but it was noted that as a direct result of the discount paid by the taxpayer on the receivables sale, it ceased to be profitable and reported a tax loss during the tax year at issue. Similarly, taxpayers' profits in later years were also significantly reduced. The Canada Revenue Agency objected to the parties' agreed-upon discount rate and reassessed the tax against the taxpayer on the grounds that, if the receivables sales agreement had been entered into by parties dealing at arm's length, the discount rate would have been 1.013%. In an appeal before the tax court, it reviewed the various components that the taxpayer and its parent company used to calculate the discount rate. Owing to a number of unexplained assumptions, it conducted its own transfer pricing analysis and concluded that the discount rate range to which parties dealing with each other at arm's length would have agreed was 0.959% to 1.17%.

While the Canada court's decision focused on the arm's length nature of the discount rate, wider issues that were not raised/pressed by the Canada Revenue Agency included the economic substance or the commercial rationality of the transaction having regard to the facts.

When the actual transaction lacks economic substance or does not possess the commercial rationality of arrangements that would be agreed between unrelated parties under comparable economic circumstances, it can lead to non-recognition of the controlled transaction. As non-recognition can be contentious and a source of double taxation, the evaluation of the commercial rationality/economic substance of a controlled transaction assumes significance.

2.3 Selection of the Most Appropriate Transfer Pricing Method

Once the question of whether any compensation for the intra-group factoring arrangement could be charged has been addressed and answered positively by performing the two steps indicated above, the next step is to determine the arm's length amount of the compensation which at first requires a selection of the most appropriate transfer pricing method.

In general, there are two methods that are most commonly used to determine the arm's length amount of the compensation for intra-group factoring arrangements, specifically, the CUP method and the methodologies embedded in the CPM/TNMM. The first can be employed when comparable transactions/arrangements between unrelated parties exist either in the market of the provider or that of the recipient. The CPM/TNMM can be utilized instead when the CUP method is not appropriate (e.g., when comparables are missing or accurate adjustments cannot be made for the differences) and, most probably, when one related party (e.g., the factor-related party) is acting as a general service provider.

However, it would be worthwhile to note that the application of each of the methods mentioned previously to benchmark factoring arrangements has some inherent limitations. For instance, when adopting CUP method, it is very difficult and often not possible to achieve comparability of credit risk associated with a related party client and its customers with that of third-party clients and its customers. Under such circumstances, one of the most important factors for comparability remains unaddressed when adopting the CUP method. However, the limitation discussed earlier does not exist in cases when the related party factoring arrangement is one with a recourse option or when adopting an internal CUP with transactions between a related party client and an unrelated factor constituting the CUP. Similarly, the adoption of the CPM/TNMM is also limited to cases for which the related party factor provides value-added services in addition to receivables financing as a part of factoring arrangement.

Thus, given the limitations of each of the transfer pricing methods mentioned above, good judgment should be exercised in determining the most appropriate method having regard to the specifics of the case.

2.4 Application of the Most Appropriate Transfer Pricing Method

CUP Method

The CUP method could be applied in the following ways:

- internal CUP method: research of discount rates applied to similar transactions in comparable circumstances between one of the related parties and an unrelated party; and
- external CUP method: the same research but between unrelated parties. In some cases, this method is applied by researching discount rates that would have been applied to similar transactions in similar circumstances between unrelated parties. Its application would require the use of information contained in publicly available databases[32] for identification of discount rates between unrelated parties.

Example

Company A located in Country X and Company B located in Country Y are part of ABC Group. Company A (having huge accounts receivable balances) and Company B (with idle cash) conclude an intra-group factoring agreement. Company B takes over part of the accounts receivable of Company A (without assuming the customer credit risk) at a discount of its face value and provides the necessary cash to Company A.

32. For example, the Securities and Exchange Commission LivEdgar Database.

Company A has also entered into a factoring agreement with a third-party factor for the balance of accounts receivable with the same conditions as those agreed with Company B. If the two factoring agreements are comparable (i.e., considering all of the economically relevant characteristics), Company A and Company B could consider using the discount rate applied to Company A by the unrelated party factor to identify the arm's length intra-group discount rate.

Example

Company A located in Country X and Company B located in Country Y are part of ABC Group. Company A (having significant accounts receivable balances) and Company B (with idle cash) conclude an intra-group factoring agreement. Company B takes over part of the accounts receivable of Company A (without assuming the customer credit risk) at a discount of its face value and provides the necessary cash to Company A.

Based on a search in publicly available databases, information can be sourced about the discount rate charged between unrelated parties on comparable factoring arrangements (i.e., considering all of the economically relevant characteristics).

Company A and Company B could use the discount rates applied in the unrelated party comparable factoring arrangements in order to identify the arm's length intra-group discount rate.

If there are significant differences in the terms of the third-party factoring arrangements identified in the search process, then the discount rates in an external factoring contract will need to be adjusted for such differences before the same are used as a benchmark.

When applying the CUP method, it is essential to verify that all of the economically relevant characteristics (or comparability factors) that are illustrated before are taken into account. Hence, the resulting discount rate might also need to be adapted by means of comparability adjustments in order to reflect such factors. Table 6.1 illustrates the impact on discount rates of certain specific characteristics of a factoring arrangement.

Table 6.1 Indicative Impact on Discount Rates of Specific Characteristics of a Factoring Arrangement

Characteristics of Factoring	*Increase Discount Rate*	*Decrease Discount Rate*
Type	Non-recourse	Recourse
	Advance factoring	Maturity factoring
Quality of receivables	Poor credit quality	High credit quality

Characteristics of Factoring	*Increase Discount Rate*	*Decrease Discount Rate*
Ratio of advance to reserve	High	Low
Volume factored / No. customers	Low	High
Term length	Short term	Long term
Float	Money transferred immediately to the client	Money transferred to the client after a lag
Days outstanding in receivables	More	Less

CPM/TNMM

When the CUP method cannot be applied, the CPM/TNMM may be used in some cases (e.g., when the related party factor also provides additional accounts receivable support services) to analyse and determine the profit to be retained by the factor entity. An arm's length profit should consider the following:

- arm's length return for the service element determined/benchmarked based on comparables performing routine administrative services; and
- arm's length return for the financing and risk element determined based on the opportunity cost and probability of loss considering the risk profile of underlying account debtors.

An alternate/corroborative approach under the CPM/TNMM involves the identification of functionally comparable uncontrolled factoring firms. This entails applying appropriate quantitative and qualitative filters and benchmarking the profit earned by the related party factor against such comparables having regard to the costs – servicing costs,[33] financing costs, cost of default,[34] and dilutions.[35] However, there must be careful consideration of the disadvantage/limitation of the CPM/TNMM approach as it takes only one side of the transaction into account. While a certain discount rate might result in a reasonable/arm's length return for the factor, it does not allow for the implications for/alternatives available to the client.

Other Method

The possibility of adopting a pricing model to support the arm's length pricing of the factoring arrangement can also be evaluated. Experts in the field can help to benchmark the terms and conditions of the related party factoring arrangement against similar contracts in the market and validate the assumptions and methodologies in the pricing model having regard to the facts. This approach is much like obtaining an

33. This includes administrative, legal, bookkeeping, and dunning expenses.
34. This includes the bad debts and insurance cost, if any.
35. This includes cost associated with rebates and chargebacks.

expert valuation. The advantage of this pricing approach is that it takes into account all of the facts/specifics of the transaction from both the factor's and the client's perspectives. Additionally, it considers the options that are realistically available to each of them to provide a robust arm's length pricing. Appropriate quotations from third-party factors could also be considered to evidence the arm's length dealing. In placing reliance on quotations, it is important to be mindful of the OECD's comments[36] on the use of opinions from independent banks as the basis for interest rate benchmarking, *inter alia* that such an approach would represent a departure from an arm's length approach. This is because it is not based on a comparison of actual transactions and the fact that such letters do not constitute an actual offer to lend. However, considering the unique nature of pricing with regard to a factoring arrangement, quotations might provide a corroborative basis to substantiate the arm's length dealing.

3 CONCLUSION

Factoring arrangements are inherently very factual, and it is imperative to analyse the economic and commercial aspects of the arrangement in detail in order to determine the appropriate arm's length nature of the transaction. As with any other financing arrangement, the recognition of related party factoring arrangements is as much a challenge as the determination of arm's length pricing. Principles established in the OECD TPG on financial transactions hold significance and should be applied having regard to the facts and circumstances of the case. Given the many ways and circumstances in which factoring services can be availed, it is extremely important that a thorough functional and risk analysis and an analysis of the circumstances surrounding the transaction is undertaken. As a consequence, such analyses contribute to the determination of the economic value added and in turn an arm's length reward for the factoring function. The transfer pricing aspect of related party factoring arrangements is a global issue, and any instances of non-recognition or inappropriate characterization and benchmarking/valuation of discount rate could result in an increased risk of transfer pricing adjustments. This could subsequently lead to economic double taxation. Consequently, it would be helpful if the OECD developed specific guidance on globally accepted methodologies and approaches in light of what has been done in relation to other financial transactions. Further, as each of the approaches to determine the arm's length pricing in relation to a related party factoring arrangement suffers from certain drawbacks/limitations, applying several methods simultaneously could be considered as a pragmatic approach. Although the OECD TPG do not require an economic analysis under more than one method, it is recognized that for difficult/complex cases, where no one approach is conclusive, a flexible approach would allow the evidence of various methods to be used in conjunction.[37] Such approach will also take care of the different perspectives of the factor and client and the

36. OECD, *supra* note 11, para. 10.107.
37. *Ibid.*, para. 2.12.

OECD requirement to analyse a financial transaction from the perspective of both of the parties involved. In the issue at hand, both have an objective to limit their individual burden and maximize their benefit from such a transaction. Hence, a potential approach that may be evaluated and considered is to use two benchmarking methodologies in parallel that analyse the transaction from the perspective of the factor (e.g., the CPM/TNMM method) and from the client (e.g., internal CUP where one party is the client), respectively, to determine the minimum and maximum discount rate. Such a floor and ceiling rate would provide a bargaining range to the transacting parties at the time of the transaction or reflect the bargain undertaken by the parties to the transaction at the stage of documenting the arm's length nature. The arm's length discount rate will thus be a rate between the results provided by both methods.

CHAPTER 7

Captive Insurance

Stanley J. Hales & Lucie Hovorkova[*]

* This chapter focuses solely on transfer pricing and does not provide a detailed review of the corporate tax law governing captive insurance nor a summary of the court case law on the subject. The views are solely of the authors and not those of Deloitte Touche Tohmatsu Limited and its member firms.

1 INTRODUCTION

This chapter examines the transfer pricing principles governing captive insurance companies that can be defined as fully owned affiliates of non-insurance groups that are created to underwrite risks for the parent company and/or its operating subsidiaries.[1] Captives are designed as a long-term risk mitigation strategy that provides alternatives to commercial insurance which enables greater control over the risk programmes and the risk financing. A captive insurance company is typically created by a single multinational group. It can also be established by several unrelated parties with common risk mitigation needs that are not insurable on the traditional insurance market or can be insured in a more favourable manner through the captive arrangement. Essentially, rather than insuring risk with a third-party insurance company, the corporate enterprise decides to self-insure it and cover future losses should it materialize into an actual liability.

Why bother to self-insure the risk? The bottom-line benefit is usually a greater return on capital (ROC) employed for the enterprise that self-insures losses when managed well within expected limits. Additional benefits include reduced insurance costs,

1. Sebastian Ma'ilei et al., *Captive Insurance Companies of Non-insurance Groups: Key Transfer Pricing Considerations* (Deloitte 2020).

increased profit/capital retention within the group, risk solutions to the unavailability of coverage from the commercial insurance market, and potential direct access to the reinsurance market.

Various jurisdictions implemented specific tax and transfer pricing rules that were aimed at preventing non-arm's length outbound premium payments for captive insurance without actual commercial substance. In February 2020, the OECD released new Transfer Pricing Guidelines on Financial Transactions that provide a framework for the application of the arm's length principles to captives.[2] These OECD principles coincide with many previously applied local laws and standards and are broadly implemented across not only the OECD but also some non-OECD countries that are part of the separate United Nations transfer pricing protocol.

This chapter provides a summary of the basic captive insurance arrangements. Section 1 provides a brief insight into the types of captive insurance arrangements, the definition of insurance in the commonly accepted sense, history of captive insurance, and the development of transfer pricing principles for captives in order to provide context for the OECD principles. Section 2 will discuss the application of the arm's length principle based on the OECD TPG and provides two practical examples on the use of different transfer pricing methods and benchmarking approaches for the support of arm's length captive insurance pricing between related parties.

1.1 Types of Captive Insurance Arrangements

Captive insurance arrangements may be organized in different ways. The most common of these arrangements are explained below.

1.1.1 Pure Captives

Pure captives are owned directly or indirectly by the insured and include both single parent captives and group captives.

(1) Pure/single parent captive is an insurance or reinsurance company usually formed as a subsidiary of the insured company. It primarily insures the parent's and/or its affiliates' risks. It may provide coverage directly or reinsure the risks of another insurance company. A single parent captive is currently the most common form of self-insurance (Figure 7.1).

2. For further details, *see* OECD, *OECD Transfer Pricing Guidelines for Multinational Enterprises and Tax Administrations 2022* (OECD Publishing 2022), Ch. X. The separate third edition of UN TPM issued in 2021 does not specifically address captive arrangements, although it acknowledges their existence. *See* United Nations, *Practical Manual on Transfer Pricing for Developing Countries 2021* (2021), para. 9.3.8.

Figure 7.1 Graphic Example of Single Parent Captive

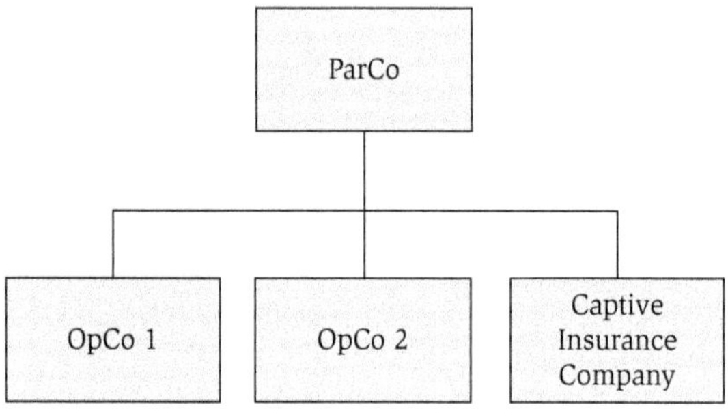

(2) Group/association captive is a structure in which several parties join to use a captive insurance programme. This can be organized through a trade group or a formal association or operate as an informal arrangement. A group or association captive usually allows the insureds to obtain coverage or coverage limits for non-standard risks beyond what is available to them through traditional commercial insurance programmes (Figure 7.2).

Figure 7.2 Graphic Example of Group Captive

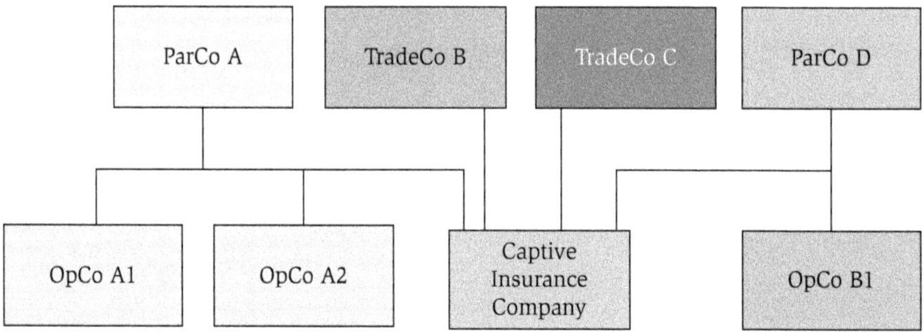

An example of a group captive is the Oil Insurance Limited established in 1972 by seventeen major energy companies as a response to a lack of pollution liability coverage.[3] The Oil Insurance Limited had more than fifty members and USD 2 trillion of insured risks in 2015.

Even though group/association captives will be established and owned by two or more unrelated parties, transfer pricing rules may apply to the arrangements in certain circumstances. This will mostly depend on the definition of related parties for transfer

3. Hugh Rosenbaum, *History of Captives*, https://www.captive.com/captives-101/history-of-captives (last visited 1 August 2022); Hugh Rosenbaum, *The Early Days of Captives*, https://www.captive.com/captives-101/history-of-captives (last visited 1 August 2022).

pricing purposes in each jurisdiction and the specific arrangements within the particular captive structure. The applicability of transfer pricing rules is not always limited to arrangements between parties related through capital. For example, some countries may apply them for related parties under common control to unrelated third parties that have been found to be acting in concert with the common objective of obtaining a tax advantage.[4]

1.1.2 Sponsored Captives

Sponsored captives include rental captives and cell captives owned and controlled by unrelated parties that may or may not have their own capital at risk:

(1) A rental captive is used as an alternative to establishing an owned captive insurance company, e.g., for cost or timing reasons or when the programmes are too small to run an owned facility. The insured uses an existing captive insurance programme of another entity that provides 'captive' facilities to others for a fee. This can be operated by a commercial insurance or reinsurance company as well as another company.

(2) Protected cell captive is a form of a rental captive that separates each participant's underwriting account so that the risks of different cells are not pooled together nor are under common risk management.

(3) Agency Captive is a company owned by an insurance company or brokerage firm to reinsure a portion of their insurance client's risks. Unlike other captive types, these are not designed to provide underwriting profits directly to the insured.

This chapter focuses on single parent captive arrangements because this is the most common form entered into by large multinational groups and covers a high level of the transfer pricing aspects and risks. However, the transfer pricing principles discussed further in this chapter would analogously apply to the related party transactions of other captive forms.

1.2 Principles of Insurance and Captive Insurance

Before examining the transfer pricing principles for captives, the question is posed of what constitutes insurance. A number of the key commonly accepted elements of insurance must be present in the captive operation for a captive insurer to be respected by revenue authorities as having a bona fide insurance operation.

4. Per US law, 'acting in concert' means knowing participation in a joint activity or parallel action towards a common goal whether or not pursuant to an express agreement. *See* section 238.31(b)(2)/section 303.81 (a) of Code of Federal Regulations.

1.2.1 Insurance

The OECD defines the insurance business as accepting liabilities and obligations in respect of uncertain losses that can arise from events occurring beyond the insured's control. Insurance companies can pool the risk of a large number of risk-averse individuals' or entities' potential losses against the payments of insurance premiums. The insured receives some form of compensation for the loss when a specified event occurs and a loss is incurred (Figure 7.3).[5]

Figure 7.3 General Insurance Arrangement

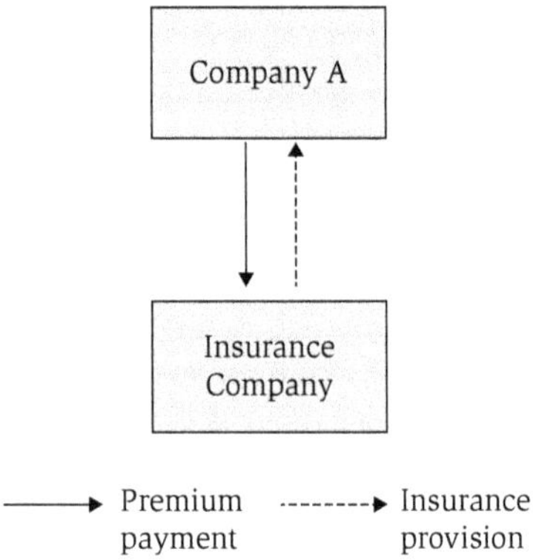

1.2.2 Premium

An insurance premium is the fee that the insured entity pays for the policy issued by the insurer. From the perspective of the insurance company, this amount represents an income and establishes a liability to provide coverage of future claims if realized for the covered risk.[6]

Insurance companies employ actuaries to determine risk levels and premium prices for specific insurance programmes. These have a unique mix of mathematical, analytical, communication, and management skills that help measure the probability and risk of future events. These skills predict the financial impact of potential events on a business and its clients.[7]

The pricing of the premiums generally takes into consideration a combination of the following aspects:

5. OECD, *Report on the Attribution of Profits to Permanent Establishments* 181 (July 2008), para. 5.
6. Stephen Morris et al., *Economic Analysis in Health Care* (John Wiley & Sons 2d ed. 2012).
7. Institute and Faculty of Actuaries, *What Is An Actuary?*, https://actuaries.org.uk/qualify/become-an-actuary/what-is-an-actuary (last visited 1 August 2022).

- insurer's expected costs of claims and the time when claims are expected to be paid;
- ratio of expected operating expenses to premiums; and
- insurer's return from the invested premiums.[8]

1.2.3 Reinsurance

To manage the assumed insurance risk, the captive insurance company may rely on an external third-party reinsurer; alternatively, the captive might operate as the reinsurer of risks already insured by the market. This is usually more essential in the early years of the captive arrangement while the captive insurance company is accumulating its capital from the underwriting profits.

The primary insurance company reduces the risks assumed by ceding one or more insured risks to reinsurers and mitigating the capital requirement for the insurance programmes that it provides. Reinsurers diversify their risk portfolio by pooling the risks ceded to them by a large number of insurance companies. This should result in reduced reinsurance premiums compared to the separate premiums charged by the primary insurance company.[9] Primary insurers free up capital through reinsurance arrangements which consequently permits more underwriting capacity for additional risks or an increased number of customers.

1.2.4 Underwriting Profits

The profit generated by the captive insurance company is known as the underwriting profit and is the difference between the collected premiums and the paid claims.[10] The actuary calculations seek to find an optimal proportion between the price of insurance premiums and the probability of claims with the intent to maximize the underwriting profits. Underwriting losses may occur when an excessive number of claims exceed the income received from the premiums such as those occurring when there is a significant insurance event such as an ecological disaster. To mitigate this risk of loss, insurance companies include both a diversification and a pooling of risks in their risk management strategies, e.g., from a geographical or policy point of view.[11]

1.2.5 Investment Activities

As a part of their business strategy, captive insurance companies typically invest premiums and part of their equity in the financial markets in order to achieve extra investment profits. Every insurance company has its own investment policy with the objective of achieving the best value from the available funds. The company can invest in various fixed-income assets with diversified risk and liquidity levels; however, it

8. OECD, *supra* note 5, at 181, para. 6.
9. *Ibid., at 183,* para. 18.
10. *Ibid. at 182,* para. 12.
11. Jean Francqis Outreville, *Theory and Practice of Insurance* 228 (Kluwer 1998).

must be able to fully meet its clients' obligations at all times. The investment activities are regulated in the insurer's residence country and set the amount of obligatory reserves that the insurer must retain and the level of liquidity needed to pay expected claims depending upon the risk profile of the investment portfolio. The insurance regulation attempts to ensure that the insurance companies have the capacity to pay out claims and protect the market against bankruptcy.

1.2.6 Income and Capital (Surplus) in the Insurance Business

Profit generated from insurance premiums and investment activities that forms the basis of an insurance business is illustrated in Figure 7.4.

Figure 7.4 Income Capital (Surplus) in the Insurance Business

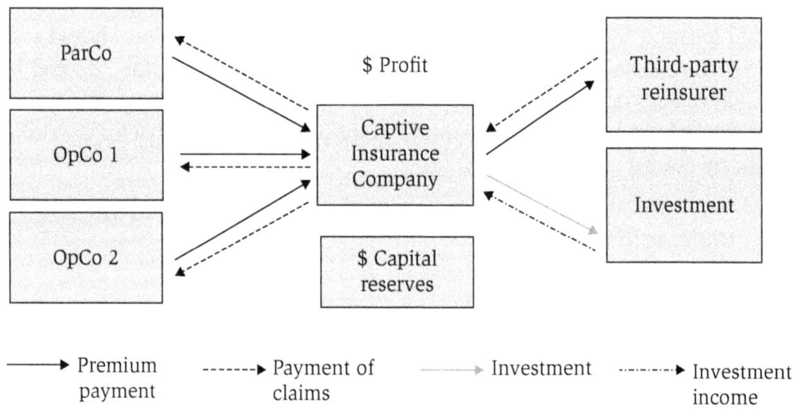

1.2.7 Fronting Arrangements

The captive insurer in a fronting arrangement does not issue the insurance policy to the insured company directly but does so through a licensed insurer. The primary insurance contract is concluded between the insured company and an unrelated licensed insurer (the fronting company) who then reinsures all or most of the assumed risks with the captive (re)insurer from the same group as the originally insured company. This arrangement is often used in cases when the captive insurance company is not able to underwrite insurance policies in the same manner as traditional insurance companies, in most cases, for local regulatory reasons. The fronting company retains administrative fees or a commission to cover its costs and the portion of the retained risk (Figure 7.5).[12]

12. OECD, *supra* note 2, para. 10.214.

Figure 7.5 Fronting Arrangement

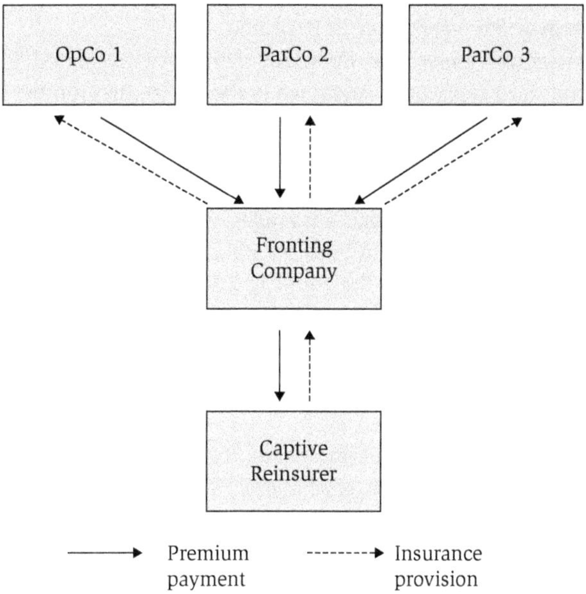

It is important to emphasize that some tax authorities may likely view the chain of transactions as a related party arrangement for transfer pricing purposes even though an external licensed insurer may be involved in the fronting arrangement.

This approach, for example, derives from the Australian Taxation Office's (ATO's) local file guidelines that specifically mention that if an entity engages an intermediary for arranging its reinsurance contracts, it is considered to be acting on behalf of that entity even if he acts as an independent agent. Transactions performed by the intermediary on behalf of the reporting entity are therefore considered related party transactions.[13]

1.3 History of Captive Insurance

The origins of co-insurance arrangements predate the nineteenth century when shippers began agreeing to share their risk from voyages, and some textile companies formed mutual funds for rebuilding after fires. The first European single owner captives and co-insurance arrangements were initiated in the 1920s and 1930s as a reaction to the inability to obtain coverage of some important risks from commercial insurance

13. Australian Taxation Office, *Local File Instructions 2021: Other Kinds of IRPDs of a Financial Nature* (March 2022).

companies. However, the actual growth of the captive industry and the move of captives offshore can be traced to the early 1950s when Frederic Reiss founded Steel Insurance Company of America in 1953 and established the first offshore captive insurance company a few years later in Bermuda.

Whereas the Captive Insurance Company Directory estimated that there were approximately hundred captives in existence in the 1960s, the number reached almost three thousand in the late 1980s.[14] Since then, there has been significant growth in the industry. Business Insurance indicates that around six thousand[15] of them are currently operating worldwide, and Marsh estimates that the number of new formations will remain high with new types of risk coverages, such as cyber, increasingly being introduced.[16] Approximately 90% of Fortune 500 companies currently have a captive insurance arrangement; however, the trend is also spreading to medium and small companies, non-profit organizations, and municipalities.

1.4 Domiciles

A captive domicile is the jurisdiction where the captive insurer is registered for business and subject to insurance regulations. There are currently approximately seventy jurisdictions with captive insurance legislation.[17] The factors considered when selecting a captive domicile include financial infrastructure, related professional services, political and economic stability, regulatory framework and conditions, and the costs of establishment.

Bermuda is traditionally the largest jurisdiction based on the number of insurers, reinsurers, and captive domiciles (approximately seven hundred captives in 2021) and is closely followed by the Cayman Islands, Delaware, Utah, and Vermont. In Europe, Dublin, Guernsey, the Isle of Man, and Luxemburg are the largest and the most favourite domiciles.[18] Asian countries such as Hong Kong, Labuan, and Singapore are rapidly developing and comprise approximately 3% of the total number of captives worldwide.[19]

---

14. Hugh Rosenbaum, *History of Captives, supra* note 3; Hugh Rosenbaum, *The Early Days of Captives, supra* note 3.
15. Andy Toh, *Research & Rankings: Captive Insurance*, Business Insurance, https://www.businessinsurance.com/article/20220304/STORY/912348170/Research-&-Rankings-Captive-Insurance?ticks=637814727524365808&ticks=637814727524365808 (last visited 1 August 2022).
16. Marsh, *The 2021 Captive Landscape Report: Captive Formations Almost Double* 2, 7 (September 2021).
17. National Association of Insurance Commissioners, *Captive Insurance Companies*, https://content.naic.org/cipr-topics/captive-insurance-companies (last visited 1 August 2022).
18. Toh, *supra* note 15.
19. Halter Adrian et al., *Asian Captive Domiciles Positioned for Growth*, Captive International, https://www.captiveinternational.com/contributed-article/asian-captive-domiciles-positioned-for-growth (last visited 1 August 2022).

1.5 Regulatory Framework

Each jurisdiction has different statutory regulations and may have alternative captive regimes when compared with large commercial insurance and reinsurance providers.[20] However, the regulatory requirements for captives will typically include the core insurance requirements such as accounting and reporting requirements, a minimum solvency ratio and minimum liquidity requirements (to pay claims), minimum capital requirements, and minimal required functions (e.g., actuary services).

For example, the European Union (EU) issued a Solvency II Directive that entered into effect in 2016.[21] The objective of the Solvency Directive is to unify the insurance and reinsurance market in the EU and enhance consumer protection with a set of uniform regulatory requirements. The regime equally applies to captives domiciled in the EU and places them in a similar regulatory, governance, and reporting position as the large commercial insurance companies.

Bermuda as the market leader for captive domiciles also has a highly developed legislative regime that is compliant with the Solvency II regulatory framework, although the capital requirements for the captive are lower.

1.6 Tax Legislation

Historically, the applicable tax rate was one of the many significant factors that companies considered when selecting the domicile for their captive insurance company. This raised concerns for tax authorities and led to increased scrutiny of captive insurance arrangements located in lower-tax-rate countries. Tax authorities implemented various regulations to prevent intentional profit shifting of which examples are provided below and are also relevant for captive arrangements.

With the recent implementation of BEPS and other tax legislative measures including the newly proposed OECD Pillar One and Pillar Two initiatives, captives are potentially becoming exposed to additional taxes in jurisdictions beyond their location of domicile. Consequently, the profits arising from the captive insurance arrangements may be, and often are, captured in the tax base of the parent company under certain circumstances.

Various corporate income tax and residency measures have been implemented across countries, such as the UK's diverted profits tax (DPT) or Australian central management and control test (CMAC), that seek to tax profits earned by group affiliates that are actually controlled or managed from the local country. This must be taken into account when considering taxation of captive arrangements, especially in cases when there would be lack of substance in the captive's domiciled country.

Additionally, controlled foreign company (CFC) rules are relevant for captive arrangements and may result in taxation of the captive profits in the parent entity's country. CFC rules have been in place in many jurisdictions for some time and are further being introduced across the European countries based on the EU Anti-Tax

20. OECD, *supra* note 2, para. 10.192.
21. *Directive 2009/138/EC on the Taking-Up and Pursuit of the Business of Insurance and Reinsurance (Solvency II)*, No. 2009/138/EC.

Avoidance Directive.[22] CFC rules are aimed at the taxation of profits that were diverted to a foreign subsidiary in a low-tax jurisdiction by attributing the income back to the controlling entity's country.[23]

In the US, the majority of eligible companies use section 953(d) of the Internal Revenue Code (IRC)[24] for their captives. This allows them to elect to be taxed as if they were a US corporation. US shareholder(s) of non-US captive insurance companies that do not volunteer to be taxed in the US would likely pay US tax on the foreign income under the US CFC rules assuming other criteria are met.[25]

Section 831(b) of the IRC[26] is another relevant US tax regulation. It includes special income tax rules for small insurance companies, including captives. To be eligible for this regulation, the company must be a genuine insurance company, a US domiciled tax-resident or taxpayer under 953(d) election, and meet a premium income threshold (USD 2.2 million).[27] If these criteria are satisfied, the insurance company can be taxed on investment income and not underwriting income. Micro-captives have long been at the centre of the inland revenue's attention as potentially abusive arrangements. This was confirmed in several court cases with the latest court decision being in *Caylor Land & Development v. Commissioner, T.C. Memo 2021-30*[28] from March 2021. In this decision, the tax court disallowed the application of section 831(b) IRC as the micro-captive arrangement failed to qualify as genuine insurance due to not satisfying the risk distribution requirement. As a result, the captive could not use the special income tax rules. Caylor was also the first US tax court case that applied penalties on a micro-captive.[29]

As there is a substantial number of captive owners domiciled in the US, the applicable tax laws are considered to be one of the most advanced systems, and, hence, many well-known tax court decisions covering captives have been issued in the US courts.

1.7 Transfer Pricing Legislation

Transfer pricing also became an area of concern in relation to captives in many countries in close association with the corporate tax measures mentioned above.

22. The Anti-Tax Avoidance Directive (EU) 2016/1164 adopted by European Council on 20 June 2016 laying down rules against tax avoidance practices that directly affect the functioning of the internal market and further amended on 25 October 2016.
23. Ma'ilei et al., *supra* note 1.
24. Section 953(d) of the Internal Revenue Code (IRC).
25. Saren Goldner & P. Bruce Wright, *953(d) Elections: The Basics*, Captive.com, https://www.captive.com/articles/953(d)-elections-the-basics (last visited 1 August 2022).
26. Section 831(b) of the Internal Revenue Code (IRC).
27. Saren Goldner et al., *The Basics of the 831(b) Election for Captives*, Captive.com, https://www.captive.com/articles/the-basics-of-the-831(b)-election-for-captives (last visited 1 August 2022).
28. *Caylor Land & Development, Inc., Et al., 1 Petitioners v. Commissioner of Internal Revenue*, No. 17204-13 (United States Tax Court 10 March 2021) (T.C. Memo. 2021-30).
29. Ma'ilei et al., *supra* note 1.

Whereas the general transfer pricing rules apply to captive arrangements, the captive-specific transfer pricing guidance was historically established mainly via local case law or rulings and other administrative guidance by revenue authorities. Application of the local transfer pricing regulations may have a broader international impact, and some cases can stand as an inspiration for the issuance of various guidelines in countries where the tax laws have not yet been promulgated. In some instances, local case law was also a significant source of influence for the development of the OECD transfer pricing approach related to captives.[30]

The OECD issued two reports as a part of the 2015 BEPS Action Plan that were most relevant for further shaping the OECD transfer pricing approach to captive insurance, i.e., Limiting Base Erosion Involving Interest Deductions and Other Financial Payments (Action 4)[31] and Aligning Transfer Pricing Outcomes with Value Creation (Actions 8–10).[32]

In July 2018, the OECD issued a public discussion draft with respect to financial transactions that included a section on captive insurance.[33] This draft contained many concepts from local country case law in the United Kingdom, the US and the EU, and case law from many different countries also influenced much of the discussion draft commentary.[34]

The OECD released new Transfer Pricing Guidelines on Financial Transactions based on the Public Discussion Draft in February 2020 which formed a new Chapter X of the OECD TPG. Section E is specifically dedicated to the application of the arm's length principle on captive insurance. The OECD Guidance covers two focus areas for insurance and reinsurance: (1) commerciality of circumstances and appropriate delineation of transactions and (2) determination of the arm's length price.

An example can be taken from Australia. The ATO issued formal alerts that address some specific non-resident captive arrangements that may be a matter of concern for the ATO and indicate the tax and transfer pricing measures likely to apply to such arrangements.[35] Even though these alerts were issued prior to the OECD BEPS initiative, similar principles are described in Chapter X of the OECD TPG. Tax Alert 2009/15 mentions arrangements that result in excessive premiums being paid to low-tax jurisdictions or payments of premiums to a company when there is no significant transfer of insurance risk as areas of concern.

30. Stanley J. Hales & John Henshall, *Chicken or the Egg: TP, BEPS, and Local-Country Legislation*, International Tax Review (February 2019).
31. OECD, *Limiting Base Erosion Involving Interest Deductions and Other Financial Payments, Action 4: 2015 Final Report* (OECD Publishing 2015).
32. OECD, *Aligning Transfer Pricing Outcomes with Value Creation, Actions 8–10: 2015 Final Reports* (OECD October 2015).
33. OECD, *Public Discussion Draft: BEPS Actions 8–10 – Financial Transactions* (July 2017).
34. Hales & Henshall, *supra* note 30.
35. Australian Taxation Office, *Taxpayer Alert: TA 2009/15 Payment of Inflated Insurance Premiums to a Related Party* (June 2009); Australian Taxation Office, *Practice Statement Law Administration: PS LA 2007/8 Treatment of Non-resident Captive Insurance Arrangements* (April 2007).

Example

ATO's TA 2009/15

XY Aus Co pays insurance premiums to related XY Captive domiciled overseas either directly or via a third-party intermediary. XY Aus Co takes a tax deduction for the premium paid. The ATO is concerned that the premium amounts may be excessive, and/or there may be no significant transfer of insurance risk (Figure 7.6).

Figure 7.6 Excessive Premium Amounts

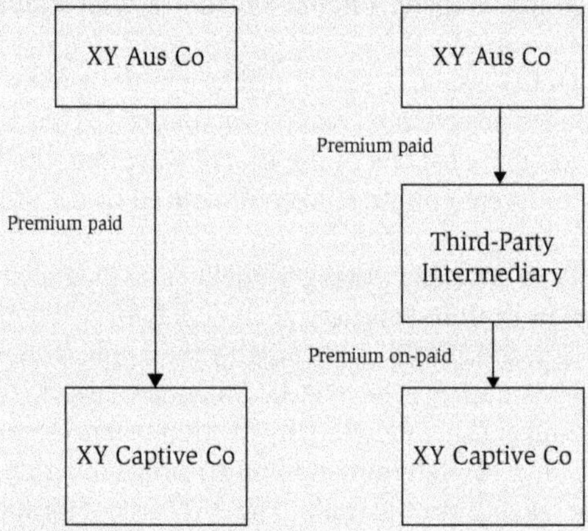

The ATO confirms that both arrangements would be subject to transfer pricing provisions and the relevant double tax treaty provisions. The arrangements may also be captured under CFC rules, residency provisions, and the general anti-avoidance rules. Consequently, administrative penalties up to 50% of the scheme's shortfall and other civil penalties may apply.

2 THE ASSESSMENT OF THE ARM'S LENGTH NATURE OF INTRA-GROUP FINANCIAL TRANSACTIONS

To examine the arm's length nature of a related party transaction under the OECD TPG Chapter X, a taxpayer must demonstrate that the terms and conditions of that related party transaction are similar to those that would have been entered into by unrelated parties in similar circumstances. This comparison covers the consideration of the commerciality of the arrangement and the assessment of the applied transfer price.

A transfer pricing analysis of a captive insurance arrangement adheres to the same general OECD transfer pricing principles even though the analysis may be applied in a slightly specific manner. Following the structure of Chapter X of the OECD TPG, the first two questions to be asked are whether the arrangement represents a genuine insurance arrangement and whether it was structured in a way that makes commercial sense for the entities involved. This is a question of the accurate delineation and recognition of the insurance arrangement and the transactions involved (i.e., application of sections D.1 and D.2 of Chapter I of the OECD TPG). Once the substance of the captive insurance arrangement is properly delineated, Chapter X requires a further analysis of whether the individual transactions covered by the captive insurance arrangement are priced in a way that would be agreed between unrelated parties. The analysis must evaluate if the transactions lead in totality to an arm's length transfer pricing outcome for the parties involved (in accordance with Chapter II of the OECD TPG).

This section will describe the application of the general transfer pricing principles to the particular circumstances of captive insurance as described in the OECD TPG. The authors do not address country-specific regulations or transfer pricing practice in individual local jurisdictions unless cited by example. Although the OECD TPG summarize the internationally accepted general principles, it is essential to check the compliance with the individual local tax laws when evaluating a particular case of a captive insurance arrangement as they may differ in each jurisdiction involved.

2.1 Accurate Delineation of Captive Insurance Arrangement

Similar to any type of related party dealings, the accurate delineation of the actual relations in the captive insurance arrangement is the first step in the transfer pricing analysis. The objective of this process is to define the economically relevant characteristics of the transaction so that appropriate comparable transactions and transfer pricing methods can be used when evaluating the arm's length character of the premiums and other payments involved in the arrangement.

The analysis is based on the actual conduct of the parties involved as opposed to the provisions summarized in the written agreements that may not always reflect the economic allocation of functions, risks, and assets (and contribution to value creation). It requires preparing a thorough functional analysis. The actual conduct of the parties is compared with the terms of the relevant written agreement between the related parties. If it does not reflect the economic allocation of functions, risks, and assets (and the parties' contribution to value creation), the transaction should be delineated in accordance with the characteristics of the transaction reflected in the parties' conduct.

When considering the above transfer pricing aspects for captive insurance, the core question to be asked is whether the arrangement in question represents a bona fide insurance transaction, i.e., whether there is an actual transfer of a commercial risk to the captive insurance company. The OECD TPG[36] mention the following features that should demonstrate the commercial legitimacy of the insurance arrangement and indicate that it involves a bona fide insurance business:

36. OECD, *supra* note 2, para. 10.199.

- there is diversification and pooling of risk in the captive insurance;
- the economic capital position of the entities within the multinational group has improved as a result of diversification, and there is therefore a real economic impact for the entire group;
- both the captive insurer and any reinsurer are regulated entities with broadly similar regulatory regimes and regulators that require evidence of risk assumption and appropriate capital levels;
- the insured risk would otherwise be insurable outside the multinational group;
- the captive insurer has the requisite skills, including investment skills, and experience at its disposal; and
- the captive insurer has a genuine possibility of suffering losses from claims.

Court Case[37]

The above OECD principles are analogous to the decision made in the *Harper Group* case which concluded that all captives must comply with the following three factors: (1) the arrangement involves the existence of an insurance risk, (2) there is both risk shifting and risk distribution, and (3) the arrangement is for insurance in its common accepted context. US Tax Court decisions have brought clarity over time to captives established in a compliant manner.

Should the tax authorities conclude that the criteria for assessing a captive arrangement as actual insurance are not sufficiently met, there is a risk that the transaction could be recharacterized and repriced for tax purposes as an arrangement other than insurance (e.g., provision of services, provision of funding, return of capital) in line with its actual delineation.

Court case[38]

The *US Tax Court* concluded in the *Avrahami* case that the captive insurance arrangement entered into by Mr and Mrs Avrahami was not genuine insurance although the captive was organized and regulated as insurance company in compliance with the applicable laws in the domicile country (St. Kitts) and met the required minimal capitalization requirements. This was due to a combination of various non-commercial features such as the risk covered by the insurance was vaguely described, some aspects of the actuary calculations were difficult to understand, and the insurance premiums were found to be excessive compared to previously agreed commercial insurance of the same kind with a small number

37. *The Harper Group and Includible Subsidiaries v. Commissioner of Internal Revenue*, No. 33761-85 (United States Tax Court 24 January 1991) (96 T.C. 45).
38. *Benyamin Avrahami and Orna Avrahami v. Commissioner of Internal Revenue*, No. 17594-13 (United States Tax Court 21 August 2017) (149 T.C. No. 7).

of claims from the insured over the lifetime of the captive arrangement. As a consequence, the Avrahami companies were not entitled to certain deductions and tax benefits,[39] and the premiums paid to the captive were not considered tax-deductible expenses. Finally, the back-to-back loan to Avrahami was reclassified as a return of premium subject to US taxation.

It is noted that the same principles as those for captive insurance apply for the insurance and reinsurance transactions in a fronting arrangement even though these typically involve participation of a third party with risk flowing-through to the group captive. However, as discussed earlier, the mere fact that the fronting company is not related to the insured group entities and/or the captive would usually not prevent application of the transfer pricing rules if the facts and circumstances indicate non-commercial arrangements such as the parties acting in concert with each other.

Court Case[40]

Again, in the *Syzygy* case, the US Tax Court did not find the insurance and reinsurance transactions as insurance in the commonly accepted context. The captive was organized and regulated as an insurance company and met Delaware's minimum capitalization requirements. However, there was no evidence to substantiate the existence of genuine actuarial calculations to achieve a reasonable premium. The fronting carriers charged unreasonable premiums and late-issued policies with conflicting and ambiguous terms. There was only one single claim paid during the existence of the arrangement, whereas other eligible claims were not submitted from the insured company. This also contributed to the conclusion of the court that there was no actual risk transferred to the captive. As a consequence, the insured company was not entitled to certain deductions and tax benefits,[41] and the premiums paid to captive were not considered a tax-deductible expense.

Each of these six OECD features of commercially realistic bona fide insurance arrangements is examined with a few examples below.

2.1.1 Diversification and Pooling of Risk

Risk diversification is one of the most important tools for maximizing the underwriting profits used by large commercial insurers and reinsurers. This can be achieved by pooling risks such as covering a large number and a diverse structure of insured entities using a variety of insurance programmes or a large geographic coverage.

39. Section 831(b) of the Internal Revenue Code (IRC) for micro-captives and section 953(d) of IRC allowing taxation of insurance income as if they were domestic company.
40. *Syzygy Insurance Co. v. Commissioner of Internal Revenue*, No. 2140-15 (United States Tax Court 10 April 2019) (T.C. Memo. 2019-34).
41. Section 831(b) IRC for micro-captives and section 953(d) IRC allowing taxation of insurance income as if they were domestic company.

The OECD TPG[42] suggest that captive insurance companies may achieve risk diversification by providing insurance to external companies outside of the multinational group. However, this is not often seen in practice as the multinational groups usually prefer to limit their captive insurance activities to internal dealings. A few commercial examples from the past exist that showed the commercial risk of such an arrangement when captive managers were underwriting both related party and third-party commercial reinsurance on a large scale. They became subject to the speculations of professional insurance brokers that placed underpriced risk with the commercial captives which ended in losses.[43]

The group would therefore typically diversify risk in a portfolio by selecting various insurance programmes that have less correlated risks and using the advantage of geographical diversification over various affiliates within the group. The group might also utilize a reinsurance programme to cede away certain risks or risk layers to other reinsurers to help diversify the portfolio's expected claims recoveries. The OECD recognizes the possible use of reinsurance arrangements for risk diversification and mitigation, considering that the insurer further diversifies the risks of loss by ceding away a portion of risks to the reinsurer.[44] There will be different circumstances and challenges for various captive insurance arrangements. In some industries with small companies, achieving diversification of risk may be more difficult. The operating subsidiaries are likely to also bear similar business risks when they have similar functional and asset profiles. An example would be an original equipment manufacturer (OEM) supplier in the automotive industry with several manufacturing operations situated across Europe which would typically be serving a few major local car producers (or, potentially, one vehicle manufacturer). The operational subsidiaries of the OEM supplier would all face similar EU-centric economic circumstances and risks (EU property/asset risks, trade unions and employee claims, market curves), and the geographical diversification would not be a contributing factor for risk pooling. However, the OEM supplier might manufacture many diverse products with each subject to different warranty terms and product liability laws in the various jurisdictions. In this case of product liability and product recall risk, the ability to pool these different risks into a single captive insurer may prove beneficial to the OEM supplier. The question is then what would be the sufficient evidence that the criterion of risk diversification has been met for transfer pricing purposes?

In order to prove that a sufficient quantum and variety of risks are covered by the captive insurer in the particular facts and circumstances, initiating an actuarial analysis may be very effective. In commercial insurance, actuary calculations are based on large number calculations and the use of probability functions to model expected losses from prior claims experience. Even though the particular circumstances of the multinational group may not allow for comparable quantum and variety, the actuarial model should

42. OECD, *supra* note 2, at 10.205.
43. Hugh Rosenbaum, *History of Captives*, *supra* note 3; Hugh Rosenbaum, *The Early Days of Captives*, *supra* note 3.
44. OECD, *The Contribution of Reinsurance Markets to Managing Catastrophe Risk* (OECD Publishing 2018).

provide evidence that all options realistically available were appropriately considered and that the selected arrangement represented the most suitable and commercially rational solution.

Example

Company A is a large multinational group active in the life science industry. It has subsidiaries located in more than sixty different countries that are represented by research companies, manufacturers, and distributors of medical equipment. Since the company has been impacted by increased insurance premiums on its property insurance for inventory and finished equipment, it established a captive to self-insure this risk. Moreover, it considers extending the insurance programme to cover other business risks once appropriate cash reserves are accumulated over time in the captive. It is expected that all subsidiaries will participate in the insurance programmes. The actuary calculation proved that the number of insured parties and diversified geographical coverage together with the group claim history is sufficient to ensure acceptable profitability models with reduced premiums compared to the previously used commercial insurance. Despite the existence of just one insurance programme, these facts indicate that the diversification and pooling of risk criteria are met.

2.1.2 *The Economic or Capital Position Has Improved*

The arm's length principle is based on the assumption that every independent party enters into a business transaction with the intent of obtaining a benefit in any form (e.g., achieving profits, lower costs, new opportunities). Such a party would consider all options realistically available and seek the most suitable alternative. As such, it can be assumed that it would not enter into an insurance arrangement unless its economic or capital position would improve in comparison to using a commercial insurance or any other form of risk mitigation alternative (including retaining the risk).

If the simple prerequisite of the captive insurance programme is to enhance the group's economic or capital position and excessive claims cause losses, this fact alone may indicate that the arrangement lacks commercial sense. However, this one factor must be evaluated in combination with the other commercial reasons and benefits from the perspective of the entire group (profit retention, group costs of insurance, retained capital) and of each individual participant in the arrangement.

There are various other business reasons why multinational groups enter into captive insurance arrangements. The following items would be the usual benefits that the insured entity and the group establishing a captive as a whole may realize (assuming the captive is well managed, sufficiently capitalized, and operates as a bona fide insurance company):

- reduced insurance costs;
- profit retention within the group;

- improved cash flow;
- risk retention within the group;
- availability of risk cover that is not insurable on the commercial market;
- effective risk management of risks, claims, and losses using internal data and information known within the group; and
- the captive's access to the reinsurance market.

2.1.3 *Both the Captive Insurer and Any Reinsurer Are Regulated Entities*

Captive insurers and reinsurers are typically established in countries with internationally recognized regulatory frameworks, government bodies to monitor compliance with local insurance law, and capital adequacy requirements. From the transfer pricing perspective, this condition is therefore usually easily met. The transfer pricing documentation may include the evidence of the insurance regulator's periodic regulatory review, financial statement audits, as well as capital and reserves reported to the local regulator.

It should be noted, however, that this criterion on its own does not provide full substance for the captive insurance to be treated as a genuine insurance arrangement as demonstrated, for example, in the *Avrahami* case above. Although the captive company met the regulatory requirements in its domicile country, the other factors such as excessive premiums and non-commercial features prevailed and resulted in the conclusion that the arrangement does not represent genuine insurance.

2.1.4 *The Insured Risk Would Otherwise Be Insurable Outside the Group*

This criterion may represent another challenge for captive insurance as one of the reasons why multinational groups can select to use a captive arrangement is exactly the difficulty or impossibility of obtaining sufficient insurance in the commercial market. Such insurance may be extremely expensive, or not commercially available, due to the excessive administrative burden associated with insuring unique or special risks with third parties.[45]

The OECD TPG mention that it may be difficult to claim the arrangement's commerciality and determine an arm's length price if related parties insure such unique risk through captive insurance company.[46] However, in practice, it may be absolutely reasonable and it is in the insured parties' best interests to purchase captive insurance coverage for risks that are not externally insurable. As mentioned with the OIL group captive example, the captive may exist because the third-party insurance market lacks a risk solution at a reasonable price. In a similar context, it may be commercially justifiable to provide insurance for such specific risks if the feasibility study supported

45. Jeremy Brown et al., *Captive Insurance Companies Put under Pressure by Tax Authorities*, International Tax Review (Jul. 2020).
46. *See also* OECD, *supra* note 2, para. 10.194.

by actuarial calculations shows the appropriateness of such an arrangement from the captive company's and the entire multinational group's perspectives.

It is also important to refer to paragraph 1.142 of the OECD TPG where it admits that an uncommon transaction between independent parties can still be recognized for transfer pricing purposes. This is because related parties have the ability to enter into a much wider variety of arrangements than independent parties and transactions of a specific nature.[47]

2.1.5 The Captive Insurer Has the Requisite Skills and Experience

Chapter I of the OECD TPG makes it clear that a party must have control over the risks and financial capacity to assume them if it is to be considered as able to assume the relevant business risks. Risk control is exercised through decision-making roles and important people functions (company directors and actuaries) with an appropriate level of expertise and experience to actually make the relevant decisions.

The OECD TPG define risk management as the function of assessing and responding to the risks associated with a particular matter. The decision to accept or reject a risk-bearing opportunity and responding to the consequences of that decision as well as creating and implementing related risk-mitigating strategies are components of the risk management function.[48]

The underwriting function is the key function in the insurance business and includes activities such as setting up insurance contracts or policies, classifying and selecting the insured risk, determining premiums, analysing the retention of risk, and finally accepting the insured risk.[49] From the transfer pricing perspective, the company that performs the underwriting function should be principally treated as the 'economic owner' of the insurance policy and be entitled to participate in the underwriting profits.[50]

The same principles generally apply to the premium investment activities of the captive insurance company and the entity that performs the key investment decisions (e.g., analysing the investment opportunities, selecting the investment instruments, and evaluating the related risk; and making decisions regarding the assumption of the risk and determining the amounts invested) should be entitled to participate in the profits from the invested premiums. In the world of insurance, these two functions are usually closely related and performed by the same entity.

If the captive is not able to demonstrate control over the economically significant functions and risk related to the transaction (particularly, the insurance risk) or does not have the financial capacity to cover the respective risks, the latter should be allocated to the relevant related party that actually exercises the control and has the financial capacity. Essentially, the transaction may be reconstructed by revenue authorities based on the actual conduct of the parties, and the transfer pricing

47. *Ibid.*, para. 1.142.
48. *Ibid.*, para. 1.61.
49. *Ibid.*, para. 10.211.
50. OECD, *supra* note 5, at 223, para. 193.

arrangement would subsequently have to be adjusted accordingly with profits flowing to the actual entity controlling this risk.

The allocation of profits between the captive insurance company and other group entities will depend on the actual allocation of functions and risks between the parties:

(1) If the captive insurer can demonstrate that it assumes the central management and control over the significant functions and risks, it should be entitled to retain the residual profits arising from the insurance activity.
(2) If, however, the captive insurer can be characterized as more of a service company rather than the actual insurer (service provider or administrator of the captive insurance function), it would only be eligible for a routine remuneration for its specific activities. The residual profit should be attributed to the group entity assuming control over the significant functions and risks.[51]

Tax authorities are likely to scrutinize captives with outsourced operating models and those that are supported by offshore risk management. In many countries, the local regulatory standards prohibit the outsourcing of some activities connected with the underwriting function. However, when this is possible and any underwriting or investment activities are outsourced, it is very important to analyse who retains control over the decision-making functions and the related risks. In this context, the general principles from the OECD TPG regarding outsourcing apply and confirm that the mere outsourcing of certain function-related activities does not imply the transfer of the function itself.

According to the OECD TPG, day-to-day mitigation of a risk can be outsourced without losing control over the risk. However, to maintain this control, it is necessary to be able to determine the objectives of the outsourced activities and the ability to manage them. This includes having the discretion to choose who performs the risk mitigation functions and being able to assess said performance to ensure it is satisfactory and making adjustments where necessary.[52]

However, when a captive insurance company would outsource all aspects of the underwriting or investment functions without actually controlling the process, it would not be considered as assuming the relevant insurance and investment risks. Consequently, the underwriting profits and the return derived from the investment of the premiums should be allocated to the party that is actually controlling and assuming the risk.[53]

In practice, captive insurance companies employ captive managers that are in charge of the day-to-day management of the insurance business, including legal representation, primary contact with a regulator, financial reporting, secretarial duties, and many more. The manager may accomplish a management role but would not usually make

51. OECD, *supra* note 2, para. 10.212.
52. *Ibid.*, para. 1.65.
53. *Ibid.*, para. 10.213.

the final executive decisions related to underwriting risks or investments of reserves outside of operating procedure limits.

2.1.6 *The Captive Is Exposed to a Real Risk of Loss from Claims*

The basic principle of insurance is the risk being transferred from the operating company to the insurer in exchange for the payment of a premium. The insured entities are then entitled to claim compensation from the captive if the insured event occurs (to the pre-agreed policy limit).

The multinational group should be able to demonstrate the transfer of risk in the following ways:

- captive is exposed to genuine risk of suffering losses and has paid claims; and
- captive has the financial capacity to cover the losses from claims.

The OECD TPG state that the captive insurer can be considered as having assumed the insurance risk if it is exposed to its unfortunate outcome and the possibility of losses.[54] To accurately delineate a captive insurance transaction, it must be also identified whether the captive insurer controls other significant economic risks corresponding to the underwriting function such as commercial risk or investment risk.[55]

Per the OECD TPG, the activities that form part of the underwriting function include setting the underwriting policy, risk classification and selection, pricing or setting the premiums, performing the risk retention analysis, and the acceptance of the insured risk.[56] These are considered control functions that predetermine the financial capacity to assume the risk and would lead to its allocation to the captive insurer.[57]

Insurance risk can only be assumed if the captive insurer has the ability to satisfy claims out of reserves and invested capital in the event that the risk event materializes.[58] In order to conclude if the captive insurance company has sufficient financial capacity, the tax authorities would analyse the capital structure and solvency ratio as well as the investment strategy and liquidity of the reserves for claims payments.

Example

PS LA 2007/8 from the ATO provides an example in which the captive insurer will not be considered as a genuine insurer due to the lack of capacity to cover the claims:

54. *Ibid.*, para. 10.202.
55. *Ibid.*, para. 10.210.
56. OECD, *supra* note 5, at 187, para. 34.
57. OECD, *supra* note 2, para. 10.211.
58. *Ibid.*, para. 10.209.

Aus Co sets up a captive insurance entity, Captive Co, and concludes a contract for USD 200 million insurance cover against a USD 20 million premium. Captive Co retains a USD 17 million premium and a USD 170 million insurance risk. It further concludes a reinsurance contract with a third-party reinsurer for USD 30 million coverage and pays a USD 3 million premium (arm's length price). Captive Co does not have any other financial capacity to cover the USD 200 million policy than the retained premiums (USD 17 million), investment income, and the USD 30 million reinsurance capacity. Actuaries have determined that the probability for the claims to exceed USD 30 million is very low (Figure 7.7).

Figure 7.7 Captive Insurer and Lack of Capacity

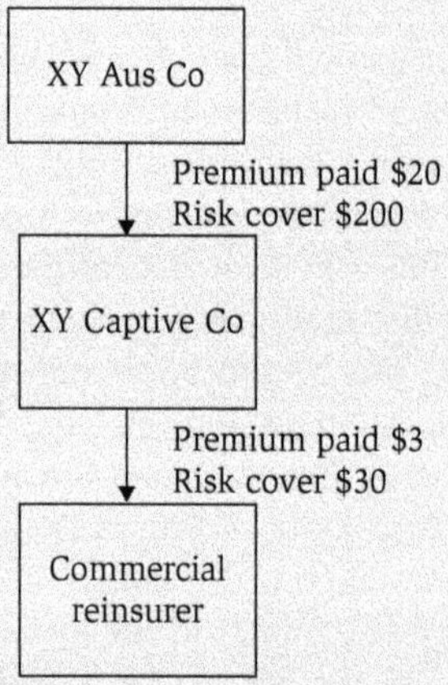

Per the ATO, this scenario would not be accepted as a captive insurance arrangement for the following reasons:

- the remote probability that Captive Co would need to fund claims from sources other than reinsurance;
- due to a much lower probability of claims in excess of USD 30 million, the arm's length premium should likely be less than the commercial premium (10%); and
- the captive insurance entity does not have the financial capacity to satisfy the USD 200 million coverage provided.

The above considerations demonstrated that the six OECD features supporting the commercial rationale and substance of the controlled transaction must be considered in their entirety and not on an individual basis. The specific facts and circumstances of every particular case need to be evaluated as these can be reflected in the fulfilment of the criteria.

2.2 Recognition of the Accurately Delineated Transaction

After the transactions are accurately delineated for the transfer pricing purposes, it needs to be further analysed if the related party arrangement makes commercial sense and would be likely entered into by unrelated parties in comparable circumstances. If this cannot be proved or concluded, the non-recognition principles described in section D.2 of Chapter I of the OECD TPG may apply. In specific circumstances, the transaction could be disregarded as a whole; however, the OECD TPG[59] mention that this should be done only in exceptional circumstances.

It is noted that the questions of accurate delineation and commerciality of the arrangements for captive insurance arrangements are closely interrelated. In this sense, they are addressed in a mutual context in section E.2 of Chapter X of the OECD TPG. Many of the recognition aspects have therefore been implicitly discussed in the previous section.

Overall, in order for the arrangement to be fully recognized, the facts and circumstances of the captive insurance should prove that:

(1) the multinational group considered all options realistically available (including traditional external insurance, balance sheet retention, and various other self-insured options) to select the most appropriate approach to insurance. This can be evidenced by various documents that were considered in the decision-making process, such as feasibility studies, expert advice, or internal documents prepared for board meetings;
(2) the transaction makes commercial sense for the multinational group and for all participants under a group retention approach. This can be evidenced, for example, by comparing the insurance policy in a previously used commercial insurance policy with the current conditions of the captive insurance;
(3) the captive insurance company has the functional and financial capacity to fulfil its insurance obligations by paying claims.

Once the bona fide nature and the commerciality of the captive insurance arrangement are proved, the taxpayer can proceed to a transfer pricing analysis in order to select a method for benchmarking and supporting the premiums, profits, or losses that can occur at arm's length for the captive.

2.3 The Selection of the Most Appropriate Transfer Pricing Method

The most common cross-border related party transactions involved in the captive insurance arrangements subject to the transfer pricing rules are the payments of insurance premiums, premium returns,[60] and the actual allocation of the underwriting

59. *Ibid.*, paras 1.141–145.
60. Per the International Risk Management Institute, the return premium can be defined as the amount payable to the insured if the actual cost of insurance policy was less than what was anticipated when the paid premium was set – e.g., the limits were reduced, the estimated

and investment profits. Separate management services, administration of claims-related services or capital loans might also be relevant depending on the operation.

One of the features to be documented in a captive insurance arrangement is whether the amounts paid as a premium may be excessive when compared to insurance coverage provided by a third-party insurer. This could indicate a non-commercial arrangement, and appropriate adjustments would be made in the pricing of the transaction for tax purposes.

The OECD Guidance discusses which transfer pricing methods may be appropriate to use for pricing of the premiums including the comparable uncontrolled price (CUP) method and transactional net margin method (TNMM). In addition, the OECD TPG also acknowledge the use of an actuarial analysis as an appropriate (other) method for determining the premium. The method selection and benchmarking examples below focus on the premiums paid by an insured related party to the captive insurer.

The premium's pricing must take into account the insurer's expected costs of claims and the time when claims are expected to be paid. The captive insurer will also have to consider the ratio of expected operating expenses to premiums. He will invest premiums to earn a return, and it will be taken into account in the calculation of the appropriate level of premium.[61]

2.3.1 CUP Method

Paragraph E.3.1 of Chapter X of the OECD TPG outlines the use of either the CUP method or an actuarial analysis Other Method as possible approaches to the pricing of captive insurance policies.

The CUP method may be applicable especially in cases when internal comparable transactions are available, i.e., when the captive insurer provides similar insurance programmes to unrelated parties. However, like in every transfer pricing analysis using the CUP method, this requires a very high level of comparability of circumstances.

Example

A captive insurer domiciled in a relevant country within the group of related party operating companies is a new single parent captive insurer established by the parent company headquartered in the United Kingdom (UK Group). The UK Group operates in the consumer retail business with a global supply chain. Products and inventory are manufactured, shipped, stored, and supplied around the world in different countries. It decides to self-insure certain risks of product and inventory loss within the global supply chain with 2022 being the first year

exposure was found higher in an audit, or the policy was cancelled. *See* International Risk Management Institute, *Return Premium*, https://www.irmi.com/term/insurance-definitions/return-premium (last visited 1 August 2022).

61. OECD, *supra* note 5, at 181, para. 6.

of the captive insurer operation for which the transfer pricing analysis is being prepared. The insured risk cover includes property and casualty (P&C) insurance for which the premiums were determined using standard actuary calculations. The captive insurer is an insurer in a single parent captive arrangement established by the manufacturing company. The multi-line risks covered by the insurance programmes are: (a) business interruption from property damage, (b) professional indemnity liability, (c) key man (employee loss), (d) trade credit loss, and (e) product recall/product liability. Related parties within the global group, referred to as related party insureds (RPIs), pay premiums to the captive insurer for the insurance coverage offered by the captive insurer.

The CUP method in this example was not selected as the most appropriate and reliable method for identifying the arm's length conditions for the following reasons:

(1) An internal CUP for premium pricing is not available as the captive insurer does not provide insurance services to unrelated parties.
(2) An external CUP may be difficult to apply as policy pricing data is often not publicly available, and comparability adjustments may need to be made to account for any potential differences between the controlled and uncontrolled transactions, including differences in terms of business volume and the level of capital between the captive insurer and the potential comparables.

An alternative approach to assessing the arm's length pricing for insurance of a particular risk is the use of an actuarial analysis. The price of an insurance premium is expected to cover insurer's underwriting and administration costs, the expected losses on claims, and the reasonable ROC as well as considering any expected investment income.[62]

While actuarial analyses do not represent actual transactions between third parties, the analysis is analogous to a CUP as it reflects what independent parties would agree to in comparable circumstances. Usually, an unrelated party actuary applies industry-accepted models and data from insurance brokers for similar lines of insurance in the premium pricing analysis.

Based on a strict interpretation of the OECD TPG, this method corresponds to an 'Other Method' under the OECD TPG. As noted in paragraph 2.9 of the OECD TPG, taxpayers retain the freedom to apply other methods to establish prices in order to satisfy the arm's length principle. The use of an actuarial analysis as an Other Method may be assumed to be the most appropriate and reliable one for assessing the arm's length nature of the insurance premiums paid by the insured related party to the captive insurer.

62. OECD, *supra* note 2, para. 10.219.

2.3.2 TNMM Method

Under the OECD TPG, a TNMM with an ROC profit level indicator (PLI) may be the primary transfer pricing method or instead offer corroborative support for the related party pricing of the captive. The TNMM could provide corroborative support for the above actuarial analysis.

Return on Capital (also known as return on investment (ROI) or return on capital employed (ROCE)) is a commonly used profit level indicator in financing sector that indicates how effectively a company has used the invested capital. The ratio can be computed as earnings before interest and tax (EBIT) divided by the capital employed. The higher the ratio, the more efficient the company is in turning the invested capital into profits.

$$\mathbf{ROC} = \frac{\mathbf{EBIT}}{\mathbf{Average\ CE}} \mathbf{x\ 100}$$

ROC – Return on Capital
EBIT – Earnings before Interest and Tax
CE – Capital Employed

The capital employed refers to a total amount of equity (including share capital, reserves, accumulated losses) and non-current liabilities (including long-term loans). It can also be calculated by deducting the business' current liabilities from its total assets.

CE = Total Assets – Current Liabilities = Equity + Non-current Liabilities

The general transfer pricing practice works with the average annual capital employed which takes the average of the opening and closing balances from the balance sheet to consider for variations over the financial year. However, when this is not possible (e.g., a newly established captive insurer/new insurance programmes), an alternative multiyear approach could be assumed.

Simply stated, the TNMM compares the ROC for the captive insurer to a range of ROC ratios from third-party insurers. Hypothetically, the latter could write similar insurance risks as the captive insurer for a similar industry. If the captive insurer's ROC falls within the range of benchmarked ROC ratios from other insurers, this evidence then supports the arm's length nature of premiums paid to the captive insurer by the insured related party relative to the capital base. Practically, selecting a set of reasonably comparable insurers in a similar broad sector who are operating in a comparable geographical location with publicly available financial data is not always easy and is the art of applying the TNMM.

2.4 Application of the Most Appropriate and Reliable Method

This case study illustrates the application of the most appropriate and reliable transfer pricing method(s) to assess the arm's length nature of the insurance premiums paid by an RPI to a captive insurer wholly owned within the same group of companies based on the UK Group example provided above.

During 2022, the captive insurer provided insurance to the insured entities and invoiced the insured related party for insurance premiums. These were determined based on an independent actuarial analysis performed by an actuarial consulting firm. The actuarial analysis presented a range of premia for different lines of insured risks. Different claims experiences, retention rates, and coverage limits set by the captive insurer impacted the premium estimates.

In accordance with the Chapter X of the OECD TPG, the following aspects were first considered in the transfer pricing analysis to assess the accurate delineation of the transaction:

- whether the insurance transactions between the insured related party and the captive insurer can appropriately be regarded as a bona fide insurance transaction; and
- the economic and commercial rationale for entering into the transactions.

2.4.1 Are the Insurance Transactions Bona Fide Insurance Transactions?

Chapter X of the OECD TPG considers whether the transaction is one of insurance. Specifically, the analysis of an insurance transaction requires consideration of whether the relevant risk has been assumed by the insurer and if risk diversification has been achieved.

To consider the transfer pricing implications of a transaction with a captive insurance, it is first necessary to identify the commercial or financial relations between the related parties as well as the relevant conditions and economically relevant circumstances in order to ensure that the actual transaction is accurately delineated. The initial question will therefore be whether the transaction under consideration is one of insurance as defined above.

The following factors provide support that the captive insurer operates a genuine insurance business and that the transaction in question is one of insurance:

(1) Risk transfer: There is a transfer of risks from the insured related party to the captive insurer. Under the insurance contracts entered into between the parties, the captive insurer is exposed to the possibility of significant loss in the event that the insured risk materializes and a claim is made.
(2) Pooling: The captive insurer engages in risk diversification and pooling of risk. The former is achieved by the captive insurer by insuring a variety of different risks and pooling them across different insureds in the group other than the insured related party.

(3) Claims paying ability: The captive insurer has the insurance reserves and financial capacity to assume the risk. He has sufficient funds to satisfy claims and has paid claims in the past that were submitted by the insured related party.
(4) Regulation: In accordance with insurance regulatory requirements in the captive insurer's domicile country, he maintains a capital reserve, including the investment returns on owned premiums out of which claims by the insured related party are paid.
(5) Governance: The captive insurer has employees and access to appropriate skills, expertise, and resources at its disposal to assume and manage insurance risk. For example, many captive insurers might engage a third-party actuarial firm to perform the role of an insurance manager. The captive insurer's employees or directors have sufficient expertise and experience to review the actuarial work undertaken by a third-party actuarial firm (e.g., to evaluate and price risk with arm's length insurance premiums).

2.4.2 Economic and Commercial Rationale for Engaging with a Captive Insurer

Engaging a captive insurer to provide insurance allows the insured related party to manage insurance coverage for the insured entities in a more economical manner. The key commercial benefits achieved from this insurance arrangement would include the following:

(1) The primary benefit is the purchase of group insurance by self-insuring the risks without engaging a third-party insurance carrier. Cash remains within the corporate group, and investment returns on the premiums are retained by the captive insurer. The retention of the risk and the premiums permits the captive insurer to generate an incremental ROC for the group.
(2) Efficiency in the entire insurance process through the elimination of a large part of the administrative costs of the traditional external insurance market (such as brokerage fees) and reduction in the cost of using intermediaries. In the absence of this arrangement, the insured related party would be required to employ a broker or approach independent insurance companies and negotiate the contracts independently which would reduce operational efficiencies and increase the costs for the company.
(3) A tailor-made group insurance policy would be implemented and provide a common standardized cover to the insured related party and other affiliates in the group.
(4) Visibility and transparency of group insurance accounting procedures providing for underwriting and cost information flow to the corporate group to better manage future claims and reduce expected losses.

Once the transaction is appropriately delineated, the most appropriate transfer pricing method under the OECD TPG Chapter X is applied to assess the arm's length nature of the insurance premiums paid by the RPI to the insured related party to the captive insurer.

2.4.2.1 Application of CUP Method

The application of the CUP method requires a comparison of the premiums charged between the related parties with the premiums that would have been charged between unrelated parties in similar circumstances. As discussed above, as neither internal nor external comparable uncontrolled transactions were available for comparison in the transfer pricing analysis, an actuarial analysis was selected as an alternative method in this example.

Table 7.1 compares the actual premiums paid by the RPI to the captive insurer in the fiscal year 2022 with the premiums for each line estimated in the independent actuarial analysis. The range of premiums by line occurs due to different options for retention, limits of coverage per customer, actual claims paid, and limits on the coverage. Each of these factors impact the expected loss amount of each policy for each risk. As the expected loss for any specific policy and the risk increases or the value of cover, the insurance premium subsequently increases. The insured related party initiated an expensive recall of one product manufactured in the year of coverage due to a defective component which resulted in claims paid by the captive insurer. As a result, the actuary estimated higher premium rates for the product recall and liability coverage than those that were paid based on prior year claims as illustrated in Table 7.1.

Table 7.1 Premiums Paid by RPI to CI Versus Estimated Premiums

Insured Risk	*Premium Paid by RPI to CI (CU)*[63]	*Premiums Estimated by Actuary (CU)*	
		Minimum	*Maximum*
Business interruption	1,000	950	1,250
Professional indemnity	650	630	750
Key man	5,000	4,000	6,000
Trade credit	6,000	5,000	7,000
Product recall/liability	8,200	9,400	10,500

As outlined in Table 7.1 for the 2022 fiscal year, the premiums paid by the insured related party to the captive insurer for each line of coverage fall within the range of premium options recommended by the actuary except for the product recall/product

63. CU = Currency.

liability risk. The exception for product recall risk arose out of large claims for a component in the product produced by Company A. The actuary estimated an increase in premiums for the higher product recall risk and the potential for future recalls.

Therefore, on the basis that the third-party independent actuarial analysis reflects what independent parties would agree to in comparable circumstances, with an additional data analysis, the average or median amount of insurance premiums paid by the insured related party to the captive insurer generally conforms with the arm's length principle.

2.4.2.2 Application of TNMM

As discussed above, the TNMM may be applied as the primary transfer pricing method or can provide corroborative support for the CUP or actuarial analysis. The ROC is used as the appropriate profit level indicator in most cases.

To apply the TNMM per the OECD TPG, the basic process to support the insurance premiums paid by the related party to captive insurance involves two steps:

(1) First, the annual ROC (the profit level indicator) of the captive insurer from the insurance programme(s) under analysis is calculated. The data for the ROC is identified in the captive insurer financial statements for the fiscal year in question or, when not available, in other financial data, a general ledger, or an enterprise resource planning (ERP) system documents.
(2) Second, the ROC ratios are determined from a sample of unrelated third-party insurers in a comparable geographical location, timeframe (bracketing the same fiscal year of the captive insurer), and sector (life or P&C) that may underwrite risks similar to the captive insurer.

For simplicity with the numbers, assume in this example that the TNMM is used as the primary method for an entire captive operation covering different business risks from P&C risks. If, as in the example for UK Group above, one line of insurance appears to be priced outside of the relevant range from an actuarial analysis due to the future expectations of additional claims, a TNMM over all of the insurance operations will capture both the underpricing and overpricing into an average or median ROC result over the insured risks.

For the UK Group example, using the P&C industry characterization to confirm the arm's length character of the actuarially derived premiums, a TNMM analysis using the ROC was selected as the most appropriate profit level indicator. Assuming the captive insurer earns an ROC in the range of ROC ratios for other functionally comparable unrelated insurers, the related party insurance premium income may be deemed to be at arm's length.

2.4.3 *Calculation of the ROC for Captive Insurer*

To calculate the ROC for the captive insurer, it is first necessary to consider both the profit (in the example in this chapter defined as premiums less expected claims) that the captive insurer expects from writing insurance for UK Group and the capital that the captive insurer is required to hold to insure these risks.

2.4.4 *Estimation of Expected Profit*

The captive insurer performs an annual pricing exercise with a third-party actuarial firm using loss models to forecast the UK Group claims for the following financial year. The analysis uses historical loss data for the UK Group and market loss data when required to derive a projected distribution of losses for the following financial year. The mean loss cost derived through this exercise can be used in conjunction with the expected premiums for the UK Group for cover provided by the captive insurer in the financial year in order to arrive at an expected profit (Table 7.2).

Table 7.2 TNMM: Expected Profit

Insurance programme	*Allocated Premium (CU)*	*Mean Loss Cost (CU)*	*Expected Profit (CU)*
Property & Casualty	20,850	18,050	2,800

In practice, a number of other factors would normally be taken into account for the ROC calculation such as any additional insurance-related expenses (which would decrease the expected profit) and the captive insurer's investment returns (which would increase the expected profit). In this simple example, it is assumed that any additional expenses and investment returns in an era of low interest rates are not expected to be material. In an actual analysis, additional financial data inputs for these investment revenues and costs would be included in the expected profit estimates.

2.4.5 *Capital Requirement*

To estimate the amount of the capital employed to be used in the calculation, the following existing hypothetical data were considered in determining the captive insurer's capital requirement:

(1) The captive insurer regulatory capital requirement calculated under the Solvency II Standard Formula, referred to as a solvency capital requirement (SCR), indicates the required regulatory capital of CU 40,000.

(2) The captive insurer-specific model from the actuary to determine an alternate capital requirement for writing the covered insurance risk indicates an estimated required capital of CU 36,987.
(3) The actual available capital contributed to the captive insurer by the parent is CU 42,424.

Without an extensive analysis, it may be assumed that a comparable third-party insurer operating in a Solvency II jurisdiction would be required to hold capital based on the standard formula or an approved internal actuarial model. As an up-to-date SCR capital figure was available for the captive insurer (also prepared by the actuary), this figure was used as the primary basis for the ROC calculation in this chapter.

The actual amount of the captive insurer's capital was not selected as the most appropriate value for the calculation as this amount was contributed by the UK Group and therefore did not represent a fully independent value in a third-party context. However, additional ROC calculations have been made to confirm that this level of capital results in a solvency ratio in accordance with expectations for a similar type of insurer. As such, it was used in supplementary testing.

The actuary model was not used in this simple ROC example as the conservative approach is to attribute greater capital (and costs) to the captive business. However, the important point is that the actuary model attributes the lowest amount of capital to the captive for covering the same expected losses with the modelled premiums. This indicates that the captive is well capitalized against unexpected future claims.

Consequently, the expected ROC for the captive insurer was calculated as shown in Table 7.3.

Table 7.3 TNMM: Expected ROC of CI

Item	*Primary Testing (CU)*	*Supplementary Testing (CU)*
Expected profit	2,800	2,800
Capital (regulatory versus contributed)	40,000	42,424
ROC	7%	6.6%

2.4.6 *Benchmarking*

A search would typically be conducted to identify potentially comparable insurance companies for the identification of the arm's length range of the ROC. The captive insurer primarily provides direct insurance to the UK Group. Functionally, the former does not require an extensive sales, marketing, or distribution platform in the same way as a primary insurer accessing the retail or wholesale market. In practice, adjustments to the EBIT data to remove these expenses would be relevant to increase comparability of the captive insurer to the industry ROC ratios. In this example, assume that the search identified ten comparable insurance companies for which publicly available data published by Bloomberg (or another third-party database with publicly available financial information) were used to benchmark the estimated prospective ROC returns in 2021–2022. This resulted in hypothetical weighted average ROC ratios as summarized in Table 7.4.

Table 7.4 TNMM: Identification of the Arm's Length Range

2021–2022	*Minimum*	*Q1*	*Median*	*Q3*	*Maximum*
ROC	3.4%	5.8%	6.2%	7.1%	12.8%

While these illustrative ROC ratios may appear to be low, an ROC less than 10% could be a possible result for some insurers at that time due to the general environment of low interests, low average cost of capital, the higher claims from natural disasters and the pandemic economic circumstances. The ROC for the captive insurer calculated from the SCR and contributed capital falls within the interquartile range of results. It can therefore be concluded that the premiums paid by the UK Group were set at arm's length. The ROC calculated from the actual contributed amount of capital employed by the captive insurer also falls within the arm's length range which provides additional support for the amount of capital and premiums being compliant with the arm's length principle.

It is noted that the ROC figures calculated for the third-party insurers would usually be estimated using reported available capital from the financial statements rather than regulatory capital. It is, however, usual for insurers to hold a buffer of capital above the SCR for covering their view of the expected future risks to the business or to maintain a premium credit rating. Using the SCR at a minimum regulatory capital level (assuming this data is publicly available) would therefore likely result in an increased arm's length range of ROC ratios than those identified in the analysis. This might be used as a supportive argument in the conservative interpretation of benchmarking results.

2.5 Transfer Pricing Documentation

Most countries now require some form of transfer pricing documentation as that described under the OECD TPG or local tax law. The OECD country-by-country reporting requirements for large multinational groups would also impose additional reporting and documentation standards. For captive insurers, the transfer pricing documentation would support the bona fide nature of the insurer as described in Chapter X of the OECD TPG and include a benchmarking analysis of the premiums paid to the captive insurer. Additional elements to the standard transfer pricing documentation for a captive insurer may also include:

- an actuarial feasibility study for the capital savings, risks transferred, and other benefits;

- legal agreements describing the insurance services;
- insurance policies issued to the insureds defining the insured risks, limits on coverage, and premiums due to the captive insurer;
- an analysis of the optimal ratio between the risks to be retained in the captive and reinsured;
- providing annual governance reviews of the business' risk management performance for the board and management to help the business develop a risk strategy that better protects its assets; and
- determining the reserves to hold and invest in the captive such that the owner maintains key management functions and oversight of the risks insured.[64]

The vagaries of compliant transfer pricing documentation and the expectations of different revenue authorities around captive insurance transactions are beyond the scope of this chapter and left to a future publication.

3 CONCLUSIONS

Captive insurance plays an important role in risk management. Self-insuring risks provide coverage for certain events that may be more difficult to insure on the market and cost savings if the claims risk is better known and managed by the insureds and the captive insurer as a group.

Multinationals must adhere to various transfer pricing and other tax rules for revenue authorities to accept the insurance arrangements as arm's length from a tax perspective. The purpose of the transfer pricing analysis is to support the arrangement as bona fide insurance and document that the premium amount is appropriate for the risk transferred through a robust functional analysis, economic analysis, and benchmarking analysis.

Governance of the captive insurer is essential for ensuring the bona fide nature of the insurance transactions. The captive insurer will be regulated by a sovereign authority with a minimum capital base covering policies and claims paid with financial statement audits.

As noted in the OECD TPG, the captive insurer must ultimately demonstrate a reasonable level of economic substance. The insurance transactions must be commercially realistic, cover actual risks transferred to the insurer, and the insurer should pay claims when an insured event occurs. Essentially, taxpayers should ensure that the captive insurer functions as an insurer, has the assets (or reserves) of an insurer to pay claims, and bears the risks of loss as an insurer. Substance, functions, assets, and risks each contribute to the bona fide nature of the commercially viable captive insurer.

64. John Talley & Alan B. Cantor, *Business Risk and the Captive Insurance Company*, Captive.com, https://www.captive.com/news/business-risk-and-the-captive-insurance-company (last visited 1 August 2022).

CHAPTER 8

Asset Management

Georg Dettmann

1 INTRODUCTION

Intra-group financial transactions have become an increasingly important transfer pricing topic in recent years. Within the intra-group financial transactions, the asset management industry plays a major role because the relevant players are globally established and interconnected. These large groups thus have many intercompany transactions.

This chapter analyses the arm's length nature of intra-group financial transactions within the asset management industry. Specific emphasis will be attributed to the pricing of fund and investment management as well as distribution services since they typically comprise the bulk of the fees within this industry. This will be highlighted in the stylized example of a value chain in the asset management industry in the next section. Other activities such as back- and middle-office services are also considered, but will be covered less extensively since many of them are less value adding or of a routine nature. However, some of them can be high value adding (such as trading).

Section 1.1 provides a broad overview of the asset management industry and its changes and developments in recent years. Section 1.2 provides a comprehensive view of the types of intra-group financial transactions that typically occur, while section 1.3 outlines the regulatory background that is applicable. Section 2 identifies the commercial relations within this sector and subsequently discusses the recognition of the delineated transactions. It further investigates how they can best be assessed (section 2.3). An analysis to assess the arm's length nature of a transaction is described separately for the transactions identified in section 2.4. This section also provides a variety of examples on the practical applications of the arm's length principle within the asset management industry. Finally, section 3 presents the author's conclusions.

1.1 The Asset Management Industry

The asset management industry grew exponentially in recent years albeit unevenly. The characteristics of the assets being managed and the nature of marketing and distribution channels also significantly vary. This section provides an overview of the primary characteristics of this sector in general terms and on a worldwide basis.

1.1.1 Function-Specific Overview

In general, the value chain of the asset management industry can be depicted as in Figure 8.1.

Figure 8.1 Value Chain of the Asset Management Industry[1]

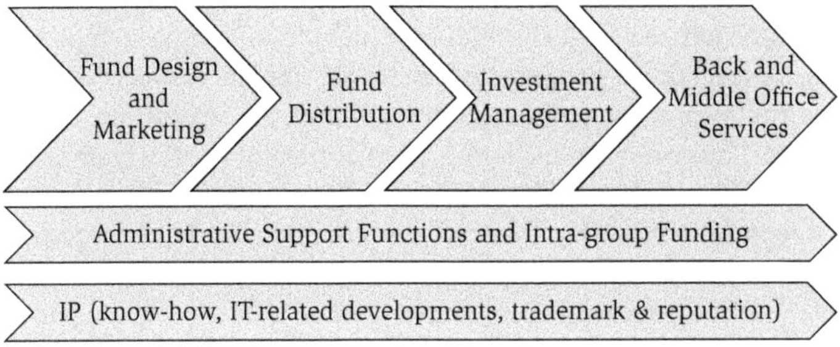

The functions along the value chain may interplay as in the following example. The distributions team may encounter an increased demand for certain products among their clients (e.g., for sustainable investments). They thus ask the investment management team to design a certain fund product, e.g., a sustainable investment fund. Once this fund is created, the distribution team collects funding, and the investment management team selects promising targets for its investment. The investments are subsequently processed by the back- and middle-office teams. In all of the steps along the value chain, some reliance may be placed on intellectual property, e.g., a strong trademark and a good reputation make it easier for the distribution team to find investors.

As can be seen from the example above, the core functions along the value chain are performed by the fund distribution and investment management teams. Fund design and marketing are typically done in close collaboration with the investment management team (which investments are feasible in the current market situation?) and the distribution team (what do customers demand?). The high value-adding aspects of fund design and marketing are thus typically remunerated as part of investment management and fund distribution. These functions are supported by a variety of back- and middle-office as well as administrative services that are compensated separately. Section 1.2 provides a detailed discussion.

1.1.2 Global Overview

The global financial crisis in 2008 led to a number of changes in regulations and consolidation in certain segments that reshaped the asset management industry. However, it recovered quickly and was characterized by significant growth in subsequent years. This even continued in 2020 and 2021 despite the global pandemic that affected the world economy during this period. The BCG Global Asset Management report confirms the strength position of the asset management industry that emerged from the global pandemic during which assets increased by 11% in 2020 and ending the year at USD 103 trillion. Retail portfolios that represented 41% of the global assets

1. Author's own illustration.

with a USD 42 trillion value grew at the same 11% rate in 2020, whereby institutional investments followed a similar pace and reached USD 61 trillion, i.e., 59% of the global market.

The main entry barriers into the industry include obtaining a capital investment infrastructure (especially regarding distribution), human resources and know-how (especially portfolio management), technology, and the realization of economies of scale and scope. Thus, when considering the historically relatively limited number of entry barriers and the players in the market, it can be noted that the great majority of companies operating within the financial services industry have targeted asset management for growth and future competitive development.[2]

This inter- and intra-sectoral competition makes the asset management industry relatively ambitious. Additionally, the level of the industry's competition has only been increasing as a greater number of non-traditional players such as fintech companies offer these services.[3]

Changes in the regulatory framework together with the dispersing of new technologies and a general change in consumer habits of new generations are leading analysts to predict that many retail clients will purchase their funds directly via online user-friendly fund platforms. They will consequently be less dependent on traditional forms of distribution.[4]

Proceeding forward, some of the upcoming changes suggest that the clientele of wealth management services will broaden in terms of both geographical area and extraction as more middle-wealth households with adequate levels of disposable income may invest. It is likely through a short-term focus that business models will hope to harness high-growth opportunities in the competitive framework and investment in innovative technologies allowing data and analytical services to offer customers digital tools that feel familiar.[5]

The main types of asset management service providers in the market can be summarized as:

- commercial and universal banks;
- investment banks;
- trust companies;
- insurance companies;
- private banks;
- mutual fund companies; and
- various types of specialist firms.

2. Strategic groups can be defined as commercial and universal banks, investment banks, trust companies, insurance companies, private banks, mutual fund companies, and various types of specialist firms.
3. Anna Zakrzewski et al., *Global Wealth 2019: Reigniting Radical Growth* 3 (June 2019).
4. Caceis Investor Services & PwC Luxembourg, *Reshaping Retail Fund Distribution Winning Strategies and Tactics in a Disrupted Environment* 9 (June 2015); Deloitte Luxembourg, *Europe's Fund Expenses at a Crossroads: The Benefits of Mutualizing the Cost of Distribution* 3 (2015); Brent Beardsley et al., *Global Wealth 2017: Transforming the Client Experience* 3 (June 2017).
5. Zakrzewski et al., *supra* note 3, at 20 et seq.

1.2 Types of Intra-group Financial Transactions in the Asset Management Industry

Although classic financial transactions such as loans and guarantees may be present in multinational asset managers, they are limited and small-scale transactions in most cases due to the nature of their operations.

Financing transactions are used more commonly for the purpose of liquidity management for the local entities in the context of their activities and trades in financial instruments. Thus, it is more important to understand how an asset manager operates and how its value chain is set up to trade financial assets (as briefly outlined above). This refers to the funding used and the financial instruments traded.

A financial asset can be defined in many ways. In the case of asset managers, the most common financial assets that investment funds (e.g., mutual funds) invest in are those such as equities, fixed-income products, alternative investments, etc. The Organisation for Economic Cooperation and Development (OECD) defines financial assets as assets in the form of cash, equity instruments, contractual rights or an obligation to receive cash or another financial asset or to exchange financial assets or liabilities, or a derivative. As examples, the OECD specifies bonds, bank deposits, stocks, shares, forward contracts, futures contracts, and swaps.[6]

As indicated in the stylized value chain analysis in section 1.1.1, the bulk of the profits generated with the management of those financial assets arises from the two functions at the core of the value chain: (1) the investment management function and (2) the distribution function. These functions are supported by a variety of middle- and back-office functions.

The core transactions within the value chain can thus be depicted as follows (Figure 8.2).

6. OECD, *OECD Transfer Pricing Guidelines for Multinational Enterprises and Tax Administrations 2022* (OECD Publishing 2022), para. 6.6.

Figure 8.2 Core Transaction Within the Value Chain of the Asset Management Industry[7]

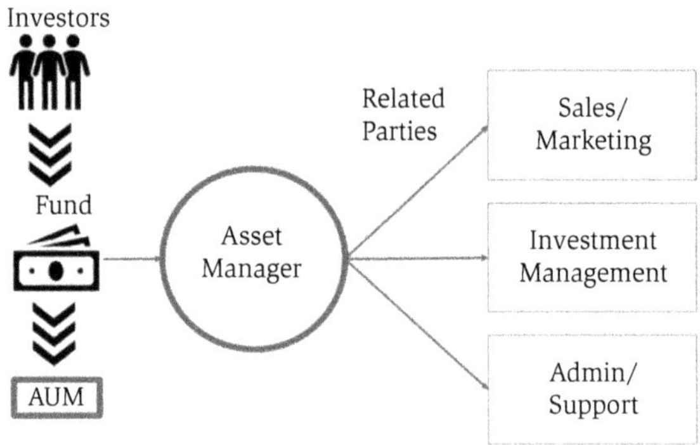

The designated entity ('fund' or 'fund manager') is responsible for collecting the necessary funding from the investors and investing it into selected assets, i.e., the assets under management (AUM). The asset manager (also 'Management Company' or 'ManCo') provides oversight functions that are typically of a routine nature such as compliance and regulatory matters. It generally delegates the higher value-adding functions to other (related) parties. The functions performed by the ManCo are low value adding; thus, they will not be within the focus of this report. While technically comparable prices for these tasks can be found, they are often remunerated by the residual of the fund fees that remains after all other parties are compensated.

The majority of the higher value-adding functions are thus typically not performed by the asset manager itself within its own capacities. These elements of the value chain are transferred to related parties that are often located in other jurisdictions (and also to external third parties to some extent). The asset manager thus typically delegates the following functions:

- sales/marketing (distribution activities);
- investment management (sub-delegated portfolio management); and
- administration/support (middle- and back-office services and other support).

The asset manager is thus involved in intercompany transactions for the above-listed functions as part of its value chain. For each of these transactions, an arm's length price needs to be determined in an intra-group context.

1.2.1 Sales/Marketing

The sales and marketing function is one of the core value drivers within the value chain of asset managers. Having access to a large quantity of either institutional or retail

7. Based on Philippe Neefs et al., *Transfer Pricing for Asset Management* 1 (2018).

clients that potentially invest in the managed funds is enormously important for the profitability of asset managers.

However, the functions performed by the sales teams can vary enormously from country to country and thus affect the asset manager's overall value chain. While fund distribution in some countries (e.g., Italy) is a classical retail function that encompasses sales personnel that have direct access in many cases to retail clients and also provide some advice to the customers, this might be completely different in other countries and, e.g., involve more direct sales via online platforms. In countries where this is typically the case (e.g., in the UK), the distribution relies less on customer networks and more on user-friendly online platforms.

The distribution function also varies by the type of company. In private banking organizations, for example, the distribution function can usually rely on networks of branches and independent agents and advisors that are promoting the funds to potential investors.

In general terms, distribution activities may entail:

- distribution of fund prospectuses;
- managing client relationships and providing client care in relation to investments;
- managing and setting up contractual arrangements internally and with external parties, including clients;
- monitoring internal fund and wealth management processes;
- monitoring and managing activities of the distribution network that performs the actual sales of the products to clients;
- distributing and marketing a number of third-party funds; and
- functioning as a liaison of information on market demands on new products to the investment management part of the business.

In terms of overall value creation, this is an important activity for asset managers that may have a relatively large network of agents to assist in the distribution activities.

1.2.2 Investment Management

Generally speaking, investment management encompasses the analysis, selection, and evaluation of investment projects while considering their risks and upside opportunities. It is one of the core activities of asset managers and potentially the key value driver in their groups' value chain. It is an activity that vastly relies on the development of know-how and its application. It is thus crucial to build up, maintain, and utilize experienced personnel (i.e., portfolio managers) within the company. This expertise can also be sold to external parties in situations of spare capacity, e.g., in the form of managing a sub-delegated portion of a third-party fund.

The investment management activities include:

- fund design;
- asset management, including acting as an investment manager;

- investment research; and
- the provision of advice on financial investment strategies.

In practice, investment management activities first involve defining portfolio management strategies. Once they have been developed, the fund is created and managed by the investment manager (or sub-investment manager).

The investments are then selected, and portfolio allocations are decided by the relevant investment manager or client. The trading desk is then responsible for execution, and the commissions involved in this are usually included in investment management fees. The executed trades are passed to the middle office where they are matched up with the confirmation letters/notices provided by the counterparty. Once this matching is completed, it is forwarded to the back office where it is settled.

1.2.3 Middle- and Back-Office Services and Other Support

This function includes all operations related to support, such as transaction processing, settlement, custody and stock lending, performance measurement, investment accounting, regulatory compliance, and customer service. In general, a substantial proportion of the back-and middle-office functions on the market tends to be outsourced to external third parties.[8]

Other support services may include functional services provided to the group entities as part of their day-to-day operations. These include:

- accounting, tax, and audit services;
- routine and investment compliance management;
- information technology (including day-to-day support, technology development, and software maintenance);
- data quality control;
- application management;
- financial reporting;
- business community management;
- project management;
- creation and maintenance of technical infrastructure; and
- operational and financial risk management.

1.2.4 Summary

In asset management, the three main transactions identified above can be characterized as follows regarding the services rendered, assets used, and risks assumed.

8. Oxera, *The Future of UK Asset Management: Competitive Position and Location Choice* 41 et seq. (May 2005).

Table 8.1 Assessment of Functions, Assets and Risks[9]

Function	*Service Rendered*	*Assets Used*	*Risks*
Distribution (Sales/Marketing)	- Client acquisition/ retention - Sale of fund products - Marketing activities	- Customer lists, - Best practices - User-friendly platforms (more relevant for some markets)	- Market Risk - Strategic Risk - Human Resource Risk - Reputational Risk
Investment Management	- Portfolio management - Stock selection/Investment research - Fund design - Risk control	- Investment strategies, know-how	- Market Risk - Strategic Risk - Human Resource Risk - Reputational Risk
Middle- and Back-Office Services and Other Support	- Transaction processing, settlement, custody and stock lending - Performance measurement, investment accounting, regulatory compliance, and - Customer service	- IT and reporting systems	- No significant risks are typically taken

1.3 Regulatory Background

Concerning regulatory changes, many asset management firms are still adapting to the MiFID II regulations[10] that came into effect on 3 January 2018. Some of the modifications to this industry include further transparency in pricing and execution, improvements in reporting, and an expansion to the exchange traded funds sector.[11]

The OECD is the main governing body for the applicable transfer pricing legislation besides the national legislation that exists. The most relevant aspects of international

9. Author's own illustration.
10. MiFID II (an EU directive) stands for Markets in Financial Instruments Directive 2.
11. Deloitte, *MIFID II - What will be its impact on the investment fund distribution landscape?*, https://www2.deloitte.com/content/dam/Deloitte/dk/Documents/finance/MIFID2.pdf; and *ETF market in Europe*, https://www2.deloitte.com/ie/en/pages/financial-services/articles/etf-market-in-europe.html.

transfer pricing are covered in the OECD's 2022 Transfer Pricing Guidelines.[12] They define the arm's length principle as the basis of all transfer pricing analyses. Its application is defined by the OECD as being based on a comparison of the conditions in a controlled transaction with those that would have been made between independent parties undertaking a comparable transaction under similar circumstances.[13]

For the specific treatment of financial transactions in an intercompany context, the OECD issued its specific Transfer Pricing Guidance on Financial Transactions[14] in 2020 that reflected the increased importance of the topic and ultimately became Chapter X of the 2022 OECD TPG. The OECD thereby provided a coherent framework for the first time to analyse the commercial and financial relations among related parties involved in a financial transaction.[15] It emphasizes the need for an analytical framework in this approach to effectively document financial transactions.

The OECD further defines two key aspects of such an analysis:[16]

(1) the *identification of the commercial or financial relations* between the associated enterprises and the conditions and economically relevant circumstances attaching to those relations in order *that the controlled transaction is accurately delineated*; and
(2) to *compare the conditions and the economically relevant circumstances* of the controlled transaction as accurately delineated with the conditions and the economically relevant circumstances of comparable transactions.

The transaction thus first needs to be accurately delineated before assessing the arm's length nature of a transaction. In a second step, comparable transactions can be considered that are based on the same conditions and economically relevant circumstances.

2 ASSESSMENT OF THE ARM'S LENGTH NATURE OF THE INTRA-GROUP ASSET MANAGEMENT TRANSACTIONS

2.1 Identification of the Commercial or Financial Relations

The commencement of each economic analysis is the assessment of the respective assets, functions, and risks. The same principles apply as those for any other controlled transaction when determining the arm's length conditions of financial transactions.[17]

The accurate delineation of financial transactions thus requires an analysis of the factors affecting the performance of businesses in the respective industry sector in

12. OECD, *supra* note 6.
13. *Ibid.*, para. 1.33.
14. OECD, *Transfer Pricing Guidance on Financial Transactions: Inclusive Framework on BEPS: Actions 4, 8–10* 46 (OECD 2020).
15. For certain aspects of financial services transfer pricing, the 2010 Report on the Attribution of Profits to Permanent Establishments can be an additional source of information.
16. OECD, *supra* note 6, para. 1.33.
17. *Ibid.*, para. 10.14.

which the Multinational Enterprise group operates. The OECD stipulates that this should begin with a thorough *identification of the transaction's economically relevant characteristics.*[18]

This means identifying the commercial or financial relations between the parties and the conditions and economically relevant circumstances attached to those relations. The recognition includes:

- an examination of the contractual terms of the transaction;
- the functions performed, assets used, and risks assumed;
- the characteristics of the financial instruments;
- the economic circumstances of the parties and of the market; and
- the business strategies pursued by the parties.

When differences exist between the tested transaction and any proposed comparable, it will be necessary to consider whether they will have a material impact on the price. If so, it may be possible to *make comparability adjustments* when appropriate to improve the reliability of a comparable.[19]

The previous section has shown a variety of intercompany transactions that are common in the asset management industry. The following might be considered as an example of the accurate delineation of a transaction.

Example

The OECD requires identifying all economically relevant characteristics of the transaction as a first step when attempting to estimate the fee that a distribution entity should receive as remuneration for its distribution activities from a related party asset manager. This includes a review of the distribution agreement and an analysis of, e.g., the market in which the distributor operates. Fund distribution in Italy can be completely different from that in the UK. The corresponding fees will thus not be directly comparable; thus, the OECD requires adjustment calculations for these (and other) differences.[20]

More precisely, the taxpayer must analyse and document the characteristics of a controlled transaction. This assessment needs to be based on the terms and conditions of the case. In the asset management industry, the following terms and conditions are typically economically relevant:

- asset class;
- asset size;
- investment objective;
- functions performed; and
- any relevant difference in the nature of the relationships.

18. *Ibid.*, para. 10.15.
19. *Ibid.*, para. 10.20.
20. These adjustments will be outlined below in section 2.4.

This initially means that a transaction incorporating a distribution agreement needs to be priced completely differently from an investment management agreement. It also indicates that the type or number of assets being distributed or managed and the country in which the related parties operate have an impact on the way the transaction is priced.

These characteristics need to be reflected in an economic analysis in order to adhere to the arm's length principles outlined by the OECD. Adjustment calculations should also be performed to enhance the comparability between the controlled and uncontrolled transactions whenever the comparable or methodology relied upon does not fully reflect these characteristics. The sections below meticulously describe the analyses undertaken to perform the necessary adjustments.

Identifying the commercial or financial relations also includes a determination of the factual substance of a transaction. As outlined by the OECD, there might be material differences between a transaction as agreed upon in the (intercompany) contracts (i.e., the contractual terms) and the actual conduct involved for the transaction, i.e., the functions that the parties involved actually perform, the assets they actually use, and the risks they actually assume.[21] If the actual conduct differs substantially from the contractual terms, tax authorities might reclassify the transaction accordingly. The following court case provides an example in which a lack of substance leads to a reclassification.

Court Case

A Swiss court decision concerned the transfer pricing set-up of a private equity structure (*Verrechnungspreiskorrektur einer Private-Equity-Struktur*) in the financial years of 2008 and 2009.[22] It was established relying on a Jersey-based investment manager and a Switzerland-based advisor. The contractual agreement between the two entities stipulated that the advisor would make recommendations on investment targets that the investment manager would review and subsequently make a decision. The investment manager would also assume all risks. In return, the investment manager should receive 33 % of the overall fees that the fund would earn, and the remaining 66 % would go to the advisor (revenue split).

Given the contractual terms, it does not seem unreasonable to assess that both entities perform high value-adding activities with the advisor having a larger share of the workload but a lesser share of the risk. From a quantitative perspective, a participation of 33 % in the revenue for the investment manager

21. OECD, *supra* note 6, para. 10.20.
22. *A AG v. Staat Zürich and Schweizerische Eidgenossenschaft*, No. SB.2018.00094 (Administrative Court of the Canton of Zurich 18 December 2019).

could be supported by a benchmarking study. The investment manager, however, did not have any employees.[23]

In a tax audit, the Swiss tax authorities assessed that, given the lack of personnel, it would be difficult to believe that the decision-making actually took place at the investment manager in Jersey and that it therefore would also not be in a position to assume the risks. The tax authorities thus concluded that the investment manager could not be considered as performing more than routine functions (fund administration, net asset value calculations, etc.) for which it should receive a fixed mark-up of 10% on the costs it incurred. After being reassessed in several instances, it was ultimately confirmed by the *Verwaltungsgericht* of Zurich in 2019.

The court decision shows that deviations between what was stated in the contractual agreements and the substance of the actual arrangement can lead to a requalification of a transaction by the tax authorities even if the transfer price can be supported quantitatively. This potentially leads to fewer profits for one of the parties involved.

2.2 Recognition of the Accurately Delineated Transaction

After the process of identifying the commercial or financial relations and the accurate delineation of a transaction, the recognition of the transaction forms the next step. This is built on the question of whether it accords with a commercial rationale that would also be agreed upon between unrelated parties under comparable economic circumstances.[24] This does not necessarily mean that the transaction as such needs to be observable between third parties but that it is economically feasible.

If an entity has entered into a commercially irrational transaction, it can be concluded that there is no price that is acceptable for the transaction. It might therefore not be recognized by the tax authorities, and the price paid may thus not reduce the profits of the company paying for the service provided. This can easily lead to double taxation.

It is therefore crucial for the taxpayer to demonstrate that the transaction is economically viable for the parties involved in it. It should be possible in most cases to demonstrate that a market for the respective transaction exists, considering the broad availability of price data for financial services. Academic literature can be an additional source for determining the economic rationale behind a transaction.

23. It should be noted that there were two directors who each received CHF 15,000 as a salary that was recorded under 'audit charges' in the P&L.
24. OECD, *supra* note 6, para. 1.143.

2.3 Selection of the Most Appropriate Transfer Pricing Method

As in any transfer pricing assessment, the choice of the most suitable transfer pricing method depends on the specific facts and circumstances of a particular transaction.

The OECD does not apply a strict hierarchy of methods and indicates that the taxpayer should apply the method that is most suitable to the specific facts of a transaction. The OECD opines that this does not mean that all the transfer pricing methods should be analysed in depth or tested in each case in arriving at the selection of the most appropriate method. This should, however, be evidenced along with the comparables.[25] It is further based on the availability and comparability of independent transactions that could serve as benchmarks for determining the arm's length nature of controlled transactions in the scope of the analysis.

The OECD refers to the following methods when assessing whether a transaction between related parties conforms to the arm's length principle:

Traditional Transaction Methods

- Comparable Uncontrolled Price Method (CUP);
- Cost-Plus Method (CPM); and
- Resale Price Method (RPM).

Transactional Profit Methods

- Transactional Net Margin Method (TNMM); and
- Profit Split Method (PSM).

Each company is required to choose the transfer pricing method that is most suitable to the character of the tested function or transaction.

Table 8.1 describes the three main identified transactions. Based on that assessment, Table 8.2 qualifies them as either routine or entrepreneurial and suggests an applicable transfer pricing method to them that is typically chosen for the evaluation of the arm's length nature of their remuneration:

25. *Ibid.*, para. 2.8.

Table 8.2 Choice of Transfer Pricing Method per Functions[26]

Function	*Assessment*	*Qualification*	*TP Method(s) Typically Relied Upon*
Distribution (Sales/Marketing)	Valuable intangibles used, significant risks taken	Entrepreneurial contribution	CUP[27]
Investment Management	Valuable intangibles used, significant risks taken	Entrepreneurial contribution	CUP/PSM
Middle- and Back-Office Services and Other Support	Few risks assumed, few valuable intangibles	Routine contribution	TNMM/CUP

While this chapter will not entail a general discussion on the available transfer pricing methods, the remainder of this subsection will briefly discuss the methods most commonly applied to the transactions identified above as the most common intercompany transaction in the asset management industry.

2.3.1 The Comparable Uncontrolled Price Method

There is a slight preference for the CUP method by the OECD even though there is no hierarchy of methods. The OECD Guidelines recognize that the CUP method is the most direct and reliable way to apply the arm's length principle whenever it is possible to locate comparable uncontrolled transactions and that the CUP method is preferable over all other methods in such cases.[28] It compares prices charged on the transfer of goods (or provision of services) in group transactions with those imposed in uncontrolled transactions. Moreover, the OECD describes this method as comparing the price for property or services transferred in a controlled transaction to that for property or services transferred in a comparable uncontrolled transaction in similar circumstances. The OECD further elaborates that any difference between these two prices may be an

26. Author's own illustration.
27. The remuneration of the distribution function could also be established relying on the PSM. This would mean splitting the overall profits generated by an asset manager between the main contributors to the value creation, i.e., between distribution and investment management (and potentially other services). The PSM is typically not applied in practice due to the broad availability of CUPs for the distribution function.
28. OECD, *supra* note 6, para. 2.15.

indication that the conditions of the commercial and financial relations of the associated enterprises are not at arm's length. Additionally, the price in the uncontrolled transaction may need to be substituted for that in the controlled transaction.[29]

This method uses the most direct level of comparison and is regarded by the OECD as preferable to the other methods if it is practicable.

The uncontrolled transactions should be goods or services of a similar type, quality, and quantity to those being tested. Other factors that should also be comparable, for example, are the time at which the transactions took place and the level in the production/distribution chain.

In practice, it is often difficult to find exact comparables. However, if there are differences such that an adjustment to the CUP can be made with reasonable accuracy, it may still be possible to use this method. When differences exist (such as in the quality of the product, the geographic markets, the level of the market, or the amount/type of intangible property) for which it is not possible to quantify adjustments, it will generally not be appropriate to use the CUP method.

There are generally two categories of transactions that can be used to conduct a CUP analysis:

(1) The first is often referred to as an 'internal CUP' and relies on the analysis of transactions entered into by group entities with external third parties; i.e., it relies on the price charged by the controlled party to an independent third party.
(2) The other category is known as 'external CUP'. It typically relies on the use of publicly available data on third party to third-party transactions, i.e., the (documented) price that independent third parties would charge on the market in a similar transaction.

As indicated above, the CUP is the method mostly applied to estimate a price for (sub-delegated) *investment management* and *distribution* (sales/marketing) services. A number of data providers exist that can be relied upon for investment management services. Data on the distribution function can typically be found in respective databases.

In certain cases, both internal and external CUP transactions can be identified, and the respective data is available for comparability purposes. In those cases, the reliance should be on both of them. A distribution agreement that the group has with external providers (internal CUP) can, for example, be considered as a reference point within a range of distribution fees that is derived from reviewing transaction data between unrelated parties (external CUP) that are obtained from a data provider.

Therefore, both CUP approaches are typically used to assess the arm's length nature of the proportion of fees to be paid to the group entities for these services rendered. The application of this approach and simplified examples for the application of the CUP

29. *Ibid.*, para. 2.14.

method to tested transactions are described in detail in the next section. Additionally, section 2.4.1. provides an example for the application of an internal CUP.

2.3.2 *The Profit Split Method*

While the CUP method is the most commonly applied transfer pricing method when assessing the arm's length remuneration within asset management companies, it should be noted that the profit split method is also applied occasionally, in particular for the split of the profits attributable to the investment management function.

In the case of the distribution function, specific teams cover the markets in which they are situated, whereas the investment management function can be split across various jurisdictions (e.g., a UK-based asset manager might have a small team in Japan dedicated to the selection of Asian equity within a fund's investment portfolio). The PSM provides an appropriate method in these situations, to split the investment management fees among the contributing teams and jurisdictions.

The OECD points out in its 2022 Transfer Pricing Guidelines that the main strength of the transactional profit split method is that it can offer a solution for cases when both parties make unique and valuable contributions to the transaction (e.g., they both contribute unique and valuable intangibles). In such a case, independent parties might effectively price the transaction in proportion to their respective contributions.[30] The OECD further stipulates that the transactional profit split method can also provide a solution for highly integrated operations in cases for which a one-sided method would not be appropriate.[31]

As a further indication for the use of the PSM, the OECD points out the shared assumption of risk in relation to a transaction.[32] To summarize, the profit split is the most appropriate method when one or more of the following parameters are relevant:[33]

- each party makes unique and valuable contributions;
- the business operations are highly integrated such that the contributions of the parties cannot be reliably evaluated in isolation from each other; and
- the parties share the assumption of economically significant risks or separately assume closely related risks.

This is the case within the management of an investment portfolio from different teams and jurisdictions. The investment management of a shared portfolio is a highly integrated operation. Different teams (that might be in various locations) contribute their work to the total composition of a joint portfolio. They also make contributions that are unique (they form an investment decision or recommendation based on the information available to them) and valuable (the performance of the portfolio is dependent on the outcome of their work).

30. *Ibid.*, para. 2.119.
31. *Ibid.*, para. 2.120.
32. *Ibid.*, para. 2.121.
33. *Ibid.*, Ch. 2.C.

The profit split might therefore be considered the best method to use to split the profits arising from the investment management function. Section 2.4.2.2 below provides an example for the application of the Profit Split Method in the scenario outlined above.

2.3.3 Transactional Net Margin Method

The TNMM provides an indication of arm's length pricing by examining net profitability margins of comparable unrelated companies for similar types of transactions.[34] It is similar to other methods as it is based on an analysis of the generated operating profit (net margins) but is less sensitive to product differences. The OECD Guidelines[35] state that the TNMM may afford a practical solution to otherwise insoluble transfer pricing problems when used sensibly with appropriate adjustments to account for any material differences. It further elaborates that this method examines the net profit relative to an appropriate base (e.g., costs, sales, assets) that a taxpayer realizes from a controlled transaction.[36]

A strength of the TNMM is that net profit indicators are less affected by transactional differences than the prices used in the CUP method.[37] However, it must be insured that the comparability standards are met, i.e., that the profits relied upon as benchmarks derive from companies that have a sufficiently comparable functional profile to the functions performed in the tested transaction. The comparability standards can go beyond product and functional similarity, e.g., the competitive position, management efficiency cost structures, or differences in the cost of capital.

An analysis under the TNMM should also only consider the part of profits that is attributable to the particular controlled transaction. It cannot be applied on a company-wide basis if the company engages in a variety of different controlled transactions (as is usually the case in the asset management industry) but only to specific transactions. In the asset management industry, the TNMM may therefore be relevant for traditional support functions (such as accounting and human resources) and some of the less complex middle- and back-office functions.[38]

For the application of the pricing of middle- and back-office services or other support services within the asset management industry, it would be necessary to identify the profitability of companies that solely provide similar services and operate under comparable economic circumstances. To the extent possible, functional differences can be compensated for in adjustment calculations. Section 2.4.3 provides an example on the application of the TNMM and possible adjustment calculations.

34. *Ibid.*, para. 2.64.
35. *Ibid.*, para. 2.80.
36. *Ibid.*, para. 2.64.
37. *Ibid.*, para. 2.66.
38. It may also apply to some investment research services provided that it is possible to identify functionally comparable companies that have similar risk profile.

2.4 Application of the Most Appropriate Transfer Pricing Methods

2.4.1 Sales/Marketing

The CUP method is typically applied (*see* section 2.3.1) to estimate an appropriate remuneration of the sales and marketing function (i.e., distribution). In cases of large multinational asset management companies, it is not uncommon that the related distribution entity also distributes the funds of external, unrelated asset managers. In these cases, the remuneration that is paid by the external parties for this distribution activity can be used as an indication of an arm's length remuneration for the sales and marketing function ('internal CUP').

Example

An asset manager distributes its investment funds in Italy through a related party distributor that has access to a large number of private household retail clients. This distributor also sells third-party funds to its clients. For this distribution activity, the third-party funds remunerate the Italian distributor by thirty-five basis points of the asset volume it distributes for them. Assuming that the distributed third-party funds are sufficiently comparable to those distributed for the related asset manager (i.e., regarding currency, volume, and fund type), these thirty-five basis points form a strong indication for the pricing of this intercompany transaction. The application of the internal CUP is thus a reasonable method for testing the transaction under review. In many cases, the distribution fee actually charged to external funds varies according to the specific characteristics of the product being distributed. In these cases, the fees are expressed as an interquartile range of applicable fees.

However, the exact parameters of these distribution activities might differ from the tested transaction; e.g., the amount of assets being distributed might differ substantially and thereby affect the remuneration. In these cases, adjustment calculations should be performed.

If no internal CUPs are available, then external CUPs are typically used. For this reason, publicly available databases (e.g., FITZ Partners or Morningstar) can be considered for identifying price data for similar transactions between independent third parties.[39] These databases comprise thousands of entries covering all types of funds and are managed and distributed in a variety of jurisdictions. In order to adhere to the comparability requirements established by the OECD, these databases should be filtered in order to identify the most comparable entries (e.g., concerning the amount of AUM being distributed, the country in which it is distributed, and the type of fund being distributed).

39. Due to the nature of some of the databases relied upon, it might not always be possible to identify if the distribution arrangements covered in the database are exclusively independent arrangements. This should be considered when applying the respective data.

The data can be used for the analysis once a sufficiently comparable sample of distribution agreements can be identified. The distribution fees are typically expressed in basis points (bps). Relying on a range around the average distribution fees identified within the sample typically provides some good indication for the arm's length remuneration for distribution activities.[40] In order to achieve results that are more robust, the arm's length distribution fees can also be expressed in relative terms, i.e., as a percentage of the total expense ratio (TER) or as a share of total management fees.[41] This can be particularly beneficial in situations when the comparables have considerable variety in their overall fee levels.

However, adjustment calculations should be undertaken if the identified sample (internal CUPs or external CUPs) is not sufficiently comparable. The OECD stipulates that comparability adjustments should be considered if they increase the reliability of the results.[42] In this context, the next paragraphs will discuss a number of adjustment calculations that should be performed in order to enhance the comparability of the data in the application of the CUP method.

2.4.1.1 AUM Adjustment

The funds in the relied-upon database might be fully comparable to geography or types of assets but include distributed asset amounts that are sufficiently larger (or smaller) than those in the considered transaction. This can be corrected by applying a statistical analysis.

For example, a regression analysis can be run across the total sample of distribution fee data that estimates the impact of size (i.e., the level of the AUM) on the fee outcome as one of the regressors. The resulting regression equation would then express the applicable fee level depending on the amount of assets being distributed.

Based on the outcome of the regression analysis, the total distribution fee can be estimated in relation to the level of the AUM being distributed.

Example

Several aspects might be considered when attempting to estimate the share of the TER that a Spanish distribution entity should receive as remuneration for its distribution activities from a related party asset manager. From the analysis of the asset management group's financial reporting, data arise on the distribution fees that the Spanish distributor charges to external fund managers to distribute their funds. There can be reliance upon this data (internal CUP).

40. It should be noted that it is common practice in financial services transfer pricing to build a range of one standard deviation around the average. This differs somewhat from the general transfer pricing practice that typically applies an interquartile range around the median.
41. The term 'total management fees' typically describes the combination of investment management fees and distribution.
42. OECD, *supra* note 6, para. 3.50.

However, while the amount of the (intercompany) AUM distributed via the Spanish subsidiary amounts to only approximately EUR 20 million, the third-party agreements cover amounts of EUR 500 million to EUR 1 billion each. To estimate an arm's length distribution fee for the Spanish entity, a simple regression analysis (e.g., ordinary least squares) can be performed that estimates the effect that the value of the distributed AUM has on the respective fees. Entering the distributed asset volume into the regression equation provides the AUM-adjusted fee level. Applying a range of one standard deviation around that value forms a range of applicable distribution fee levels that adhere to the arm's length standard.

2.4.1.2 Fund Type Adjustment

The distribution fees might substantially differ depending on the type of asset that is being distributed. Funds that focus on certain types of assets (e.g., equities) tend to have higher distribution fees than those pertaining to other assets (e.g., fixed-income products). The OECD recognizes that the characteristics of a financial instrument are an important comparability factor to be considered. It acknowledges in its 2022 guidelines that there is a wide variety of them in the open market, with different features that affect the pricing of those products or services. As a consequence, it is important to document the transactions' features and attributes when pricing controlled transactions.[43]

Applying what is referred to as a dummy variable to the regression adjustment described above can be an effective tool for adjusting these effects. It is a numerical variable used in a regression analysis to represent subgroups of the sample in a study.[44] These dummy variables allow using a single regression equation that encompasses a variety of different asset types and adjusting the results for each particular asset type.

Example

An asset manager distributes equity funds in Germany via its German subsidiary. Distribution fee agreements stemming from a public database that contains distribution agreements for equity funds are analysed to estimate an arm's length distribution fee for the German entity. The database also contains data on funds focusing on other types of assets such as fixed income, money markets, alternative assets, or a combination thereof. In order to derive the results for equity

43. *Ibid.*, para. 10.28.
44. This is a variable that assumes the value of 1 for certain fund types and 0 for all other fund types. They thereby can turn various parameters on and off in the regression equation.

funds, a dummy variable can be applied that 'switches off' the effects of other asset types on the final result.

While the fund type adjustment is always feasible for enhancing comparability, it should be noted that distribution fees are typically not extremely sensitive to the asset class being distributed when expressed as a percentage ratio of the TER.

2.4.1.3 Country Adjustment

The sample of applied comparable transactions does not always include promoters that are in the tested transaction's country or are in a sufficiently comparable jurisdiction to the funds distributed by the tested entity. In these situations, a country adjustment should be performed in order to make the respective entries sufficiently comparable. This can be done by identifying a subsample of entries in the sample, e.g., funds distributed in the country in which the tested distribution entity operates that differ from other characteristics such as type of fund to the tested transaction.

Calculating an average of these distribution fees within that subsample and comparing them to a subsample of funds from other countries with otherwise similar characteristics allows isolating the geographical difference in distribution fees. In some cases, it might be necessary to rely on an additional data source for this adjustment. Comparing the average distribution fees of both subsamples can quantify the difference when performing the necessary adjustment. Subject-specific literature might form an additional source to estimate the country effect on distribution fees.

Example

An example could be a UK-based asset manager that distributes equity funds in France via a related French sales entity. However, the French distribution fees in the sample are all for fixed-income funds. It would thus be possible to isolate a subset of non-French fixed-income funds in the sample and compare them to the subset of the French fixed-income funds. If it is found that the French fixed-income funds are distributed for a fee that is, e.g., on average 30 % higher, this can be used as an indication that the results derived from the (non-French) equity funds will need to be adjusted by 30 %. However, an asset type adjustment could also be considered, i.e., relying on the French fixed-income funds and adjusting them for the different distribution fees that are typically applied to equity funds.

2.4.2 Investment Management

The CUP method is usually applied to estimate the arm's length remuneration for the investment management function within an asset ManCo. One way of doing so is by analysing sub-delegated fund management agreements. Some asset managers delegate a portion of the AUM they manage to external fund managers and remunerate them accordingly. In particular, these agreements and their fee arrangement are public in the United States and can therefore be analysed.

Databases such as Morningstar, FITZ Partners, or Mercer provide detailed data on the amount of fees charged by sub-delegated advisors and the share of assets under their management. These agreements might differ depending on the investment area (i.e., geography), fund type, or other characteristics. Filtering the available data for these characteristics should allow identifying a sample of sub-delegation agreements that is sufficiently comparable.

These considerations on comparability are strictly necessary as outlined by the OECD in its 2022 Transfer Pricing Guidance. In a specific reference to investment management services, the OECD states that the features of the local market indicated above may affect the price that can be charged for certain types of investment management services and the profit margins that may be earned from providing them.[45]

However, the agreements might still encompass levels of the AUM that are vastly different from the transaction under review. A regression analysis can be used to adjust for the differences in the AUM if a sufficiently large sample of data is available.

Example

A German asset manager asks its London-based investment management team to do the investment management for its European equities amounting to EUR 30 million in total. Sub-delegation fees for a sample of European equity funds with similar characteristics are identified in order to derive the appropriate investment management fees. However, the funds in the sample have different levels of AUM. A regression analysis mapping the level of investment management fees per AUM is undertaken. The resulting equation can be used to estimate the appropriate fee level per level of AUM.

However, it should be noted that the type of fund or asset class that is managed by the investment management team can have a significant impact on the investment management fees observed in the market. In order to reflect different asset types (i.e., funds with a different investment focus) in the analysis, dummy variables might again be added to the analysis (*see* section 2.4.1.2 for the application of dummy variables).

Another slightly more straightforward approach is to apply regression equations that represent the sub-advisory fees in relation to the level of the AUM. Data providers such as FITZ Partners publish these equations for different types of assets and geographies such that the respective transactions can be priced by applying the amount of AUM managed to the regression equation that covers the respective investment type and geography.

45. OECD, *supra* note 6, para. 1.170.

2.4.2.1 *Trade Execution Cost Adjustment*

Multinational asset managers tend to centralize their trade execution function in one particular entity. This means that many of the investment management teams do not always perform execution activities themselves. This might be a difference to the data points derived from the comparable sub-advisory agreements. The bps numeration quoted in these agreements typically includes a (small) remuneration for trade execution.

To adjust for this difference, public databases are available that provide trade execution fees for different jurisdictions and asset types.[46] These would need to be deducted from the bps fee remuneration that is derived.

It should be noted that all of the above criteria and adjustments may also apply when internal comparables are used. These internal CUPs need to be filtered and adjusted to reflect the precise characteristics of the tested function (i.e., the specific asset being managed).

2.4.2.2 *Contributions from More Than One Jurisdiction*

In contrast to distribution functions in which a distributor typically covers one jurisdiction, a particularity within the investment management function is that functions are often performed from more than one jurisdiction. In these cases, the profits attributable to those functions need to be split among the contributing entities. This can be done by applying a profit split analysis (*see* above).

Based on the outcome of that split (which can be based on the weighted salary of the contributing senior personnel), the profits attributable to the investment management function can be split among the jurisdictions.

Example

The German asset manager in the example above manages its European assets from its Frankfurt-based investment management team comprising thirty staff members. However, the tranche of assets that is composed of UK shares is delegated to their investment management team in London that has five staff members devoted to UK equity. Following the CUP approach, a total remuneration of 40 bps (of AUM) has been estimated to be at arm's length for the investment management function. In order to split this, a splitting key is derived by multiplying the average salary of the Frankfurt-based staff with the total number of hours they jointly spend on their share of the portfolio. This is compared to the average salary of the five London team members multiplied by

46. Elkins/McSherry or Greenwich Associates provide trade execution data that can be used in this respect.

their total number of working hours on their share of the portfolio. The ratio of the two can be used as the splitting factor for the 40 bps that is subsequently applied to the total AUM.

2.4.3 *Middle- and Back-Office Services and Other Support*

Within a multinational asset management group, some entities might provide support services to other entities. While it is technically possible to identify external companies providing comparable services in the market (application of the CUP method),[47] in practice, these comparables can be very difficult to find. Independent players offering a particular service (e.g., custodian services) are rarely found in the market. The remuneration for these support services is therefore typically estimated by the application of a mark-up on total costs (Return on Total Costs). The TNMM is typically used to establish arm's length ranges for the remuneration of this cost-plus remuneration.

For this reason, comparable companies providing similar support services in similar countries are identified. This is accomplished by relying on, e.g., the Orbis database published by Bureau Van Dijk. Its screening process is designed to identify potentially comparable companies that are engaged in providing support services similar to those of the tested party. The following screening criteria are typically applied:

(1) *Geographical Scope:* To ensure similarity of regulatory and operating environment and background conditions to the tested party, only comparables from the same geographical region should be considered.
(2) *Selected Industry Codes*: To refine the search, industry codes (e.g., known as the NACE codes) are applied that cover certain types of industries.
(3) *Functional Review*: A functional review based on the company descriptions from the companies' websites is performed for companies that adhere to the above screening criteria.
(4) *Financial Review:* Companies that incurred losses for multiple years and start-up companies or those with different business strategies (e.g., not for profits) need to be rejected since their financial ratios may not reflect arm's length pricing or conditions.
(5) *Independence*: Companies that are part of the same group as the tested party are rejected since their financial ratios may be influenced by the group's transfer pricing policy and may not reflect arm's length pricing.
(6) *Data Sufficiency:* For the identified comparables, sufficient data for the analysis needs to be available. This typically requires at least two years of available financial data in the database.

47. Data providers, for example, such as Bloomberg, could be relied upon to identify comparable funds and download the respective fund reports. In these fund reports, the specific fees for back-office services might be stated in detail. However, in many cases, these services might be provided by related parties to the fund and thus cannot be relied upon as a CUP.

Based on the above search, a sample of comparable companies can typically be established. For this sample, the financial data for profits and costs are analysed. It can thus be determined whether the tested ROTC margin falls within the interquartile range of arm's length remuneration for comparable companies.

However, it is sometimes not possible to identify sufficiently comparable companies in the same jurisdiction. Comparable companies from other jurisdictions can be analysed in these cases, and adjustment calculations to their results can be performed.

2.4.3.1 Adjustments

As stated above, it is not always possible to identify comparables that are based in the same jurisdiction as the company for which the remuneration is established (tested party). While the comparable companies might be located in the United States, for example, the tested parties can be located in other geographical locations. Since market differences can influence the remuneration that an entity should receive for a given function, several economic adjustments as described below need to be performed.

Focus is given to two differences that may have an impact on the financial performance of companies that can be reliably adjusted, i.e., differences in the financing of the *working capital* (terms of trade) and differences in the *cost of capital*:

- *Working capital*: The profitability of each comparable is directly affected by the number of days outstanding of its payables and receivables. In many instances, accounts receivables and payables can be subject to interest payments and thus have an impact on the profitability of a firm. Different geographical locations not only have very different 'generally accepted' terms of trade varying from 30 days to 120 days but are also subject to very different interest rate levels. Thus, any cross-country comparisons of profit levels need to consider the implications that the terms of trade have on companies' profits.
- *Cost of capital:* Cost of capital refers to the cost of a company's funds using both equity and debt. It is represented by the weighted average cost of capital which takes into account both of these. It is important to note that both public and private companies issue loans and equity to finance themselves. The profitability of a company depends directly on its cost of capital which can significantly differ across locations.

Example

A multinational asset manager performs most of its back-office functions from their Swedish entity. The Swedish entity is remunerated on its costs plus a mark-up of 10% since these are considered routine functions. In order to assess the arm's length nature of the activity, a TNMM study is conducted comprising the financial data of ten comparable entities, i.e., performing similar back-office services and adhering to the criteria outlined above. However, since it is not possible to obtain sufficiently comparable data from Sweden, German companies are considered instead. The interquartile range of their profit mark-up on total costs ranges from 7.0% to 12.0%. This data for working capital and cost of capital need to be adjusted since the companies are based in a different jurisdiction. The subsequent (adjusted) interquartile range is from 7.5% to 12.4%. The 10% mark-up on total costs that the asset manager applies can thus be considered to be at arm's length.

3 CONCLUSIONS

In contrast to other aspects of transfer pricing in financial services (e.g., the interest rates on intercompany loans), there is surprisingly little literature and public debate on the assessment of intra-group transactions within the asset management industry. However, this does not mean that the general principles outlined by the OECD would not apply as rigorously to taxpayers within the asset management industry. On the contrary, given that asset management structures are mostly established in a multinational framework that often includes offshore jurisdictions, taxpayers should be prepared for a detailed scrutiny by tax authorities. For this reason, asset management companies need to proactively prepare detailed documentation on the application of the arm's length principle on their intercompany transactions.

This chapter forms a guideline on how to assess the arm's length nature of intra-group financial transactions within the asset management industry. It provides a coherent framework for the pricing of the most common types of cross-border intra-group transactions that are typically present in the asset management industry. These are particularly:

- sales/marketing;
- investment management; and
- administration and support.

After briefly outlining the regulatory background that is applicable, a comprehensive transfer pricing analysis as prescribed in the relevant OECD legislation is described. The specific terms and conditions for each transaction are analysed, and it is established how this can best be assessed in a transfer pricing framework.

The applicable transfer pricing methods are discussed, and the application of the most suitable methods is elaborated for each of the transactions including the description of possible adjustment calculations that can be relied upon to enhance comparability. Practical examples provide simplified guidance on how to assess the establishment of the appropriate transfer price for the services typically rendered within the asset management industry.

The chapter thus provides a guideline for pricing the most relevant aspect within the value chain of an asset ManCo. The methods applied form an economically reasonable assessment of the arm's length prices; however, other methods might also be feasible.

Table of Cases

Index

www.ingramcontent.com/pod-product-compliance
Ingram Content Group UK Ltd.
Pitfield, Milton Keynes, MK11 3LW, UK
UKHW020803290926
15470UKWH00003B/934

9 789403 540221